U.S. Counterterrorism

From Nixon to Trump – Key Challenges, Issues, and Responses

Michael B. Kraft
Edward Marks

CRC Press
Taylor & Francis Group
Boca Raton London New York

CRC Press is an imprint of the
Taylor & Francis Group, an **informa** business

CRC Press
Taylor & Francis Group
6000 Broken Sound Parkway NW, Suite 300
Boca Raton, FL 33487-2742

First issued in paperback 2020

ISBN-13: 978-1-4987-0615-5 (hbk)
ISBN-13: 978-0-367-77878-1 (pbk)

Library of Congress Cataloging-in-Publication Data

Name: Kraft, Michael, 1937 - author. | Marks, Edward, 1934 - author.
Title: U.S. counterterrorism : from Nixon to Trump : key challenges, issues, and responses / Michael B. Kraft and Edward Marks.
Description: Boca Raton, FL : CRC Press, [2018] | Includes bibliographical references and index.
Identifiers: LCCN 2017034020| ISBN 9781498706155 (hardback : alk. Paper) | ISBN 9781315371610 (ebook)
Subjects: LCSH: Terrorism--United States--Prevention--History--20th century. |Terrorism--United States--Prevention--History--21st century.
Classification: LCC HV6432.K689 2018 | DDC 363.325/17--dc23
LC record available at https://lccn.loc.gov/2017034020

Visit the Taylor & Francis Web site at
http://www.taylorandfrancis.com

and the CRC Press Web site at
http://www.crcpress.com

We dedicate this book to the all too many victims of terrorism around the world, and to the many thousands of men and women in the government services of many countries who work to prevent future attacks, "succor the afflicted," and "punish the wicked."

Contents

FOREWORD

National security issues are seldom simple. Many require a deep understanding of history, technology, national cultures, international law, and other subjects. Yet, even by the standards of the field, few topics are as complex as contemporary terrorism and counterterrorism. There is never a single kind of terrorist threat or a pure "type." Instead, at any one time, we may encounter a multiplicity of threats: state-sponsored terrorist groups, independent groups with no relationships to particular states, "lone wolves" with no substantive ties to particular groups but general ideological agreement with one or more, religiously motivated organizations, ethno-nationalist ones, and so on.

Moreover, since terrorism is the transnational threat *par excellence*, with groups operating across national boundaries, in the global financial system and in cyberspace, counterterrorism is also a dizzyingly complex area of activity. Practitioners speak of the need for a "whole-of-government" approach, and, indeed, the military, law enforcement agencies, the intelligence community, diplomats, finance ministries, and development agencies are all routinely involved in the effort to destroy the terrorist groups and counter individuals who would harm innocents in an effort to advance their political or ideological agenda.

For decades, the paucity of informative literature on terrorism and counterterrorism was not much noted. Then, as now, most works on terrorism were journalistic and focused on notable incidents and particularly repellent groups. Since September 11, 2001, and the emergence of terrorism as a top-tier national security threat and concern of the informed public, this dearth in literature on terrorism has been more distressing. In the years since, the scholarly literature on terrorist tactics, ideologies, and organization as well as evaluations of legal instruments, domestic policies, and international cooperation and the like has proliferated enormously. Interestingly, though, few broad-gauge histories of terrorism and counterterrorism have emerged. A few excellent works—like *Inside Terrorism*, the standout book by Bruce Hoffman—have provided a comprehensive overview of the main historical developments and trends on both the offensive and defensive sides. But histories, *per se*, are still scarce.

Consequently, even serious students of public affairs are often bewildered by news accounts of the operations of terrorist groups and the governments that fight them. Indeed, experienced reporters have often muddied the waters with imprecise use of terms such as rendition (movement of a terrorist subject from one country to another outside the formal extradition process) and extraordinary rendition (the same done without the permission of the country in which the subject was located), especially when what they really meant was rendition to torture (the movement was with the acquiescence of the host government, but the goal was to send the individual to a country where interrogation techniques outlawed elsewhere can be used).

Moreover, few outside those in the policy community directly charged with dealing with counterterrorism and a handful of scholars and journalists understand how the many parts of counterterrorism policy fit together. What does it mean when the State Department lists a group as a foreign terrorist organization? What are the implications of being designated as a state sponsor of terrorism? Who can undertake covert operations against terrorists? What kind of operations can be taken against terrorists in areas that are deemed to be under armed conflict? How have partner countries reacted in the past to the incarceration of terrorist suspects in Guantanamo and how might they react if the United States starts putting new captives in the facility on the island of Cuba? All of these issues are faced regularly by the government officials, yet they are little understood by the public that all too often sees every successful or thwarted attack as a sign that the nation is losing in the fight against international terrorism.

This is why *U.S. Counterterrorism: From Nixon to Trump—Key Challenges, Issues, and Responses* comes as an important and welcome addition to the literature on terrorism and counterterrorism. Although some of the questions are not dealt with in great depth, this work seeks to be comprehensive—to address the many facets of the conflict between those who commit terrorist attacks and those who seek to thwart them. Michael Kraft and Ambassador (rtd.) Edward Marks also take a genuinely historical perspective on this subject, something seldom attempted by other authors. This approach is vital if Americans and others wish to judge—as they should—the efforts to safeguard our population, our foreign partners, and our other interests from attack.

Making informed judgments will also require a larger sense of world events than any one volume can communicate. The upheaval of the Arab Spring, for example, swept away the security services (most of which were longtime human rights abusers) of a number of Arab countries, creating a vacuum that terrorist groups exploited. How well the United

States and its partners met that challenge is another part of the picture, and the rise in global statistics on attacks is all too often another source of complaints without a real sense of how much security has been achieved. Policymakers have too often been wary of making any claims, however justified, with regard to the achievements of various government agencies or our partnerships with different nations around the world. Thus, it is all the more vital that scholars—or in this case, scholar practitioners like Messrs Kraft and Marks with long experience in the field of counterterrorism—supply the context and so helpfully inform readers of the bigger picture. It is challenging enough that so much counterterrorism activity goes on in the dark, in operations that must be covert, far from the eyes of the press. In a world in which terrorists and counter terrorists will continue to seek an edge from the ever-changing technologies, and globalization creates challenges and opportunities for both sides, it is essential that light be shed on as much of the conflict as possible.

U.S. Counterterrorism: From Nixon to Trump—Key Challenges, Issues, and Responses is a critical contribution that will help more people reason about the threat and the steps the government is taking to confront it.

Daniel Benjamin

Norman E. McCulloch, Jr. Director of the John Sloan Dickey Center for International Understanding at Dartmouth College and former Ambassador and Assistant Secretary of State for Counterterrorism (2009–2012).

Preface

The United States and its allies have been fighting terrorism in one form or another for decades and the election of a new president is an appropriate time for an overall review of the evolution of the threats and responses.

Six years ago, in 2011, CRC Press published the authors' book on terrorism and the U.S. government response: *U.S. Government Counterterrorism: A Guide to Who Does What*. The book was the first public unclassified overall description of the many U.S. programs and agencies involved in the counterterrorism effort.

In the succeeding years, the overall strategic policy and most programs have not changed significantly, but specific programs and budgets have evolved in scale and scope in response to the expanding challenge and threat to the United States and its allies. These have occurred incrementally in some areas and rapidly in others, especially in the technological arena.

What has changed dramatically is technology—drones, the Internet, and cyber threats are the main examples. Governments such as the United States led in the development and use of these technologies, but increasingly sophisticated technology—especially the Internet—has been and is being used effectively by terrorist and insurgent groups.

While overall strategy remains more or less unaltered there has been significant reordering of programs and some changes in scale and scope. The interest in deradicalism and prevention, for instance, has led to a significant increase in Countering Violent Extremism (CVE) programs in the United States as well as in other countries, especially because of the threat of individuals, often called "lone wolves," becoming radicalized and committing attacks in the countries where they are living.

In January 2017, a new president and a new administration were sworn into office following an election campaign in which candidate Donald Trump expressed views on terrorism quite different from those of the Obama, Bush, and previous administrations. We therefore thought the beginning of this administration offers an opportunity to provide a stock-taking: to review the developments, both with respect to the terrorist challenge and in the U.S. government's response. This book, therefore, is an attempt to describe the counterterrorism situation and context at the beginning of the Trump administration.

Accordingly, most of the book is taken up with that review of the "war on modern terrorism," beginning in the Nixon administration and carrying it to the end of the Obama administration. We begin with an overview of issues, including the evolution in policy and programs as each administration faced the changing terrorist challenge, and a chronological review of the changing and evolving character of the terrorist challenges, U.S. policies, responses, and programs during this period. A key theme as we approach today is the impact of technology, such as the Internet. The discussion includes the evolution of the terrorism threat from groups, most of them secular with relatively narrow goals, to those such as ISIS, which has broader religious cum nationalist goals, including restoring an Islamic Caliphate. This includes the subject of terrorism funding, the organized crime nexus, and the concern for weapons of mass destruction.

Paired with the review of the threat, we include a chronological review of the evolving counterterrorism policy of the U.S. Government, with a special focus on the Bush administration, and its complete strategic review following the attack on 9/11, the declaration of the Global War on Terrorism, the inauguration of wars in Afghanistan and Iraq, and expanded CT programs, both domestic and foreign. Following, we discuss the Obama administration and how it both continued and modified previous USG policies and programs in dealing with the rapidly changing technological scene. We also include, for those who wish to do more research or see original texts, an extensive list of key documents, speeches, and testimony on counterterrorism issues.

All of this is intended to put in context the strategic challenge facing the Trump administration. This challenge will include specific programs and their budgets and therefore a series of decisions whether to continue, modify, cancel, or replace them. However, the first and most basic policy determination—as it is for all administrations—is strategic: what is the nature of the threat? President Bush's reaction after 9/11 was to view terrorism as an existential threat to the United States and to launch the "War on Terror," although near the end of his administration he toned down this interpretation. President Obama continued this more modest view, reflecting his judgment that terrorism is a "serious" threat but not existential.

First of all, the Trump administration, like its predecessors, must make a basic strategic judgment on the nature of terrorism and its implications. This will have basic ramifications for CT policy and programs and budget resources and potential effect on overall "traditional"

USG foreign policy. By the time the first 100 days or so of this administration had passed, it had become increasingly clear that at least rhetorically President Trump sees Middle East terrorism as an existential threat to the United States. What this means programmatically is still unclear, although President Trump authorized more aggressive military actions and his first overseas visit was highlighted by a visit to Saudi Arabia where he essentially called for an Islamic "NATO" to fight terrorism. Presumably specific details will follow.

The authors hope that this book, this overview, will assist readers—and maybe even the administration—to see the whole picture. Terrorism is now high on the security list of every government, especially with the attacks during 2017 against Britain, France, Germany, and other countries as well as by "home grown" terrorists in the United States. The past is often prologue and the world has almost 60 years of experience with modern terrorism, so no government starts from scratch. Therefore, this book is an interim report card, with the date of the final exam yet to be determined.

Michael B. Kraft
Edward Marks
Washington, DC

Acknowledgments

Few books of this nature could be written without the insights and the shared knowledge from others who also have been working in their own ways to counter the threat of international terrorism.

We, particularly, would like to thank former colleagues and other experts who helped provide their views and analysis of the developments in the counterterrorism arena over the years. They include former State Department counterterrorism coordinators Dan Benjamin and Frank Taylor, who later served as Under Secretary for Intelligence and Analysis in the Department of Homeland Security (DHS); also Michael Sheehan, who, after serving as the State Department Counterterrorism Coordinator, later became the Assistant Secretary of Defense for Special Operations and Low Intensity Conflict. The three of them span the Clinton, Bush, and Obama administrations. We also appreciate the assistance of Susan Spaulding, a former DHS Under Secretary with long experience in the counterterrorism world.

In exploring the complicated efforts to Countering Violent Extremism (CVE), we benefited greatly from the assistance of Eric Rosand, now the director of the Prevention Project: Organizing Against Violent Extremism at the Brookings Institute, who previously headed the CVE efforts in the State Department Counterterrorism Bureau. Former colleague Michael Jacobson, who supervised CT programs in the State Department's programs, also was helpful in bringing us to date, as was Rhonda Shore and others in the bureau who were helpful on this book and our earlier book *U.S. Government: A Guide to Who Does What.* That book, also a CRC publication, was the starting point for summarizing some of the programs described in this book.

Persons in other areas of the government also shared kindly their insights, including John Carlin, the recent Assistant Attorney General for National Security, Robert McBrien, a former senior Treasury Department official who contributed a section on sanctions, and Michael Rolince, a retired FBI counterterrorism specialist who is still active on the counterterrorism issue. We also wish to thank other officials still in the government for their insights but who may prefer not to be named because they were speaking informally on background or without formal approval of the "public affairs minders."

We note the very important analysis and perspectives shared over many years by three retired and experienced veterans of the CIA, Tony Porcaro, Kenneth Daigler, and Glenn Carle.

We owe a particular debt to our dedicated research assistant, Marzia Borsoi-Kelly, who was especially helpful in compiling the list of key documents and resolving some computer-related problems for the two of us of the "older generation."

We are indebted to Professor Yonah Alexander, the veteran counterterrorism academic, and Director, International Center for Terrorism Studies at the Potomac Institute. Professor Alexander was the original inspiration of the book—author Michael Kraft had coauthored an earlier book with him, *Evolution of U.S. Counterterrorism Policy,* that ended with the George W. Bush administration, but the professor had to drop out of the current project at an early stage. We appreciate the work of his interns, especially David Wiese and Andrew Coley, in helping in the early stages of our research.

We thank Joshua Sinai, a counterterrorism specialist and veteran reviewer of counterterrorism books, who helped us with our bibliography. Brian Jenkins, the veteran counterterrorism expert at the RAND Corporation, and Professors Martha Crenshaw of Stanford University and Dennis Pluchinsky of George Mason University, a former State Department analyst, provided useful comments over the years.

Finally, and perhaps most important, we thank our wives, Lisa Kraft and the late Aida Marks, who tragically died after the manuscript was completed, for their support during this long process and Mark Listewnik, our editor and guide, for his patience.

Michael B. Kraft and Edward Marks
Washington, DC

Authors

Michael B. Kraft is a Washington-based counterterrorism consultant, writer, and editor with more than 30 years of experience working on terrorism issues in the State Department, Congress, and the private sector. After retiring as a senior advisor in the State Department Counterterrorism Office, he worked on counterterrorism issues at the National Defense University Africa Center for Strategic Studies.

He coauthored with Ambassador Marks *U.S. Government Counterterrorism: A Guide to Who Does What,* also published by CRC Press. It described for the first time in one place the many unclassified USG counterterrorism program. He also coauthored with Professor Yonah Alexander a major counterterrorism reference book, *The Evolution of U.S. Counterterrorism Policy* (2008). Mr. Kraft has also contributed chapters for several other counterterrorism books, including the *McGraw Hill Homeland Security Handbook,* the Project for National Security Reform as well as articles for various journals and newspapers and the Counterterrorism Blog.

Consultant activities included projects for the Departments of Homeland Security and Defense, and a current program to help strengthen the resiliency of U.S. and foreign cities. He was an officer of the Institute for Bioscience and International Security Policy, which was formed to help counter the potential bioterrorism threat.

During his 19 years at the State Department Counterterrorism office, Mr. Kraft worked closely with the Justice Department in drafting and enacting legislation, including the material support and other provisions to counter terrorism financing and to tighten sanctions against terrorist states. Earlier, as a Congressional foreign policy specialist, he helped draft the original sanctions legislation against countries supporting terrorism. While in the State Department, Mr. Kraft also worked with the Department's Antiterrorism Training Assistance program that bolsters the capabilities of friendly governments, the interagency counterterrorism research and development program, and public diplomacy efforts.

Mr. Kraft initiated a series of seminars that the State Department and Justice Department held after 9/11 to assist 52 countries strengthen their counterterrorism laws. He conducted counterterrorism seminars for the Institute of International Law in Kampala, Uganda, and also has been a guest lecturer at a number of other institutions, including the Defense Department's Marshall Center, the Marine Corps Academy, and various civilian universities including Stanford, the University of Michigan, and George Washington University.

Before joining the State Department, Mr. Kraft served ten years on Congressional staff, including service as staff director of the Senate Foreign Relations Middle East Subcommittee and on the Foreign Assistance Subcommittee staff. Earlier, he was chief Congressional Correspondent for the Reuters News Agency. He previously worked for United Press International in Washington, London, and Central Africa, where he also reported for the BBC. He is a graduate of the University of Michigan, where he was a senior editor on the *Michigan Daily*. He is married to Lisa Rosenthal Kraft, originally from Wellington, New Zealand. Their daughter, Dina, has covered numerous terrorist attacks as a foreign correspondent in the Middle East and Africa.

Edward Marks, since retiring as a senior foreign service officer (Minister–Counselor) in 1995, has engaged in consulting, lecturing, and writing, primarily on terrorism, interagency coordination, United Nations affairs, and complex international emergencies. He has written extensively on these and other subjects.

Ambassador Marks was recalled to active duty in 2002–2005 to serve as the Department of State's advisor on terrorism to the U.S. Pacific Command.

Current activities include member, Governing Board of American Diplomacy, and Member, Association for Diplomatic Studies and Training. He is also a Founding Trustee of the Command and General Staff College Foundation. Past activities have included serving as a senior fellow at several policy think tanks, senior advisor to the Project on National Security Reform (2008–2009), a senior mentor to various military commands, member of several publication boards, and a consultant to several United Nations organizations.

Ambassador Marks was appointed into the Foreign Service in 1956 with early assignments in Kenya, Mexico, Angola, Zambia, Belgium, and Zaire. In 1976, he was appointed Chief of Mission to the Republics of Guinea-Bissau and Cape Verde. Returning to Washington in 1980, he attended the National War College, after which he moved to the Department of State as the deputy coordinator for counterterrorism. This assignment was followed by a year as a visiting senior fellow on terrorism matters at the Center for Strategic and International Studies. He was assigned to the Republic of Sri Lanka as Deputy Chief of Mission and then Chargé d'Affaires in 1986. In 1989, he was appointed

Deputy United States Representative to the Economic and Social Council to the United Nations in New York (1989–1993).

Born in Chicago, Illinois, in April 1934, Ambassador Marks attended high school in Detroit, Michigan, and graduated from the Universities of Michigan (BA in Political Science, 1956), Oklahoma (MA in Economics, 1976), and the National War College (1981). He served in the United States Army (1956–1958). He was married to the late Aida Marks (née Nercess) originally from Tehran, Iran.

CHAPTER 1

Overview of the Terrorism Threat from Nixon to Trump

The U.S. government's efforts to counter international and domestic terrorism have evolved considerably over the past decades, but the pace accelerated during the Obama administration. The acceleration was influenced both by changes in the character and scope of the threat and the impact of modern technology. Many of the challenges, issues, and programs that emerged in the past are carrying over into the Trump administration, although perhaps in a different form.

During the Obama administration, some of the key developments included the more sophisticated use of the Internet by terrorist groups to spread their propaganda and recruit activists and "lone wolves," the emergence of cyberterrorism threats and hacking, and the increasing deployment of armed drones by the United States and other governments and now even terrorist groups. On the "defensive side," the increased deployment of surveillance cameras in urban areas and airports has been useful in identifying terrorist suspects and prosecuting them in courts. Information sharing within the U.S. government, with local and state governments, and with foreign partners also became intensive.

The issues that faced the Obama administration and will face the Trump administration—as well as the basic policies and programs—have roots in previous generations, some of them dating back to the 1970s and President Richard Nixon's administration. Many programs conceived and developed during previous administrations continued, evolved, and were expanded during subsequent administrations. These programs include antiterrorism training for U.S. and foreign law enforcement officials, the interagency Counter Terrorism Financing (CTF) and Countering Violent Extremism (CVE) programs, and the ever-pressing need for improved international cooperation and intelligence sharing.

They are likely to continue in one form or another as tools in the ongoing efforts against one or another manifestation of terrorism.

Underlying all counterterrorist strategy, however, remains the fundamental question as to whether terrorism is an existential threat to the United States, with the perspective of the "War against Terrorism" initiated by the George W. Bush administration after 9/11, or a serious problem enmeshed in the wider foreign policy concerns of the United States as perceived by President Barack Obama.

In either case, the world and the United States are now in the sixth decade of the modern era of terrorism and, as the Trump administration came into office, the 15th year of the current era of terrorism that began with 9/11. These have been frustrating as well as tragic years, as the terrorist challenge has metastasized within the broader problems of a dramatically changing and increasingly violent international environment. The terrorist threat and challenge can be seen as primarily Middle Eastern and South Asian problems—with those regions being "ground zero" for terrorist origin and the main terrorist battleground. However, the United States is a prominent target, along with people in the Middle East and our Western European allies, such as Britain, France and Belgium, and some African countries. At the same time, the United States is the most prominent and historic leader of the effort to develop counterterrorist alliances.

One sober summary balance sheet of the situation was recently presented by long-time terrorism expert Brian Jenkins of the Rand Corporation:

> Measuring progress in irregular warfare without frontlines is always difficult. The various dimensions and multiple fronts of the US' ongoing campaigning against terrorists make it an exceptional challenge. And much has changed since that campaign began 15 years ago. There not been another 9/11-scale event. Although they attract followers, neither Al-Qàida nor its progeny have become a mass movement. The constellation of groups claiming allegiance to them is far from an effective alliance and the Islamic State's territorial control has been contained and pushed back. The leaders of AQ depend heavily on exhortation to get others to fight and the turnout is thin. On the other side of the ledger, the targeted groups have survived, their determination seems undiminished, and their ideology remains powerful. They are deeply imbedded in a number of fragile, divided, conflict-ridden states. Persistent foes, they are able to operate underground and capable of comebacks if pressure on them subsides. The conflict will go on.[1]

[1] Jenkins, Brian Michael. Fifteen Years On, Where are We in the "War on Terror." *CTC Sentinel*, September 7, 2016. https://www.ctc.usma.edu/posts/fifteen-years-on-where-are-we-in-the-war-on-terror (accessed May 8, 2017).

A primary theme of the past 15 years, indeed of the past 50 years, has been the evolving character of the terrorist threat, from the so-called boutique terrorists of Western Europe to today's "Islamic State." Earlier terrorist groups usually had relatively specific targets and goals, such as trying to free their imprisoned colleagues or specific nationalistic/territorial demands. However, with al-Qaeda, the Tamil Tigers, and Hamas, we saw the emergence of more ambitious goals and related suicide and larger attacks designed to kill and wound as many people as possible. The terrorists' goals keep moving and will continue to do so. There has been a significant and dramatic change in the numbers, character, and capability of the terrorists themselves, from the 50 or so core Red Brigade members in Germany during the 1980s to the estimated 40,000 Jihadists of ISIS. In addition, the global environment has changed in significant ways.

"The West failed to predict the emergence of Islamic terrorism in general and al-Qaeda in particular across the Middle East and North Africa. It was blindsided by the ISIS (also known as ISIL or Daesh) sweep across Syria and Iraq, which at least temporarily changed the map of the Middle East. Both movements have skillfully continued to evolve and proliferate—and surprise," Jenkins observed.[2]

The technological developments since 9/11 have especially complicated the situation by further empowering both governments and nonstate terrorist groups. The Internet, drones, and cyber warfare, with the latter even producing its own form of terrorism—cyber terrorism—have changed the landscape for terrorism and countermeasures. For these and other reasons, the international character of terrorism and counterterrorism has become more marked. There are few countries now untouched by the threat.[3]

Politically and environmentally, the collapse of meaningful governance and governmental organizations in the Arab Middle East has created a zone of anarchy. In the ungoverned areas of Afghanistan, Syria, Iraq, and Yemen, a complex mix of religious, ethnic, national, ideological, and political combatants struggle for power "where ignorant armies clash by night." In the process, they have drawn in their neighbors and other players as far distant as the United States. The same is true in parts of Africa, where the French have played a major role in helping their former colonies, but the United States has also provided training and

2 *The Jihadi Threat: ISIS, Al Qaeda and Beyond*, United States Institute of Peace, December 12, 2016. https://www.usip.org/publications/2016/12/jihadi-threat-isis-al-qaeda-and-beyond (accessed May 8, 2017).

3 For a summary of the role of the Russian invasion and Bin Laden's activities, see Martha Crenshaw and Gary LaFree, *Countering Terrorism*, Brookings Institution Press, Washington, 2017, pp. 7–9. https://www.brookings.edu/book/countering-terrorism-no-simple-solutions/ (accessed May 8, 2017).

FIGURE 1.1 French soldiers stand guard in Mali as part of Operation Barkhane; Barkhane is centered in the African Sahel. France has increased its involvement and support of countries' counterterror measures in Africa in recent years. The United States has been working closely with France and other countries to counter various terrorist groups in Africa. French Ministry of Defense photo. (Courtesy of U.S. Department of Defense.)

other assistance (Figure 1.1). Major geographic regions are in turmoil and the violence has an impact abroad, even indirectly, with the movement of hundreds of thousands of refugees from Syria and Afghanistan to Europe and elsewhere.

A cottage industry has developed in trying to analyze terrorist movements in general and Islamic jihadist movements in particular. The experts pretty much agree that terrorist movements are produced by a confluence of factors. A key point in the emergence of the Islamic jihadist movement was the rallying of Muslims to fight the Russian occupation of Afghanistan in the 1980s. Subsequently, some individuals were motivated to join jihadist movements by a variety of reasons: ideology, the desire for meaning in their lives and belonging to a greater cause, anger at the West, even just a desire for adventure and "action." Other conditions enable jihadism to flourish. They include the volatile mix of shifting demographics, notably a surge of youth, higher literacy, and greater social aspirations intersecting with economic woes, growing unemployment, and deepening political malaise or disillusionment. The mix of personal motives and enabling conditions has become even more combustible since the Arab uprisings of 2011. These drivers of extremism are rampant in the Middle East. They differ in local contexts. Six conditions are particularly pivotal today.

1. The fragility of states
2. Ideological upheaval
3. Conflict zones
4. Foreign intervention, for example, by the United States, Russia, Iran, and Saudi Arabia
5. Socioeconomic factors
6. Technology

All of these developments are impacting the international environment. Terrorism kills and wounds people, contributes to refugee problems, threatens both national governments and the traditional international order. Countering terrorism effectively puts a premium on global, regional, and bilateral cooperation and alliances.

These developments and the consequent analysis have also made it increasing clear that the global community cannot simply kill its way out of the problem by attacking terrorist leaders and followers. This is despite the key role played by military force in attacking and weakening terrorist groups such as ISIS that control territory and are able to extract taxes and other payments from locals and sell oil or other resources. Until the ideology underpinning jihadism is defeated, or at least effectively countered, it will continue to be used to recruit new—sometimes very young—men and women. This realization is increasingly influencing strategic calculations, including the effort to reduce the territory controlled by such groups and undercut the image they try to project of being the wave of the future.

A basic question affecting strategic approaches is the perception of Islamic extremist violence or terrorism. This question can be posed in a fairly simple form: is Islamic jihadist terrorism a "serious" threat or an "existential" threat? The answer that governments and officials give to this question significantly influences the response. Just as the threat has been evolving, so has the response of governments, notably that of the U.S. government. Although counterterrorism had been evolving in various ways, from the 1980s' focus on European and Japanese terrorist movements toward the increasing importance of Islamic-based movements from the Middle East, U.S. Government policy remained essentially the same during that period, albeit increasing in scale and scope, and especially undergoing a significant expansion of military and intelligence community capabilities.

THE BUSH ADMINISTRATION

The attack on 9/11, however, dramatically changed the scene. President George W. Bush, and the country, now saw a different and more serious threat. To use a word that became common later, the Islamic jihadist terrorist threat was now seen as "existential," that is, a fundamental threat to the continued existence of the United States and its traditions.

With that viewpoint, President Bush announced a Global War on Terrorism (GWOT), putting the country on a war footing in attitude and behavior if not technically in legal terms, that is, a Declaration of War by Congress. The Authorization for Use of Military Force against Terrorists became law on September 14, 2001, authorizing the use of U.S. Armed Forces against those responsible for the attacks on September 11, 2001 (see Chapter 2).

The GWOT signaled two shifts in USG policy: a war footing against an existential threat, and a concentration on Middle East/Islamic terrorism. The War on Terror (WOT) or the GWOT was a metaphor of war referring to the international military campaign that started in Afghanistan and Iraq after the 9/11 attack. The Bush administration and the Western media used the term to describe a global military, political, legal, and conceptual struggle against both designated terrorist organizations and regimes accused of supporting them. It was originally used with a particular focus on countries associated with Islamic terrorist organizations, including al-Qaeda and like-minded organizations. President Bush and Vice President Cheney, at the same time, tried to make clear that this was not a war against Islam itself.

The GWOT produced a number of titled military campaigns. Operation Enduring Freedom, Operation Iraqi Freedom, and Operation Active Endeavor were the major operations.

Operation Enduring Freedom was the official name for the war in Afghanistan, together with three smaller military actions, under the umbrella of the GWOT. These global operations are intended to seek out and destroy any al-Qaeda fighters or affiliates. Under this general rubric, the United States conducted operations in North Africa, the Horn of Africa, and the Philippines, working with and supporting local governments and sometimes allied countries. The activity in Africa spread into other countries and eventually resulted in the creation of a new U.S. regional combatant command—AFRICOM.

Operation Iraqi Freedom began in March 2003 with an air campaign, which was immediately followed by a U.S.-led ground invasion. The Bush administration stated the invasion was the "serious consequences" spoken of in the UNSC Resolution 1441, partially on the basis of Iraq possessing weapons of mass destruction. The Bush administration also stated the Iraq war was part of the WOT.

To pursue these programs, the Bush administration oversaw a significant increase in the military services and intelligence services, especially the Army and the CIA's paramilitary forces. Between 2001 and 2017, $1.778 trillion was spent on or budgeted for the WOT. This amount includes spending on the WOT in the Department of Defense base budget and supporting departments (Homeland Security, the Veterans Administration, and the State Department). It reflects both increased personnel and related costs, as well increased operational and acquisition expenses.[4] By some estimates, the United States spends up to $100 billion annually on various counterterrorism efforts.[5] However, the exact amount is hard to pinpoint because some expenditures, for aircraft or strengthening embassy security, can serve dual purposes, such as protecting an embassy against violent protestors. Details of the intelligence community's budget are classified. As part of the WOT, the Bush administration created additional structures and new policies for dealing with prisoners and suspected terrorists captured as part of the various military and intelligence operations. A detention center was created at U.S. controlled facilities at Guantanamo Bay, Cuba (Figure 1.2),

FIGURE 1.2 November 14, 2006: U.S. Army soldiers stand guard on a cell block inside Camp Five at the Joint Task Force Guantanamo detention center at Naval Base Guantanamo Bay, Cuba. The Obama administration tried to close the controversial facility but was blocked by Congress. The Trump administration is keeping the facility open.

---

4 Belasco, Amy. *The Cost of Iraq, Afghanistan, and Other Global War on Terror Operations since 9/11*, Congressional Research Service, December 8, 2014. https://fas.org/sgp/crs/natsec/RL33110.pdf (accessed May 8, 2017).

5 Adams, Gordon, a former Office of Management and Budget (OMB) Defense budget expert, quoted in *The Cost of Fighting Terrorism* by Jeanne Sahadi @CNNMoney, November 16, 2015. http://money.cnn.com/2015/11/16/news/economy/cost-of-fighting-terrorism/ (accessed May 8, 2017).

and detention and interrogation procedures were established. Among the latter were "enhanced interrogation procedures", such as waterboarding, under presidential authority, which came under criticism from those who considered them to be torture and were eliminated in the last years of the administration.

In addition to military efforts abroad, in the aftermath of 9/11, the Bush administration increased domestic efforts to prevent future attacks. Various government bureaucracies that handled security and military functions were reorganized. A new cabinet-level agency called the U.S. Department of Homeland Security (DHS) was created in November 2002 to lead and coordinate the largest reorganization of the U.S. federal government since the 1949 consolidation of the armed forces into the Department of Defense. It brought 22 agencies or offices, even the Coast Guard, under one tent. DHS, with its cabinet-level department responsibilities for public security, is roughly comparable to the interior or home ministries of other countries. Its stated missions involve antiterrorism, border security, immigration and customs, cyber security, and disaster prevention and management (see Chapter 4).

In the wake of 9/11, the Bush administration also pushed through the USA PATRIOT Act of October 2001, which dramatically reduced restrictions on law enforcement agencies' ability to search telephone, e-mail communications, medical, financial, and other records during terrorist-related investigations; eased restrictions on foreign intelligence gathering within the United States; expanded the Secretary of the Treasury's authority to regulate financial transactions, particularly those involving foreign individuals and entities; and broadened the discretion of law enforcement and immigration authorities in detaining and deporting immigrants suspected of terrorism-related acts. The act also expanded the definition of *terrorism* to include domestic terrorism, thus enlarging the number of activities to which the USA PATRIOT Act's expanded law enforcement powers could be applied. Global telecommunication usage, including those with no links to terrorism, is being collected through the NSA electronic surveillance program for possible use in investigations. The PATRIOT Act is still in effect (see Chapter 2).

The Intelligence Community (IC) has always been a major element in USG counterterrorism policy and was called upon to provide critical support to the GWOT. In addition to the expanded overseas intelligence and paramilitary operations mentioned above, the IC's working relations with domestic agencies, notably the new Department of Homeland Security, were intensified. New lines of communication and collaboration were opened between the IC and the law enforcement and counterintelligence communities, and with state and local officials through fusion centers in major cities. The IC also built upon long-standing foreign partnerships and established new partnerships to aid in the WOT. All elements of the IC, including the Treasury Department and its comprehensive attack on terrorist financing, directed greater emphasis to counterterrorism and homeland security issues, focusing on producing actionable intelligence and timely warnings in support of military forces and law enforcement. These were primarily a continuation and intensification of previous efforts rather than innovations. The FBI meanwhile shifted its emphasis from civilian crimes to counterterrorism, including preventive measures, investigations, and apprehension of terrorist suspects.

THE OBAMA ADMINISTRATION

President Barack Obama redefined the terrorist threat from an existential threat (GWOT), returning USG counterterrorism policy to a broader foreign policy perspective, albeit at the same if not higher operational level. This was part of the effort to rebalance the United States' role because he felt that the country had overextended itself and bogged down in fighting wars on the ground in the Islamic world, particularly Afghanistan and Iraq. It was also reflected in his reluctance to become more deeply entangled in the Syrian civil war by establishing no-fly zones to protect Syrian civilians from President Assad's bombers, as proposed by many.

Near the end of his administration, President Obama reviewed his counterterrorism policy in a speech at MacDill Air Force Base in Tampa, Florida, on December 6, 2016:[6]

> First of all, a sustainable counterterrorism strategy depends on keeping the threat in perspective. The terrorist threat is real and it is dangerous.
>
> Today's terrorists can kill innocent people, but they don't pose an existential threat to our nation, and we must not make the mistake of elevating them as if they do.

Or, as John Cassidy put it in an article in the *New Yorker*:

> Constructed in response to the disaster that was the Iraq War, the Obama doctrine abjures direct U.S. military intervention in countries that don't represent a direct security threat to the United States, such as Syria. It favors working quietly through allies and proxies, such as Kurdish Peshmerga forces, and even, where necessary, Iranian militias, to attack America's enemies, and also through deploying U.S. military

[6] The White House. *Remarks by the President on the Administration's Approach to Counterterrorism*, MacDill Air Force Base, Tampa, FL, December 6, 2016. https://obamawhitehouse.archives.gov/the-press-office/2016/12/06/remarks-president-administrations-approach-counterterrorism (accessed May 8, 2017).

> and technological assets that can be operated from afar, such as cyber-spying systems, reconnaissance planes, and drones.[7]

Based on this perspective, the Obama administration shifted its military focus from the deployment of regular troops overseas to a greater use of unmanned aerial vehicles, or *drones*, as well as the increased deployment of Special Operations Forces (SOF) (Figure 1.3). The drone program not only reflects an administration's desire to cut back and avoid extensive use of ground forces in what was perceived as another quagmire—but also the dramatic technological increase in drone capability. Although the use of drones began during the Bush administration, the Obama administration greatly stepped up the number of attacks, targeting not only ISIS bases and units but also individual terrorists, especially key leaders.

The expanded use of SOF also met a perceived policy objective: how to attack ISIS and other terrorist groups, while utilizing a unique U.S.

FIGURE 1.3 July 31, 2015: The 2-week Black Dart counter-UAS (counter drone) demonstration seeks to improve technologies, tactics, and techniques used by the Defense Department and its partners. The Black Dart project officer is speaking to the media in front of a MQ-9 unmanned aircraft system, at Naval Base Ventura County and Sea Range, Point Mugu, California. (Courtesy of U.S. Department of Defense/Lisa Ferdinando.)

---

[7] Cassidy, John. How Much of the Obama Doctrine Will Survive Trump? *The New Yorker*, December 8, 2016. http://www.newyorker.com/news/john-cassidy/how-much-of-the-obama-doctrine-will-survive-trump

capability and avoiding large numbers of U.S. "boots on the ground." This approach combined U.S. military SOF forces with CIA paramilitary resources. The expansion of SOCOM (U.S. Special Operations Command, a joint combatant command) continued during the Obama administration, in personnel, finances, and in mission. Apart from the initial campaign in Iraq, SOCOM has been charged with the military lead in USG global CT operations. This has largely taken the form of kinetic operations, although there has been an effort to shift to liaison, training, and intelligence cooperation missions in support of friendly local forces, such as the Iraqi Army, Kurdish units, some relatively more moderate Syrian rebel forces, and some African governments.

Just as the U.S. military has shifted its strategy from boots on the ground to target-specific kills, through both SOF raids and drone strikes, the U.S. IC, specifically those involved in "humint" seems to have done likewise. Specifically, traditional resources once used to recruit and penetrate terrorist organizations seem to have been reduced, while targeting and drone killing have been significantly bolstered. Like the military, this seems to indicate some confusion regarding whether certain actions are tactical or strategic in regard to the terrorist target.

One important positive aspect of the Obama administration's focus on greater collaboration with allies was trying to ensure that the United States was not the only one bearing the share of the cost. In dealing with the terrorism and insurgencies in Afghanistan and Iraq, the United States worked to include allies such as Australia, Canada, Britain, and other European countries, as well as Jordan, Turkey, Saudi Arabia, other Gulf countries, and the Kurds.

That approach was discernable very early on. "Under President Obama, the U.S. was focused on doing things in ways that the rest of the world could understand as rooted in principle and rooted in a set of ethics that they could identify with," said one Washington counterterrorism expert, Daveed Gartenstein-Ross.[8]

The Obama administration took a strong stance against the use of the so-called enhanced interrogation techniques, labeling them as torture; it promised to close the Guantanamo Bay prisoner installation and used the civilian trial process for terrorist suspects. Congress blocked efforts to close Guantanamo but the Obama administration managed to sharply reduce the numbers by getting other countries to take over responsibility for some of the prisoners who were deemed safe to be paroled from the facility.

---

[8] Gartenstein-Ross, Daveed. Al Qaeda Assessment off the Mark. *The cipherbrief.com*, December 8, 2016. https://www.thecipherbrief.com/article/middle-east/al-qaeda-assessment-mark-1089 (accessed May 8, 2017).

The Obama administration also paid attention to immigration and visitor entry programs as well as Mexican border issues, including building barriers along the border and stepping up controls. However, they came under attack as being inadequate, especially during the 2016 election campaign. Not as part of CT policy, but of some relevance, were Obama administration refugee and immigration policies. The trend was toward relaxation of limitations, including support of the DREAM Act to allow legal status for Immigrants who were children when their illegal immigrant parents brought them into the country; lifting of the HIV immigration ban; changes in deportation policy; and an effort to increase the number of Syrian refugees let into the United States.

Meanwhile, the Obama administration continued and expanded programs to counter terrorism financing (CTF), which, like other programs in the tool kit, began in earlier administrations. This program worked to cut off fund-raising and money flow to terrorist groups. A related effort was the Justice Department's effective use of 1986 legislation developed during the Clinton administration to make it illegal to provide funds or other forms of material support to foreign terrorist organizations for terrorist attacks by individuals. The administration, also through the Treasury Department's Overseas Foreign Assets Control program, continued to impose terrorist sanctions on terrorist-supporting countries, primarily Iran.

Otherwise, President Obama continued to support most previous programs, such as those for training foreign law enforcement officials and strengthening their judicial systems and expanding the efforts to curb terrorism financing. The administration also worked to strengthen the coordination and information exchanges with local and state governments, notably the fusing of national and local law enforcement agencies, as in the Joint Interagency Task Force program and the fusion centers that brought federal and local officials together to share intelligence information. DHS also increased its program of grants and training to improve the capabilities of the first responders at the state and local level.

COUNTERING VIOLENT EXTREMISM

One of the major and particularly troublesome terrorism-related developments during the Obama administration was the emergence of increasingly sophisticated use of the Internet by terrorist groups to spread their propaganda and to radicalize and recruit new supporters, potential suicide terrorists, and other foot soldiers. They also used the Internet, often using encryption technologies, to promote operations and send instructions.

To counter this, the Bush administration started, and the Obama administration expanded and modified, a program called *Countering Violent Extremism*, or CVE. The program aimed at blunting the radicalization of persons, either through the Internet or by person-to-person recruitment efforts by al-Qaeda and ISIS organizations.

The CVE program had its genesis in the Bush administration, which revived a public diplomacy program that originally started under Secretary of State George Schultz in the mid-1980s but faded away under Secretary of State James Baker. The CVE program has undergone various changes in an effort to more effectively deal with a very difficult problem. It tries to work on domestic prevention, working with local not only law enforcement but also public health, mental health, or social services providers, parents, researchers, teachers, businesses, and women's, religious, and youth leaders (see Chapter 4 for more details).

During the Obama administration, DHS started a program of grants to local agencies to help them identify persons vulnerable to radicalization and address some of the issues that provide fertile ground for radicalization such as estrangement from society, resentments, and personal problems. DHS and the FBI are both involved in CVE efforts, and during the early stages there were some coordination and overlap problems. The Obama administration subsequently formed an interagency task force to foster coordination and prevent these issues. Meanwhile, the State Department and other agencies developed a CVE program for export to help other countries cope with their domestic radicalization problems. There were even activities to counter the radicalization chat-rooms on line.

CYBERSECURITY

Another example of the impact of the increasing sophistication of technology emerged in the form of growing cyberterrorism and cyber hacking threats. As with other issues, these threats predate the 2008 elections that brought in the Obama administration. The Bush administration even had a National Security Council (NSC) coordinator for dealing with the problem, Richard Clarke, a veteran NSC counterterrorism expert. However, the scope stepped up in the past 8 years, with hackers breaking into various USG websites, banks, corporations, and even the Democratic National Committee during the 2016 elections, traced by U.S. intelligence agencies to Russia. Most hackers appeared to be criminals; however, culprits have been traced to China, Russia, and North Korea, among others.

Overseas, government websites had been attacked in a number of countries, for example, Estonia and Ukraine, which have been under pressure from Moscow, and in the Arab–Israeli dispute. Israeli press reports in April 2017 said some Israeli sites were hacked by Iranian operatives. The Obama administration and Israel meanwhile were reported in the press to have inserted a virus (named *stuxnet*) into Iran's centrifuges to slow down its nuclear weapons program. There also have been press reports that the

United States has managed to interfere electronically with some of North Korea's missile launches, causing them to fail after only short flights.

IMPENDING POLICY QUESTIONS FOR THE TRUMP ADMINISTRATION

The CT policy and program structure of the U.S. government is a result of evolution and innovation to respond to an evolving challenge. Over the years and from administration to administration, there has been a great deal of continuity in policies and programs, although new programs have been initiated and some modified. The overall trend has been to expand in scope, variety, and cost. At least one knowledgeable veteran expert notes:

> The United States is better organized and equipped to combat terrorism, but its citizens remain fearful. The United States' frightened, angry, and divided society remains the country's biggest vulnerability. Progress in degrading al-Qaeda's capabilities or dismantling the Islamic State is almost completely divorced from popular perceptions. Rather than appeal to traditional American values of courage, self-reliance, and sense of community, our current political system incentivizes the creation of fear.[9]

Others are less sanguine about the USG performance.

> But strategically, the U.S. faces the most parlous international security situation in terms of terrorism, at least since the immediate aftermath of the 9/11 attacks. According to the National Counterterrorism Center (NCTC), despite our ongoing efforts in Iraq and Syria over the past two years, ISIS has expanded geographically. The NCTC reported that in 2014, when the U.S.-backed campaign against ISIS began, the group had branches in seven countries. By 2015, they had branches in 13 countries, and by 2016, this number had increased again, now to 18. So clearly the Obama Administration's strategy hasn't stopped the spread of ISIS.[10]

However, various allies on the ground, with U.S. support, have rolled back ISIS from its early successes and greatly reduced the amount of territory it controls in Iraq and Syria; actions that also undercut the terrorist group's revenue (see Chapter 4).

A core question, therefore, that faces the new president and the new administration with respect to the terrorist threat is the one that all new administrations face—what to keep and what to change.

---

[9] Jenkins, Brian Michael. *Fifteen Years On, Where are We in the "War on Terror.* CTC Sentinel, September 7, 2016. https://www.ctc.usma.edu/posts/fifteen-years-on-where-are-we-in-the-war-on-terror (accessed April 27, 2017).

[10] Hoffman, Bruce. Comprehensive Terrorism Strategy Needed, *The Cipher Brief*, December 8, 2016. https://www.thecipherbrief.com/article/middle-east/comprehensive-terrorism-strategy-needed-1089 (accessed May 8, 2017).

This will require a strategic decision as to the nature and gravity of the threat. The two previous administrations differed, with Bush at first seeing it as existential and hence the GWOT. Obama, on the contrary, saw it as a serious problem to be integrated into and balanced with other U.S. foreign policy interests.

The first fundamental policy determination for the Trump administration, therefore, is to decide this question for themselves and then, if deemed necessary, to implement appropriate changes in USG policy and programs. Various remarks and comments by then-candidate Trump and his supporters indicated that they would take a new approach. This may not be in the form of a formal statement of policy but rather in the import and direction of presidential and administration decisions taken over time. For instance, candidate Trump's use of the phrase "radical Islamic terrorism" marked a departure from the Obama administration, which, along with most counterterrorism professionals, felt the appellation antagonized millions of peaceful Muslims. President Trump used it after his inauguration but his national security advisor, Lt. General H.R. McMaster (Figure 1.4), departing from President Trump's rhetoric, indicated he also shared the concerns of the other professionals.[11] Which term is "official" USG usage remained unclear as the administration reached its 6-month mark.

President John F. Kennedy once used a metaphor of an aircraft carrier to describe the U.S. government—a mammoth creature that only with difficulty and time can be moved into a very different direction. Its inertia is enormous. Every single subject in the president's in-box, such as counterterrorism, involves a broad range of government responsibilities and authorities all subject to the influence of inertia.

The issues involving U.S. government policy counterterrorism activities fall into three general areas, all involving hotly contested aspects of government policy and programs:

1. National security law involves important questions of constitutional law, including the extent of government surveillance and secrecy, and the perpetual question of balancing national security interests and citizen's rights, including privacy rights.
2. Domestic counterterrorism policy concerns law enforcement, including the use of sting operations, immigration, visa entry procedures, refugee policy, CVE, and domestic intelligence. Operationally, it involves the management and direction of the mammoth DHS, with its myriad of domestic agencies and the organizational and management problems that continue to beset

[11] Denver Post Editorial Board. Trump should listen to McMaster on "radical Islamic terrorism," March 3, 2017. http://www.denverpost.com/2017/03/03/trump-should-listen-to-mcmaster-on-radical-islamic-terrorism/ (accessed May 8, 2017).

FIGURE 1.4 U.S. Army Lt. General and the Trump administration National Security Advisor Herbert Raymond "H.R." McMaster. His immediate past military assignment was as director of the Army Capabilities Integration Center and deputy commanding general, Futures of the U.S. Army Training and Doctrine Command. (Courtesy of U.S. Department of Defense.)

this relatively new department. Immigration issues and screening of refugees, and even how many should be admitted, have become controversial issues during the 2016 election campaign and the early stages of the Trump administration, highlighted by the issuance of controversial executive orders.

3. External counterterrorism policy is the most obvious and the most media prominent. It involves first of all military policy and programs involving questions such as the deployment of U.S. troops, use of drones and air power, Special Forces, and the organization of U.S. military forces. One issue raised early in the Trump administration is to what extent the regional commands will have more authority to launch operations without referring back to the White House for clearance.[12] The issue

[12] Cooper, Helene Cooper and Eric Schmitt. Trump May Give the Pentagon More Authority to Conduct Raids, *New York Times*, March 2, 2017. https://www.nytimes.com/2017/03/02/world/middleeast/airstrikes-are-said-to-target-al-qaeda-in-yemen.html?_r=0

came up in April when the U.S. Air Force dropped "the Mother of All Bombs," the largest nonnuclear bomb in the U.S. arsenal, on an al-Qaeda terrorists' cave in Afghanistan.

Early on, the Trump administration continued the use of military operations in the Middle East. In early March, for example, in Yemen it launched 25 air strikes in two nights against al-Qaeda in the Arabian Peninsula.[13]

This followed a special operations attack in which a Navy Seal was killed, the first military casualty during the new administration. The Trump administration also continued the policy of targeting specific terrorist leaders, in early March using a drone to kill the second-in-command of al-Qaeda.[14] And in April 2016 it launched 59 Tomahawk cruise missiles against a Syrian Air Force based used by the plane that dropped a chemical bomb on Syrian civilians. These and other decisions indicate strongly that indeed there has been some loosening of controls over military operations.

Meanwhile, the Trump White House and its budget officials proposed deep cuts—about one-third—to the State Department budget and foreign assistance programs. The State Department, however, plays a major role in the development and improvement of international cooperation, which every past administration has viewed as essential to countering terrorism. The department also funds a number of programs to help train foreign officials to prevent and counter terrorist attacks as well as to identify terrorist and narcotics suspects from crossing international borders. The foreign assistance programs also help alleviate some of the economic and social problems that contribute to making persons vulnerable to the radicalization efforts by terrorist groups. A key issue to watch will be to what extent Congress goes along with the proposed budget cuts and which specific counterterrorism programs will continue. In the Initial Congressional stages of acting on the budget during 2017, key committees rejected the sweeping cuts.

An important element of diplomacy, as well as military policy and actions, is accurate and shared intelligence and the response to it. The IC is the primary source of information and analysis. Open sources and diplomatic exchanges are also important in this respect, and intelligence agencies incorporate them into their work. A key question is to what extent, in view of his past criticisms of the IC, President Trump and his

---

13 Martinez, Luis. More than 30 airstrikes in Yemen mark escalated fight against terror group, *ABC News*, March 3, 2017. http://abcnews.go.com/International/2nd-night-us-airstrikes-yemen-mark-escalated-fight/story?id=45882852 (accessed May 8, 2017).

14 Gordon, Michael R. and Eric Schmitt. Senior Qaeda Leader Is Killed in Drone Strike, *New York Times*, March 1, 2017. https://www.nytimes.com/2017/03/01/world/middleeast/drone-strike-kills-senior-al-qaeda-leader.html?_r=0 (accessed May 8, 2017).

immediate cadre will rely on the IC, especially in a time of crisis or situations where the information often is not black and white but ambiguous and grey.

Finally, all of these matters must be pursued within a strategic view, whether formally expressed or informally understood. Whether terrorism is seen as a serious or existential threat, the response has to be pursued within the context of overall U.S. foreign policy.

After the 9/11 attack, U.S. Vice President Dick Cheney appeared on *Meet the Press* and promised that the United States would use "any means at its disposal" to fight terrorism. The practical result of that statement was the GWOT, although he also said that this is not a war against Islam.[15] President Obama assumed office promising to change national security polices, including the executive power claims of his predecessor. The operational results of that perspective were changes in military and political involvement, but the jury is still out on the practical result. Evaluating the degree to which these two approaches succeeded and the resulting effect on the terrorism challenge is now in the hands of the historians.

It is now the turn of President Donald Trump. It is this history and the legacy CT structure that the Trump administration inherits, evaluates, and changes to meet its strategic view and objectives.

[15] Vice President Dick Cheney. *Meet the Press* Interview, September 16, 2001. https://www.youtube.com/watch?v=KQBsCIaxMuM (accessed May 8, 2017).

CHAPTER 2

Terrorism Definitions, Sanctions, and Legislations

Key components in the evolution of U.S. counterterrorism policies and responses, regardless of the administration, are the issues of defining terrorism and the body of sanctions and legislation that has developed over the past four decades. We therefore describe them before discussing the various administrations and time periods in more detail.

DEFINITIONS OF TERRORISM

One of the longest running legal issues in confronting terrorism is the effort to reach agreement on an internationally accepted definition of terrorism. Lawyers and various terrorism experts have chewed up countless hours of discussion and thousands of pages on the subject. The U.S. government alone uses several definitions of terrorism, reflecting the needs and perspectives of the various agencies, such as the State Department, Justice Department, and Department of Homeland Security. (See below.) Other governments, international organizations, and private and academic experts often use their own definitions, generally reflecting their needs and perspectives.

There are two basic reasons for the failure to reach a consensus. One is the difference among lawyers and practitioners in formulating the most precise wording that would work best with a nation's laws. The second is basically political, given that the legitimacy of the use of violence often lies in the eyes of the beholder and the view of the "cause" in question. As a result, scores of different definitions of terrorism have been used by various countries, UN and regional organization resolutions, and promoted by scholars. Efforts in the United Nations, led by India, to adopt a comprehensive convention against terrorism have been stalled for years over the difficulties in agreeing to a definition. The cliché that "one man's terrorism is another man's freedom fighter" encapsulates the difference some see between "politically acceptable" and "not politically acceptable" violence. One very notable example is that of Arab governments and their mainly third-world supporters who have repeatedly and successfully sought to define terrorism in terms intended to keep the terrorism label from tagging some Palestinian organizations as "terrorists."

One example of how this attitude works was the UN General Assembly resolution passed in December 1985[1] after a series of airline hijackings and a Mediterranean cruise liner hijacking that year. The resolution condemned "as criminal, all acts, methods and practices of terrorism wherever and by whoever committed, including those which jeopardize friendly relations among States and their security" but also said:

> Reaffirming also the inalienable right to self-determination and independence of all peoples under colonial and racist regimes and other forms of alien domination, and upholding the legitimacy of their struggle, in particular the struggle of national liberation movements ...

Most of the UN international treaties against terrorist acts do not define terrorism but consider such crimes as hijacking aircraft or taking hostages as crimes regardless of the motives, requiring nations to prosecute the culprits they arrest or extradite them to a country with a claim—for example, the nation whose citizens were killed or aircraft was hijacked. Somewhat of a breakthrough in defining terrorism came with the International Convention for the Suppression of the Financing of Terrorism,[2] adopted in 1999 as part of the effort to counter fundraising by al-Qaeda and other groups. It finally provided a working definition that was supported by the United Nations.

U.S. DEFINITIONS

The U.S. government has adopted several definitions of terrorism, to suit the focus and legal needs of the department involved:

The State Department definition[3] focuses on deliberate attacks targeted against noncombatants. This definition has been used for

---

1 UN General Assembly Resolution A/RES/40/61. December 9, 1985, United Nations General Assembly. http://www.un.org/documents/ga/res/40/a40r061.htm (accessed May 8, 2017).

2 United Nations. http://www.un.org/law/cod/finterr.htm (accessed May 8, 2017).

3 State Department Bureau of Counterterrorism and Countering Violent Extremism Counterterrorism. *Definitions included in the annual report*, Chapter 7. https://www.state.gov/j/ct/rls/crt/2015/257524.htm (accessed May 8, 2017).

years in the annual report on international terrorism that the State Department has made public since 1982. It is also shared by the National Counter Terrorism Center (NCTC), which prepares the statistical annex to the report. This definition of international terrorism included in Section 2656f(d) of Title 22 of the U.S. Code defines certain key terms:

1. the term "international terrorism" means terrorism involving citizens or the territory of more than one country;
2. the term "terrorism" means premeditated, politically motivated violence perpetrated against noncombatant targets by subnational groups or clandestine agents; and
3. the term "terrorist group" means any group practicing, or which has significant subgroups which practice, international terrorism.

The Justice Department, FBI, and Defense Department also have their own definitions of terrorism tailored to their focus.

The Justice Department uses a definition that relates more closely to its role in prosecuting violators of criminal laws and also emphasizes the use of violence to intimidate or coerce civilians and governments. It is similar to earlier versions except that it adds the reference to weapons of mass destruction.

In addition the Department of Justice utilizes another approach, utilizing laws that do not spell out definitions of terrorism per se but cite by reference previously enacted laws that criminalize certain actions, such as hijacking aircraft, hostage taking, etc. For example, the law enacted by the Antiterrorism and Effective Death Penalty Act of 1996, TITLE 18 U.S. Code § 2339A, makes it a criminal offense to provide material support for terrorist acts and cites a series of section numbers of existing predicate offenses.[4] A companion provision, Title 18, U.S. Code § 2339B, criminalizes material support to foreign terrorist organizations (FTOs) designated by the Secretary of State and cites the definition of terrorist activity as defined in Section 212 (a) (3) (B) of the Immigration and Nationality Act.[5]

---

[4] TITLE 18 US Code § 2339A and TITLE 18 US Code §2339B. https://www.law.cornell.edu/uscode/text/18/2339A and https://www.law.cornell.edu/uscode/text/18/2339B (accessed May 8, 2017).

[5] 8 U.S.C. § 1182: U.S. Code—Section 1182: Inadmissible aliens, Findlaw. http://codes.lp.findlaw.com/uscode/8/12/II/II/1182 (accessed May 8, 2017).

The FBI, the lead agency for investigating terrorism against U.S. targets, defines terrorism as:

> The unlawful use of force or violence against persons or property to intimidate or coerce a Government, the civilian population, or any segment thereof, in furtherance of political or social objectives.[6]

The Department of Homeland Security's definition,[7] reflecting its role in protecting the national infrastructure, says:

> The term "terrorism" means any activity that:
>
> 1. involves an act that—
>   a. is dangerous to human life or potentially destructive *of critical infrastructure or key resources* [emphasis added].

The Department of Defense Dictionary of Military Terms[8] defines terrorism as:

> The unlawful use of violence or threat of violence to instill fear and coerce governments or societies. Terrorism is often motivated by religious, political, or other ideological beliefs and committed in the pursuit of goals that are usually political.

The Defense Department also provides definitions for various programs involved in countering terrorism, or antiterrorism, which are defensive measures taken to reduce vulnerability to terrorist acts, counterterrorism (offensive measures taken to prevent [preempt], deter [disrupt], and respond to terrorism), terrorism consequence management (preparation for and response to the consequences of a terrorist incident/event), and intelligence support (collection and dissemination of terrorism-related information).[9]

To sum up, if there is any common theme in the many terrorism definitions, it is the identification of violence or the threat of violence that is deliberately directed against noncombatants for political or ideological reasons rather than robbery or other motives.

---

6 FBI Report Terrorism 2002–2005. https://www.fbi.gov/file-repository/stats-services-publications-terrorism-2002-2005-terror02_05.pdf/view (accessed May 8, 2017).

7 Homeland Security Act of 2002 Pub. L. No. 107–296—November 25, 2002 116 Stat. 2135 Sec 2 (15). http://www.dhs.gov/xlibrary/assets/hr_5005_enr.pdf (accessed May 8, 2017).

8 Department of Defense Dictionary of Military and Associated Terms. November 8, 2010 (As Amended Through March, 2017). http://www.dtic.mil/doctrine/new_pubs/jp1_02.pdf (accessed May 8, 2017).

9 Department of Defense Directive number 2000.12. March 1, 2012. Incorporating Change 2, Effective November 15, 2016. Enclosure 2, Page 21. http://www.dtic.mil/whs/directives/corres/pdf/200012p.pdf (accessed May 8, 2017).

Despite the difficulties in obtaining consensus, there has been considerable progress in the recent treaties and UN resolutions directed against terrorism fund-raising in enforcing the point that crashing airplanes into buildings or bombing a market place is a crime regardless of the motivation. Nevertheless a former State Department lawyer, Geoff Levitt, counted about 100 definitions in an article published 25 years ago entitled, "Is Terrorism Worth Defining?"[10] (Some scholars now count another 20 or so.)

The title reflected the attitude of most of the State Department's officials involved with terrorism issues during that period of discussions in the United Nations with defining terrorism. These officials generally felt that it was fruitless to spend many hours in endless discussions of definitions when such acts as hijacking or blowing up airplanes were crimes in themselves subject to criminal punishment, regardless of the motivation.[11]

Additional Resources

- The Rand Corporation's Articles on The Future of ISIL's Finances and other Terrorism financing issues, March 29, 2017. https://www.rand.org/topics/terrorism-financing.html
- Department of Defense. Dictionary of Military and Associated Terms. November 8, 2010 (As Amended Through January 31, 2011 1-02 p. 368) http://www.dtic.mil/doctrine/new_pubs/jp1_02.pdf
- Crenshaw, Martha. 2011. *Explaining Terrorism: Causes, Processes, and Consequences*. London and New York: Routledge.
- Ganor, Boaz. 2008. *The Counter-Terrorism Puzzle*. pp. 8 & 17. New Brunswick, N.J. and London, U.K. Transaction Publishers.
- Hoffman, Bruce. 2006. *Inside Terrorism*, revised and expanded. Columbia University Press. New York.
- Laquer, Walter. 1977. *Terrorism*. London, Boston, Toronto. Little, Brown and Company.
- Laquer, Walter. 1999. *The New Terrorism*. Oxford University Press. New York, Oxford
- Levitt, Matt. *How Do ISIS Terrorists Finance Their Attacks?* The Washington Institute Policy, November 18, 2015. http://www.washingtoninstitute.org/policy-analysis/view/how-do-isis-terrorists-finance-their-attacks

---

[10] Levitt, G. 1986. *Is "Terrorism" Worth Defining*? Ohio Northern University Law Review 1986. http://heinonline.org/HOL/LandingPage?handle=hein.journals/onulr13&div=15&id=&page= (accessed May 8, 2017).

[11] Observations by the authors, who served in the State Department's counterterrorism office at the time.

- McCormack, Wayne. 2008. *Legal Responses to Terrorism.* Newark, NJ, San Francisco, Ca. Matthew Bender & Company, LexisNexis.
- Pillar, Paul. 2001. *Terrorism and U.S. Foreign Policy.* Washington, D.C. The Brookings Institution.

SANCTIONS

Economic and other sanctions are an important tool in countering terrorism as well as in dealing with other issues such as nonproliferation and aggressive actions by countries attacking their neighbors. These sanctions imposed on Iran and Russia were not imposed as part of the antiterrorism legislative framework, but they have similar goals: to use economic pressures and/or travel restrictions to persuade the targeted governments to change their unacceptable behavior.

The use of sanctions has evolved considerably over the years. In the late 1970s, when Congress began enacting specific counterterrorism laws, it focused on imposing sanctions against countries that supported terrorism. Thus—in the wake of the terrorist killings of Israeli athletes at the 1972 Olympics in Munich and other terrorism overseas—one early law, enacted in 1976, cut off foreign assistance to "any government which aids or abets, by providing sanctuary from prosecution, any group or individual which has committed an act of international terrorism."[12]

Three years later, Congress enacted a broader major counterterrorism law that is still a pillar of sanctions legislation after more than four decades: the so-called terrorism list legislation. The Export Administration Act of 1979, Section 6 (j),[13] required the executive branch to notify Congress 30 days in advance before issuing export licenses for dual-use goods and services (that can be used for military or terrorism purposes as well as civilian use) to countries that the Secretary of State has determined have "repeatedly provided support for acts of international terrorism."

The legislation was initiated after learning that mid-level Commerce and State Department officials approved export licenses to Libya for 400 heavy duty trucks used for tank transports and six C-130 "civilian version" cargo planes for Syria. Both countries were involved in

[12] International Security Assistance and Arms Export Control Act, Section 303, 1976. http://www.opbw.org/nat_imp/leg_reg/US/arms_exp_cont_act.pdf (accessed May 8, 2017).

[13] Export Administration Act of 1979, Section 6 (j). Pub L. No. 96-72 (codified in 50 USC App. § 2405. http://www.law.cornell.edu/uscode/html/uscode50a/usc_sec_50a_00002405----000-.html (accessed May 8, 2017).

terrorism activities. Therefore, they contended, such sales should first be approved at high levels in the executive branch, followed by a notification to Congress with enough time for members to take action to block the sales if necessary.

Congress later added "piggy back" sanctions by amending the Foreign Assistance Act to cut off foreign or military assistance, and the Internal Revenue Code to deny foreign tax credits for income earned in terrorist list countries. Other provisions prohibited financial transactions; a measure intended to discourage business dealings as well as travel. The amendments also required the United States to oppose international banking institution loans to the terrorist countries.

In 1982, the Reagan administration touched off a controversy with Congress by removing Iraq from the list of designated terrorist supporting countries without consulting Congress or even providing advance notice. The move was widely regarded as a "tilt" toward Iraq in the Iraq–Iran war. The Reagan administration regarded Iran as the greater danger to U.S. interests and Tehran was attacking oil tankers in the Gulf. (Iraq was put back on the list in 1990 following its invasion of Kuwait. It was removed again in 2004 after the fall of Saddam Hussein and the installation of a new Iraqi government.)

Congress reacted in 1989, after the Iran–Contra scandal broke out. Oliver North, a National Security Council (NSC) staff member on detail from the Marine Corps, was charged with violating U.S. laws by selling TOW antitank missiles to Iran in attempt to free hostages held by Iranian-backed terrorists in Lebanon and using the proceeds to finance the Contras in Nicaragua. (He was convicted of three counts but later pardoned by President Reagan.) In reaction, Congress passed the Anti-Terrorism and Arms Export Amendments Act of 1989.[14] That law tightened up arms export licensing requirements. The law also included procedures that require that the president certify to Congress that the government of the country in question has not supported acts of international terrorism for the previous 6 months and has given assurances that it will not do so in the future, before he can remove a country from the terrorism list. Congress has 45 days to react, for example, by passing a resolution or amendment or just jawboning the executive branch, before the removal takes effect.

The Congressional committee report language for that legislation also described the criteria the Secretary of State should use in formally designating a government as a state sponsor of terrorism. The criteria included but were not limited to whether the country provides to terrorists sanctuary from extradition or prosecution;

[14] Pub. L. No. 101-222 (codified in 22 U.S.C.A. §§ 1732, 2364, 3371, 2753, 2776, 2778 and 2780, and 50 U.S.C.A. § 2405).

arms, explosives, and other lethal substances; logistical support; safe houses or headquarters; planning, training, or other assistance for terrorist activities; direct or indirect financial backing; and diplomatic facilities such as support or documentation intended to aid or abet terrorist activities.[15]

Countries currently on the list are Iran, Syria, and Sudan.

Another provision imposes sanctions on countries that are deemed to be "not fully cooperating" with U.S. counterterrorism efforts but whose activities are not of the nature to be placed on the terrorism list. The provision prohibits the sale or approval of defense articles or services to countries that the president has determined do not fully cooperate with the United States.[16]

Syrian officials involved in chemical warfare were targeted for sanctions in both the last days of the Obama administration and the first months of the Trump administration.

On April 14, 2017, the Trump administration's Treasury Department announced sanctions[17] against 271 employees of Syria's Scientific Studies and Research Center (SSRC). The action was triggered by the US Government's conclusion that the Assad regime had dropped a chemical weapon, reported to be sarin, on the town of Khan Sheikhoun on April 4, 2017. The Treasury said the 271 SSRC employees had worked in support of the institute's chemical warfare program since 2012. This follows the sanctions imposed by the Obama administration on January 12, 2017, against eighteen senior government officials and five branches of the Syrian military. A UN agency had determined that the Syrian government was responsible for three chlorine attacks in 2014 and 2015. The sanctions freeze any assets that these persons or military branches might have or indirectly control in the United States and prohibit U.S. persons from dealing with them.

Congress and the executive branch also took actions against nonstate actors. The Clinton administration drafted and obtained passage of legislation that made it a criminal offense to provide funds or other forms of material support to FTOs. (See Counterterrorism Legislation section below.) The White House had issued a series of executive orders

---

[15] H. Rep. No. 101–296, at 7; *also see* S. Rep. No. 101–173, at 5.

[16] Section 330 of the Antiterrorism and Effective Death Penalty Act of 1996, Pub. L. No. 104–132, 110 Stat. 1214, amending Chapter 3 of the Arms Export Control Act (22 U.S.C. 2771 et seq.). https://www.gpo.gov/fdsys/pkg/PLAW-104publ132/html/PLAW-104publ132.htm (accessed May 8, 2017).

[17] Treasury Department. *Treasury Sanctions 271 Syrian Scientific Studies and Research Center Staff in Response to Sarin Attack on Khan Sheikhoun*, Treasury Department press release. April 24, 2017. https://www.treasury.gov/press-center/press-releases/Pages/sm0056.aspx (accessed May 8, 2017).

against various entities and individuals who were involved in materially supporting or personally engaging in terrorist activities.

Sanctions Executive Orders

Executive orders are also an important tool for imposing sanctions. The following description of the complicated and little known process is provided by J. Robert McBrien, former associate director of the Treasury Department's Office of Foreign Assets Control (OFAC).

Comprehensive Sanctions. In January 1995, a new sanctions era began in the countermeasures against transnational terrorism. On January 21, 1995, President Clinton issued an executive order imposing comprehensive economic/financial sanctions against a dozen foreign terrorist groups whose activities were threatening the Middle East peace process.[18] That action, announced in the president's State of the Union address, introduced the use of comprehensive economic–financial sanctions against nonstate actors whose activities were found to pose an unusual and extraordinary threat to the national security, foreign policy, or economy of the United States. It also helped move the Treasury Department's OFAC into the central role in formulating sanctions responses to foreign threats to our national security and foreign policy.

Executive Order (EO) 12947. Between January 1995 and September 11, 2001, sanctions were imposed against 37 Specially Designated Terrorists (SDTs), including the original dozen organizations identified by the EO, those individuals and one group added in 1998 after the bombings of the U.S. embassies in Dar es Salaam, Tanzania, and Nairobi, Kenya (i.e. al-Qaeda, Usama bin Laden, and two others), and those other fronts, representatives, and agents identified by OFAC.

EO 13224. Following the terrorist attack on 9/11, a new counterterrorism executive order arose from the precedent established by the 1995 EO. That new executive order, EO 13224,[19] was a foundational authority for the financial sanctions measures in the Global War on Terrorism, and it remains basic to continuing to use financial measures against

---

[18] Treasury Department. *E.O. 12947, Prohibiting Transactions with Terrorists Who Threaten to Disrupt the Middle East Peace Process, Jan. 23, 1995, 60 Fed. Reg. 5079.* www.treasury.gov/resource-center/sanctions/ Documents/12947.pdf (accessed May 8, 2017).

[19] Treasury Department. *E.O. 13224, Blocking Property and Prohibiting Transactions with Persons Who Commit, Threaten to Commit, or Support Terrorism,* Sept. 23, 2001, 66 Fed. Reg. 49079. http://news.findlaw.com/cnn/docs/dotreas/terroristsanctions110701.html (accessed May 8, 2017).

ISIS, the mutated forms of al-Qaeda, and their networks of fronts and facilitators.

The concept embedded in those two U.S. executive orders of economic sanctions imposed through counterterrorism designations was the seed for the UN counterterrorism sanctions programs that followed EO 13224.[20]

Counterterrorism Designations Numbers. To distinguish between counterterrorism sanctions targets designated under the two EOs, the original descriptor, SDT, was succeeded by *Specially Designated Global Terrorist* (SDGT).[21] To date under EO 13224, there are 1,084 individuals, entities, and aircraft designated as SDGTs. More than 467 of those SDGT designations occurred during the administration of President George W. Bush ("Bush 43"), and they are broken down into more than 290 individuals and 177 entities.[22]

Designations under EO 13224 continued to be used robustly throughout the administration of President Obama, reaching a total of 597 SDGTs. SDGTs designated during the Obama administration include as 378 individuals, 118 entities, and 101 aircraft.

During the first 3 months since President Trump's inauguration, 20 SDGT designations have occurred, of which sixteen are individuals and four are entities. No inference about counterterrorism sanctions policies and process under the Obama and Trump administrations should be drawn from this data since SDGT designations are typically developed over several months or longer before the designation occurs.

---

[20] UN Security Council Resolution 1373 (2001) adopted on September 28, 2001. http://www.un.org/en/sc/ctc/specialmeetings/2012/docs/United%20Nations%20Security%20Council%20Resolution%201373%20(2001).pdf (accessed May 8, 2017).

[21] OFAC is the lead office responsible for implementing economic and trade sanctions based on U.S. foreign policy and national security goals. Imposition of sanctions depends heavily on the use of OFAC's Specially Designated Nationals List (SDN list) of which SDTs and SDGTs are subsets. The SDN list further defines and identifies the individuals and entities that make up the sanctioned foreign government or sanctioned nonstate entity's network. In most programs, this includes entities and individuals that are controlled by the principal targets of the sanctions, act for them, or provide services or support. The SDN list is the tool through which front companies, middlemen, facilitators, and financiers are identified and exposed to governmental authorities worldwide, the global financial and commercial world, and the public at large. The SDGT list includes all but one of the 12 terrorist groups named in the Annex to the 1995 E.O. on counter-terrorism. The SDGT list also includes the 61 Foreign Terrorist Organizations (FTOs) identified by the Secretary of State under authority of the Anti-Terrorism and Effective Death Penalty Act of 1996 (AEDPA).

[22] The number of designations that occurred during the Bush-43 years is greater than the specific numbers noted in this discussion since several of them have been removed under the standards of the designation program.

Further information on the history of comprehensive counterterrorism sanctions may be found in *Treasury's War: The Unleashing of a New Era of Financial Warfare*,[23] and in Chapter 12 of *Impunity: Countering Illicit Power in War and Transition*.[24]

COUNTERTERRORISM LEGISLATION

Just as the terrorism threat has evolved considerably since the Nixon administration, the web of U.S. laws and international conventions have grown. The pre-9/11 U.S. legal measures against terrorists and their supporters had evolved considerably from the 1970s, falling into three broad categories. The initial focus was on state sponsors of international terrorism—using a variety of sanctions—and international counterterrorism treaties and their implementing legislation. Congress also enacted legislation that allows private U.S. citizens to file civil suits against foreign governments that support international terrorism and terrorist groups. Then in the 1990s, as terrorist groups began reducing their dependency on sympathetic governments, the executive branch and Congress began focusing on legislation aimed against nonstate actors, especially at their funding. After 9/11 the focus shifted to making the U.S. government more effective in its organization and enforcement of laws, even creating a new agency, the Department of Homeland Security.

Early in the emergence of modern terrorism threats in the 1970s, most of the terrorist attacks affecting Americans and American interests were overseas, conducted by secular terrorist groups. They were usually supported by various rogue states such as Syria and Libya. As described earlier in the sanctions section of this chapter, this prompted the development of U.S. economic sanctions legislation against state sponsors of terrorism. This was accompanied by international treaties and implementing legislation against various forms of terrorism, such as attacks on aircraft and commercial shipping.

In the early 90s, the U.S. government realized that some major terrorist groups were becoming more independent from state sponsors, developing their own means of funding. This prompted the development of laws and regulations and programs aimed at stemming the flow of money and other forms of material support to terrorists from nonstate actors, so-called charities, and even individuals.

---

[23] Zarate, Juan C. *Treasury's War: The Unleashing of a New Era of Financial Warfare*, New York: Public Affairs, 2013.

[24] McBrien, Robert. *Financial Tools and Sanctions: Following the Money and the Joumaa Web*, *IMPUNITY: Countering Illicit Power in War and Transition*, ed. Michelle Hughes and Michael Miklaucic, Washington, DC: National Defense University Press, 2015.

Major terrorist attacks overseas, especially in the Middle East, gave impetus to this effort along with the 1993 World Trade Center attacks and the 1995 Oklahoma City federal building bombing. Following 9/11, the Bush administration's War on Terror and invasions of Afghanistan and Iraq forced the executive branch and Congress to grapple with constitutional, moral, and effective means of prosecuting and detaining relatively large numbers of suspected terrorists and combatants captured in foreign territory. At the same time, the United States, working with the United Nations and its own training programs, tried to strengthen foreign governments' counterterrorism efforts, including their ability to stem financial contributions to suspect terrorist groups.

Many forms of terrorist attacks, such as murder and assault, were already covered in the criminal code. However, the newer legislation, with enhanced penalties for terrorist acts and the changing nature of terrorism and legislative countermeasures, resulted in legislation that both authorizes a variety of domestic and overseas counterterrorism measures and tries to balance them with civil liberties concerns.

In strengthening the rule of law against terrorists, the United States promoted international counterterrorism treaties covering terrorist attacks such as bombings of buildings and attacks on civilian shipping.

The first phase was the development of international treaties against such crimes as hijacking aircraft and taking hostages. By 1971, there were four international conventions dealing with the security of civil aircraft, and in the 1970s three international conventions against taking hostages were enacted.

After terrorist acts against airports and the hijacking of the Italian cruise ship *Achille Lauro* in the 1980s, international conventions were negotiated to cover attacks on civilian airports, passenger vessels, and offshore platforms. In the 1990s, the United States and other countries, working together at the United Nations, successfully drafted international conventions against terrorist bombings and against funding terrorism.

These 13 counterterrorism conventions usually required implementing legislation. For example, the Anti-Hijacking Act of 1974 prohibits the hijacking of aircraft in the jurisdiction of the United States and provides jurisdiction over offenders who hijack other civil aircraft in other countries if those hijackers are subsequently found in the United States. Often, the necessary implementing legislation is tacked on as a provision of a broader vehicle bill.

Apart from the Convention for the Suppression of the Financing of Terrorism (1999),[25] the conventions do not define terrorism but consider actions such as blowing up an aircraft, a criminal act and an extraditable

[25] International Convention for the Suppression of the Financing of Terrorism. http://www.un.org/law/cod/finterr.htm (accessed May 8, 2017).

offense regardless of motivation. This approach was reflected in numerous statements by high-level U.S. government officials, including by President Reagan that "there is no political or any other justification for terrorist acts and those who commit them should be brought to justice."[26] It also reflected the realities of the difficulties in achieving an international consensus on a definition of terrorism.

The Long-Arm Statute

In October 1985, a Palestinian terrorist group, the Palestine Liberation Front, hijacked the Italian cruise liner *Achille Lauro* in an effort to enter Israel during a port call. During the hijacking, the terrorists threw overboard Leon Klinghoffer, an elderly American passenger who was in a wheelchair. Muhammad Abu Abbas, the leader of the group, was later arrested after the ship finally docked in Alexandria, Egypt. Italian authorities forced his release when the U.S. military plane transporting him to the United States landed at an Italian air base for refueling. Abu Abbas fled to Yugoslavia, then took refuge in Iraq, was eventually recaptured by U.S. forces after the 2003 invasion, and died of a heart attack while in custody.

In short, the terrorists killed an American overseas and were released by one country to take refuge in another. This prompted the Justice Department to draft a so-called "long-arm statute", making it a federal crime to murder, attempt to murder, conspire to murder, or cause serious bodily injury to Americans if the Attorney General determined that the violence was terrorism, rather than an ordinary nonpolitical criminal offense.

This "long-arm statute" legislation, enacted as Section 1202 of the Omnibus Diplomatic Security and Antiterrorism Act of 1986,[27] makes the terrorist murder of an American citizen overseas a crime punishable in U.S. courts, even if the attack did not take place on American territory, such as an embassy.

In singling out terrorist crimes from ordinary crimes, the legislation defined the criteria to be used by the attorney general as action intended to coerce, intimidate, or retaliate against a government or civilian population.

---

[26] Reagan, Ronald. *Radio Address to the Nation on Terrorism*. May 31, 1986. http://www.presidency.ucsb.edu/ws/index.php?pid=37376#ixzz1MpziZAr6 (accessed May 8, 2017).

[27] P.L. 99-399, later modified as 18. U.S.C. § 2332. U.S. Department of Justice. *Omnibus Diplomatic Security and Anti-Terrorism Act of 1986*. http://www.usdoj.gov/usao/eousa/foia_reading_room/usam/title9/crm00012.htm (accessed May 8, 2017).

Following enactment of the "long-arm statute", the Justice Department greatly expanded its assignment of legal attachés (LEGATs) abroad. The LEGATs facilitated U.S. investigations and in some cases also helped host countries pursue investigations and improve their own laws. Currently, the FBI has sixty-four legal attaché offices—commonly known as "LEGATs"—and more than a dozen smaller suboffices in key cities around the globe.[28]

Nonstate Actors

In the mid-1990s, the legislative focus shifted to countering terrorist groups that were increasingly independent from states that sponsored terrorism. Some secular terrorist groups, such as the Abu Nidal Organization, began using front companies and organizations to obtain and transfer funds rather than depend upon state sponsors. Extremist fundamentalist groups such as al-Qaeda and Hamas were emerging and raising large sums of money through so-called charities, used as front organizations. State Department Counterterrorism Office officials and lawyers in the State Department and Justice Department began drafting comprehensive legislation to take the offensive against terrorists, to curb the ability of terrorists to raise funds, not only for the weapons and actual operations but also for support networks, sometimes in the form of charitable activities, that they used to recruit sympathizers and even operatives.[29]

A major impetus was a series of major terrorist attacks in the Middle East in 1994, including an attack on a mosque in Hebron by an American-Israeli settler and bombings by Palestinians of Israeli buses and other targets that same year. After numerous hearings and meetings and some Congressional revisions, Congress passed the legislation and President Clinton signed in April 1996 what became labeled the Antiterrorism and Effective Death Penalty Act (AEDPA) of 1996.[30] The counterterrorism

---

[28] FBI website. https://www.fbi.gov/contact-us/legal-attache-offices (accessed May 8, 2017).

[29] Coauthor Michael Kraft was the State Department Counterterrorism Office's senior advisor for legislative affairs at the time and its lead official in drafting, negotiating, and obtaining passage of the AEDPA legislation.

For additional legislative history see: Alexander, Yonah and Michael Kraft. 2008, eds. *The Evolution of U.S. Counterterrorism Policy*, Westport, Conn/London, England: Praeger Security International. Volume 1, pp. 17–26.

[30] P.L. No. 104-132,110 State. 1214. https://www.gpo.gov/fdsys/pkg/PLAW-104publ132/content-detail.html (accessed May 8, 2017).

Also see Doyle, Charles. *The Antiterrorism and Effective Death Penalty Act of 1996: A Summary*. Congressional Research Service Issue Brief, June 3, 1996. http://www.4uth.gov.ua/usa/english/laws/majorlaw/96-499.htm (accessed May 8, 2017).

sections of the bill include two material support provisions, key elements in the efforts to reduce the terrorists' capabilities.

- The first provision, 18 U.S. Code § 2339A, strengthens an earlier version in the 1994 Crime Bill and makes it a criminal offense for U.S. citizens, residents, or organizations to knowingly provide material support—such as weapons, safe houses, training, communications equipment, and financial services—for specific acts, whether perpetrated by individuals or previously unknown groups.
- The second provision, 18 U.S. Code § 2339B, makes it a criminal offense for U.S. citizens, residents, or organizations to knowingly provide funds and other material forms of support, including training, to groups formally designated as an FTO by the Secretary of State with the concurrence of the Attorney General and Secretary of the Treasury. The original group of 30 designated in October 1997 had expanded to 61 as of September 2017. A dozen groups meanwhile had been removed from the FTO designation list, which changes as groups are added or removed—sometimes because they faded away—based upon analysis by State Department and intelligence officials.[31]

The Mujahedin-e Khalq Organization

The most controversial group was the Mujahedin-e Khalq Organization (MEK), which opposed the Iranian government and was placed on the original list of groups designated in October 1997. Although the U.S. government and the Iranian regime were at odds following the takeover of the U.S. embassy by militants, including MEK members, the group was later designated, after the departure of the Shah, as an FTO because of its attacks on Iranian civilians, including mortar attacks on courthouses.

As part of their lobbying campaign, MEK supporters claimed the designation was made as a gesture to the Iranian government; this assertion was based on a *Los Angeles Times* report. One of this book's authors, Michael Kraft, was involved in the State Department's preparation of the documentation for the MEK designation and attests from personal knowledge that the MEK's designation was prepared "from the bottom up" from within the department. The MEK was on the list of 30 organizations that the counterterrorism office prepared and was approved by the Secretary of State and sent to the NSC. The *LA Times*

[31] State Department Bureau of Counterterrorism and Countering Violent Extremism. *Foreign Terrorist Organizations*. https://www.state.gov/j/ct/rls/other/des/123085.htm. For additional information on related designation lists, see https://www.state.gov/j/ct/list/index.htm (accessed May 8, 2017).

reporters involved in the story two decades ago said they did not remember the source.

Over the years, MEK supporters mounted an intensive lobbying campaign to get the State Department to delist the organization and some prominent political figures and former government officials reportedly received payments for making speeches on behalf of the MEK. After the fall of the Iraqi regime, which supported the MEK, its members were confined to camps near the Iraqi border. The State Department took the MEK off the terrorist organization list in September 2012 after MEK members were disarmed and its leaders pledged to not commit future acts of terrorism.

For more background, see the Council of Foreign Affairs backgrounder, Mujahedin-e Khlaq, July 28, 2014 http://www.cfr.org/iran/mujahadeen-e-khalq-mek/p9158, accessed May 8, 2017.

The material support provisions have been a major tool in the fight against terrorists. The material support provisions do not define terrorism directly but instead cite as offenses definitions in other U.S. laws, including the Crime Act of 1994 and legislation implementing various international conventions regarding terrorism, as well as U.S. laws concerning attacks on the president, cabinet officials, members of Congress, and government property. The provision also cites the definitions used in the Immigration and Nationality Act and the Foreign Relations Authorization Act for Fiscal Year 1988 and 1989 that mandated the State Department's annual global terrorism report to Congress.[32] The Supreme Court upheld the material support bans in a June 21, 2010, decision, supporting the constitutionality of the legislation as well as the foreign policy authority of the Secretary of State to designate terrorist states.

The material support provisions have been an effective tool in prosecuting persons who have not personally engaged in actual or attempted attacks but have provided support for those individuals or groups that do. According to a Justice Department chart, 257 persons have been convicted under one or more of the material support provisions between 9/11 and December 31, 2016.[33]

---

[32] State Department Bureau of Counterterrorism and Countering Violent Extremism Counterterrorism. *Definitions included in the annual report*, chapter 7. https://www.state.gov/j/ct/rls/crt/2015/257524.htm (accessed May 8, 2017). State Department Bureau of Counterterrorism, legislative requirements and definitions for the annual report on international terrorism to Congress. http://www.state.gov/g/ct/rls/crt/2010/170265.htm (accessed May 8, 2017).

[33] The chart, obtained by the authors after repeated requests, includes only those actually convicted and whose convictions were unsealed. It does not include persons whose convictions were still under seal or who were charged but had not been convicted yet by trial or guilty plea. The list of convictions, under a variety of statutes in addition to material support provisions, runs 24 pages.

These material support provisions have been used in cases involving previously unknown and undesignated terrorist groups as well as designated FTOs.

Some of the designated FTOs such as Hamas and those in Algeria and Egypt, attracted supporters by providing schools and medical facilities or assisting the families of active members or suicide bombers. Although these are not terrorist activities per se, Congress noted in Sec. 301(7) of the AEDPA act ("Findings and Purpose") that "Foreign organizations that engage in terrorist activity are so tainted by their criminal conduct that any contributions to such an organization facilitates that conduct." Also, even a contribution intended for legitimate charitable purposes would free up funds for terrorist activities, such as buying weapons.

In response to earlier lower court decisions questioning the precision of the original language, Congress enacted Section 6603 of the Intelligence Reform and Terrorism Reform Act of 2004,[34] which clarified the meaning of *training* to include military-type training from or on behalf of a terrorist organization and training to impart specific skills as opposed to general knowledge such as lobbying Congress.

AEDPA also authorizes the Treasury Department to seize assets in the United States of a designated FTO. This provision complements executive orders issued under the authority of the International Emergency Economics Powers Act (IEEPA); such orders have been used increasingly since 9/11.

Additionally, the FTO provision tightens the Immigration Nationality Act as regards restrictions on visas for persons involved with terrorist groups. Under AEDPA, mere membership in a designated FTO was added to the grounds for denying a visa as well as previous restrictions against leaders or representatives of a terrorist group.

Civil Suits

In an expansion of U.S. law, sought by families of victims of Pan Am Flight 103 (Figure 2.1), the *Achille Lauro* hijacking, and other attacks on Americans, Congress amended the Foreign Sovereign Immunities Act to allow U.S. nationals to bring civil actions against terrorist actions

[34] Pub. L. No. 108-458 118 Stat. 3638 P.L. 108–458. Enacted Dec. 17, 2004. http://www.nctc.gov/docs/pl108_458.pdf (accessed May 8, 2017). Doyle, Charles. *Material Support of Terrorists and Foreign Terrorist Organizations*: Sunset Amendments in Brief. P.L. 108-458 118 Stat. 3638 P.L. 108–458 Congressional Research Service Issue Brief. March 17, 2006. https://fas.org/sgp/crs/terror/RS22222.pdf (accessed May 8, 2017).

FIGURE 2.1 The Pam Am Flight 103 bombing. On December 21, 1988, Pan Am Flight 103 took off from London's Heathrow Airport bound for New York City. The flight exploded enroute approximately 30,000 feet up, killing all 259 passengers and crew and 11 people on the ground. Debris rained down over 845 square miles across Scotland. Thousands of pieces of evidence were recovered; more than 10,000 individuals were interviewed. Ultimately, forensic experts from the FBI, CIA, and other agencies determined that one of the fragments found on the ground, no bigger than a thumbnail, came from the circuit board of a radio/cassette player. That tiny piece of evidence helped establish that the bomb had been placed inside that radio and tape deck in a piece of luggage. Another small fragment, found embedded in a piece of shirt, helped identify the type of timer. On January 31, 2001, Abdel Basset Ali Al-Megrahi was found guilty of the crime. The codefendant was found not guilty and released. (Courtesy of U.S. Federal Bureau of Investigation.)

supported by governments on the Secretary of State's terrorism list.[35] After 9/11, the civil suit approach was broadened to permit civil suits to also be brought against individuals, foreign nongovernmental organizations, and domestic organizations, both to provide a deterrent as well as compensate the families of victims. It was argued that those who conducted or supported terrorist operations should suffer financial losses

[35] 28 U.S.C. §1605(a) (7). https://www.law.cornell.edu/uscode/text/28/1605A (accessed May 8, 2017).

as well as running the risk of prosecution in the criminal courts system, and this might deter future terrorist actions. Another was the belief that the families of victims should receive compensation. U.S. courts have awarded large damages in some instances, although collection has been very difficult.[36]

Weapons of Mass Destruction

A growing concern over weapons of mass destruction (WMD) led to the Biological Weapons and Anti-Terrorism Act of 1989.[37] In 1992, the Weapons of Mass Destruction Act called on the Defense and Energy Departments to maintain and improve their ability to monitor and respond to the proliferation of WMD and missile delivery systems. Although the nonproliferation effort originally was directed against nations, it has since also been directed against nonstate groups, such as al-Qaeda, that reportedly are seeking to obtain or develop chemical and biological agents.

Progressively tighter legislation has strengthened controls over chemical, biological, and radioactive (CBR) agents or has authorized sanctions against countries that use CBR weapons in violation of international law and against companies that aid in the proliferation of such weapons. For example, provisions in Title V of AEDPA refine and expand the definition of possession of CBR agents to cover unlawful possession of a substance whether or not the material is in the form of a delivery system, such as a bomb or missile.

Two years earlier, Congress enacted the Public Health and Bioterrorism Preparedness and Response Act to improve the ability of the United States to prevent and respond to bioterrorism and other public health emergencies. This was followed by the Project Bioshield Act of 2004,[38] which authorized the purchase of vaccines that would be used in the event of a bioterrorist attack.

---

[36] Elsea, Jennifer K. *Suits against Terrorist States By Victims of Terrorism. Congressional Research Service*, August 8, 2008. http://www.fas.org/sgp/crs/terror/RL31258.pdf (accessed May 8, 2017).

Also see Murphy, John F. Litigation against Terrorists and the Sponsors of Terrorism: Problems and Prospects. *The University of Texas School of Law, The Review of Litigation*, 2008. https://litigation-essentials.lexisnexis.com/webcd/app?action=DocumentDisplay&crawlid=1&srctype=smi&srcid=3B15&doctype=cite&docid=28+Rev.+Litig.+315&key=df301961ed7759b82528fe845ab332a2 (accessed May 8, 2017).

[37] H.R. 237—101st Congress: Biological Weapons Anti-Terrorism Act of 1989."1989. June 28, 2017, https://www.congress.gov/bill/101st-congress/house-bill/237 (accessed May 8, 2017).

[38] Project Bioshield Act of 2004. Enacted July 21, 2004. http://frwebgate.access.gpo.gov/cgi-bin/getdoc.cgi?dbname=108_cong_public_laws&docid=f:publ276.108 (accessed May 8, 2017).

After 9/11—USA PATRIOT ACT

Shortly after the September 11 attack, Congress enacted the USA PATRIOT Act (Patriot Act),[39] "to enhance law enforcement investigatory tools" to protect the country from terrorism (Figure 2.2). The title of the act stands for *Uniting and Strengthening America by Providing Appropriate Tools Required to Intercept and Obstruct Terrorism Act of 2001*. This was followed on September 18, 2001, by the Authorization for Use of Military Force (SJ Res. 23, Public Law No. 107-40),[40] which authorizes the president to use all necessary and appropriate force against those nations, organizations, or people he determines planned, authorized, committed, or aided the terrorist attacks that occurred on September 11, 2001, to prevent any future acts of international terrorism against the United States by such nations, organizations, or people. It was later utilized by the George W. Bush administration as authority for military operations in Afghanistan and Iraq.

In mid-2011, some Republican lawmakers introduced legislation to extend and broaden the provision.

The issue reemerged in April 2017 for Congressional discussion after the new Trump administration launched a cruise missile attack against the Syrian Air Force base used by the plane that, U.S. officials said, dropped chemical weapons on Syrian civilians.

The Patriot Act gives federal officials greater authority to track and intercept communications, both for law enforcement and foreign intelligence gathering purposes. It also gave the Secretary of the Treasury new powers to combat money laundering and more detailed regulatory powers to combat corruption of U.S. financial institutions for foreign money laundering purposes. It creates new crimes, new penalties,

[39] Pub. L. No. 107-56, 115 Stat. 272, 272 (2001). Title II of the original PATRIOT Act, entitled "Enhanced Surveillance Procedures," contains a number of important amendments to the Foreign Intelligence Surveillance Act (FISA) and other laws to make national security investigations more effective and efficient. Of these Title II provisions, sixteen were scheduled to expire in 2005, but Congress made fourteen of them permanent in the USA PATRIOT Improvement and Reauthorization Act of 2005 while extending the sunsets on the roving surveillance and business records provisions.

See USA PATRIOT Improvement and Reauthorization Act of 2005, Pub. L. No. 109–177, §§ 102–03, 120 Stat. 192, 194–95 (2006). https://www.congress.gov/congressional-report/109th-congress/house-report/333/1 (accessed September 15, 2017).

See Todd Hinnen, Acting Assistant Attorney General for National Security, *Statement to the House Judiciary Subcommittee on Crime, Terrorism and Homeland Security*. April 29, 2017. http://www.justice.gov/nsd/opa/pr/testimony/2011/nsd-testimony-110330.html (accessed May 8, 2017).

[40] Pub. L. No. 107–34 115 Stat. 224. *Authorization for Use of Military Forces*. Enacted September 18, 2001. http://www.gpo.gov/fdsys/pkg/PLAW-107publ40/html/PLAW-107publ40.htm (accessed May 8, 2017).

Department of Justice

The Department of Justice's first priority is to prevent future terrorist attacks. Since its passage following the September 11, 2001 attacks, the Patriot Act has played a key part - and often the leading role - in a number of successful operations to protect innocent Americans from the deadly plans of terrorists dedicated to destroying America and our way of life. While the results have been important, in passing the Patriot Act, Congress provided for only modest, incremental changes in the law. Congress simply took existing legal principles and retrofitted them to preserve the lives and liberty of the American people from the challenges posed by a global terrorist network.

The USA PATRIOT Act: Preserving Life and Liberty

(Uniting and Strengthening America by Providing Appropriate Tools Required to Intercept and Obstruct Terrorism)

Congress enacted the Patriot Act by overwhelming, bipartisan margins, arming law enforcement with new tools to detect and prevent terrorism: The USA Patriot Act was passed nearly unanimously by the Senate 98-1, and 357-66 in the House, with the support of members from across the political spectrum.

The Act Improves Our Counter-Terrorism Efforts in Several Significant Ways:

1. **The Patriot Act allows investigators to use the tools that were already available to investigate organized crime and drug trafficking.** Many of the tools the Act provides to law enforcement to fight terrorism have been used for decades to fight organized crime and drug dealers, and have been reviewed and approved by the courts. As Sen. Joe Biden (D-DE) explained during the floor debate about the Act, "the FBI could get a wiretap to investigate the mafia, but they could not get one to investigate terrorists. To put it bluntly, that was crazy! What's good for the mob should be good for terrorists." (Cong. Rec., 10/25/01)

FIGURE 2.2 First page of the Department of Justice's information sheet on the Patriot Act. (Courtesy of U.S. Department of Justice.)

and new procedural efficiencies for use against domestic and international terrorists, including a number of legal procedures sought by the Department of Justice.

Reflecting the focus of the legislation, Title I was called "Enhancing Domestic Security against Terrorism." Many other titles also related to homeland security—for example, by facilitating investigations and surveillance. Some provisions had been drafted earlier by officials during the Clinton administration but had been rebuffed by Congress before 9/11. One example is a "roving wiretap" provision (Sec. 206), under which federal officials may get a wiretapping order that would follow a suspect to any phone he uses (previously, a wiretap order had to apply to a specific phone number). The Justice Department and FBI had sought the measure because previously in counterterrorism cases, authorities had to seek separate court approval for each electronic device carried by a suspect, from a cell phone and a BlackBerry to a home computer. Under the provision, one warrant can cover all of those communications devices. The authority already had existed for cases involving organized crime.

Other important features include a records access provision that allows investigators probing terrorism to seek a suspect's records from third parties such as financial services and travel and telephone companies without notifying the suspect, by issuing National Security Letters, and authority for law enforcement officials to subpoena personal customer records from Internet service providers, financial institutions, and credit card companies, particularly those involving money laundering and foreign individuals and entities.

In 2004, the use of National Security Letters to obtain personal email and phone data was ruled to violate the First and Fourth Amendments in *Doe v. Gonzalez*. The bill's domestic "sneak and peek" provisions were similarly found to violate the Fourth Amendment in the 2007 case of *Mayfield v. United States*. In that case, a Muslim attorney in Portland, Oregon, was incorrectly linked to the 2004 Madrid train bombing and secretly surveilled using the provisions. After ultimately being jailed for several weeks before the case against him was dismissed, Mayfield eventually received an apology from the Justice Department along with a multimillion dollar settlement.

Key provisions in the Patriot Act helped tear down the so-called Foreign Intelligence Surveillance (FISA) wall between law enforcement and intelligence. (See USA PATRIOT Act, Sections 203, 218, and 504.) The act permits the sharing of foreign intelligence (including information relating to protection against international terrorism or foreign attack, or concerning foreign activity and the conduct of foreign affairs) with officials of federal law enforcement, protective enforcement, immigration, national defense, and national security, for the performance of official duties. "The cumulative result of the elimination of the wall is better cooperation than ever before between the intelligence and law enforcement communities."[41]

Additional provisions adopted in the Patriot Act addressed the other side of the wall. For example, Section 203 revised the Wiretap Act and Federal Rule of Criminal Procedure 6(e) to facilitate sharing of Title III and grand jury material involving foreign intelligence or

[41] Doyle, Charles. *Terrorism: Section by Section Analysis of the USA PATRIOT Act.* Congressional Research Service, Issue Brief, December 10, 2001. https://fas.org/irp/crs/RL31377.pdf (accessed May 8, 2017).

counterintelligence with any federal law enforcement, intelligence, or national security official to assist them in performing their duties.[42]

In addition, the act broadened the discretion of law enforcement and immigration authorities in detaining and deporting immigrants suspected of terrorism-related acts. The act also expanded the definition of terrorism to include domestic terrorism, thus enlarging the number of activities to which the Patriot Act's expanded law enforcement powers can be applied.[43]

Commentary

The Patriot Act has been described as, unlike the 1996 AEDPA, "not adding very much to the body of antiterrorism crimes" but rather as "directed to broadening and strengthening law enforcement tools of investigation and procedures that can be used to attack terrorist groups and activities."[44] The removal of earlier legal barriers is considered by some observers a major benefit of the Patriot Act. Others, however, say that the barrier against sharing information across agency lines had resulted not from law but from perceived restrictions and operating practices within the CIA and FBI. The Justice Department originally had concluded that a bar was necessary, in part because of concerns that the right of criminal defendants to know the sources of the evidence against them could in some cases jeopardize the intelligence community's sources and methods.

The controversy also involves Section 215, which would allow federal authorities during a foreign intelligence or international terrorism investigation to obtain a FISA order for access to any tangible item no matter who holds it, including by implication library loan records and the records of library computer use.[45]

Despite the criticisms by some members of Congress and outside groups, the provisions of the Patriot Act have been extended through additional votes at various intervals, most recently in June 2015, for 4 years.[46]

---

[42] Ibid.

[43] Ibid.

[44] Abrams, Norman 2008. *Anti-Terrorism and Criminal Enforcement. Abridged Edition, 3rd Edition*. St. Paul, MN: Thompson/West. p. 10.

[45] Doyle, Charles and Yeh, Brian T. *Libraries and the USA PATRIOT Act*. Congressional Research Service Issue Brief. February 3, 2006. https://0-www.hsdl.org/?view&did=711000 (accessed May 8, 2017).

[46] Hattem, Julian. *Obama Signs NSA Bill, renewing Patriot Powers*. The Hill, June 2, 2015. http://thehill.com/policy/national-security/243850-obama-signs-nsa-bill-renewing-patriot-act-powers (accessed May 8, 2017).

Military Commissions Act of 2006,[47] Amended by the Military Commissions Act of 2009

Another major legislation enacted after 9/11 was the Military Commissions Act of 2006, amended 3 years later, which established military commissions and the procedures for trying enemy unlawful combatants—mainly supporters of al-Qaeda or other terrorist groups, captured in the Afghanistan and Iraq conflicts. The Classified Information Procedures Act[48] and provisions in the Military Commissions Act of 2006[49] authorize the use of military commissions to try enemy combatants without jeopardizing sources and methods.

The statute, signed on October 17, 2006, authorizes the president to establish military commissions and the procedures for their use in trying alien unlawful enemy combatants engaged in hostilities against the United States for violations of the law of war and other offenses to be tried by military commissions. The 2006 act defines alien *unlawful enemy combatant* as follows:

- A person who has engaged in hostilities or who has purposefully and materially supported hostilities against the United States or its cobelligerents who is not a lawful enemy combatant (including a person who is part of the Taliban, al-Qaeda, or associated forces).
- A person who has been determined to be an unlawful enemy combatant by a Combatant Status Review Tribunal or another competent tribunal established under the authority of the President or the Secretary of Defense.

Three years later, Congress enacted the Military Commissions Act of 2009[50] as part of the Department of Defense Authorization Act for FY2010, to provide some reforms the Obama administration supported

[47] The Military Commissions Act of 2006, P.L. No. 109–366—October 17, 2006. http://frwebgate.access.gpo.gov/cgi-bin/getdoc.cgi?dbname=109_cong_public_laws&docid=f:publ366.109.pdf (accessed May 8, 2011).

[48] Department of Justice. *Synopsis of Classified Information Procedures Act (CIPA)*. Criminal Resource Manual 2054. http://www.justice.gov/usao/eousa/foia_reading_room/usam/title9/crm02054.htm (accessed May 8, 2017).

[49] Pub. L. No. 109-366, 120 Stat. 2600 (October 17, 2006), enacting Chapter 47A of Title 10 of the United States Code (as well as amending Section 2241 of Title 28). https://www.gpo.gov/fdsys/pkg/PLAW-109publ366/html/PLAW-109publ366.htm (accessed May 8, 2017).

[50] Defense Department. Pub. L. No. 111–84, Defense department web site. *Title XVIII Military Commissions*, April 10, 2010. http://www.mc.mil/Portals/0/Military%20Commissions%20Fact%20Sheet%20%28April%202010%29.pdf, http://www.defense.gov/news/2009%20MCA%20Pub%20%20Law%20111-84.pdf (accessed May 8, 2017).

and to make other amendments to the Military Commissions Act. They included the use of the term *unprivileged enemy belligerent* instead of *unlawful enemy combatant* and further safeguards for the rights of the prisoners.[51]

Congress has taken a firm stand against transferring to the United States any prisoners held in Guantanamo Bay Prison, blocking President Obama's intention, declared during his election campaign and reaffirmed shortly after his inauguration, to close the controversial facility by January 2010. He was unable to do so. The 111th Congress (2009–2010) had passed nine pieces of legislation that contained a ban in one form or another. The 2011 National Defense Authorization Act,[52] which was signed into law on January 7, 2011, prohibits any Defense Department funds from being used to transfer Guantanamo detainees into the United States for any purpose and also bars such funds from being used to assist in the transfer of such persons. The legislation also bars authorized funds from being used to construct facilities in the United States to house transferred Guantanamo detainees and imposes restrictions on the transfer of detainees to certain foreign countries in order to prevent them from reengaging in hostilities against the United States.[53] (See Chapter 6, Obama Administration Policy and Program Responses.)

Other Legislation Enacted or Modified since September 11, 2001

Prosecution and Detention of Terrorists

Since 9/11, the United States has struggled to develop the laws and procedures that govern both the prosecution and noncriminal detention of terrorists and those "enemy combatants" caught on the battlefield. The unique nature of these cases has proven to be a challenge to constitutional principles of the United States and its established criminal law traditions. Practical challenges inherent to terrorism interdiction and investigation present novel legal problems for both the prosecution and detention of terrorist subjects. Many suspects are noncitizens apprehended in foreign territory by military rather than civilian personnel. Military personnel are not trained to investigate or gather evidence on terrorist suspects;

---

51 For detailed discussion see: Elsea, Jennifer K. The Military Commissions Act of 2009: Overview and Legal Issues. *Congressional Research Service Issue Brief.* April 6, 2010. http://www.fas.org/sgp/crs/natsec/R41163.pdf (accessed May 8, 2017).

52 Section 1034 National Defense Authorization Act of 2011. P.L. 111-383. 124 STAT. 4353. January 7, 2011. http://www.gpo.gov/fdsys/pkg/PLAW-111publ383/pdf/PLAW-111publ383.pdf (accessed May 8, 2017).

53 Garcia, Michael John. *Guantanamo Detention Center: Legislative Activity in the 111th Congress.* Congressional Research Service Brief. January 13, 2011. https://fas.org/sgp/crs/natsec/R40754.pdf (accessed May 8, 2017).

they do not detain witnesses in war zones or take statements for trial purposes. Even if they could do so in the heat and confusion of a battle, such witnesses usually cannot legally or reliably be summoned to the United States at a later date to testify. Further, the military as well as other national security forces do not and cannot operate on the same evidentiary basis as do civil law enforcers. In these combat zones or cities where terrorists are operating, they must have the latitude to operate without warrants and act based on hearsay, fragmented information, or evidence that comes from confidential or unknown origins.

Background

In November, 2001, President Bush issued a military order establishing the right of military courts to try and detain certain noncitizens in the war on terrorism.[54] The order specified that such persons had no recourse to federal civil courts to challenge their detention or appeal the military courts' decisions. In the landmark 2004 case of *Rasul v. Bush*, the Supreme Court specifically invalidated the provisions of the order that denied detainees access to civil courts, holding that noncitizen detainees in military custody at Guantanamo Bay, Cuba, had a right to challenge their detention in civil courts under habeas corpus law.

Congress responded with the Detainee Treatment Act (DTA) of 2005,[55] a legislative response to *Rasul* meant to strip federal courts of the ability to hear habeas corpus petitions from suspected terrorist detainees like Rasul. In place of habeas petitions, the DTA instead provided for a special process of limited review, which would be confined to the jurisdiction of the DC Circuit Court of Appeals. In a narrow holding meant to avoid direct conflict, the court answered in *Hamdan v. Rumsfeld* by interpreting DTA's jurisdiction-stripping language as not applicable to currently pending detainee habeas petitions. Yet in a separate portion of its opinion the court ruled to invalidate the military commission system established by President Bush's original military order. In doing so, the court refrained from outlining acceptable procedures, stating only that valid trial procedures must be as similar as possible to those used for military courts martial as outlined in the Uniform Code of Military Justice (UCMJ).

Congress countered with the Military Commissions Act of 2006.[56] In conformity with *Hamdan* the act established a new military commissions system with procedural rules based upon those provided in

[54] Military Order of November 13, 2001, *Detention, Treatment, and Trial of Certain Non-Citizens in the War against Terrorism*, https://fas.org/irp/offdocs/eo/mo-111301.htm (accessed May 8, 2017).

[55] 42 U.S. Code Chapter 21D—DETAINEE TREATMENT, https://www.law.cornell.edu/uscode/text/42/chapter-21D (accessed May 8, 2017).

[56] Military Commissions Act. https://www.congress.gov/bill/109th-congress/senate-bill/3930 (accessed May 8, 2017).

the UCMJ (although with significant departures). However, in a direct challenge to the court's ruling in *Hamdan*, the act once again reiterated Congress's intent to strip habeas jurisdiction from federal courts for cases involving noncitizen detainees, including jurisdiction for currently pending cases. Subsequent actions in these areas diverged after *Hamdan* and are explained further below.

Commentary

While terrorist activity may at one level seem to be simple criminal violations punishable under law, prosecutions of such cases are beset by numerous challenges: Are noncitizen terrorist subjects captured in foreign territory entitled to constitutional protections during trial? In which courts—civil or military—should the proceedings take place? Whose laws should govern? In some cases, countries have rendered suspects to the United States through formal extradition procedures. In some others, the country that found the suspect in its territory quietly informed the United States that it could take custody of the prisoner without a formal and public procedure. This was usually the case when a country had domestic political concerns and/or was worried about possible retaliation.

Even more vexing, the nature of terrorist threats and the need to interdict them before terrorist crimes and potentially major attacks with large numbers of casualties occur arguably counsels for a need to detain select suspects indefinitely and without trial. Britain and some other countries allow for preventive detention, though usually for a fixed period of time.

Military and national security personnel cannot risk waiting for incidents to occur in order to launch investigations or detain suspects. The fact that a suspect is a member of a terrorist organization or has attended terrorist training camps, for example, may signal they are a dangerous, if not an imminent threat, but there is not yet court admissible evidence that they have committed a criminal violation. Further, the evidence or intelligence used to reach conclusions about terrorist subjects may be sensitive or simply inadequate to obtain a reliable conviction. Therefore it is argued that despite our inability to successfully convict suspects in these gray areas, their preemptive and potentially indefinite detention is nonetheless essential to U.S. security. A challenge is how to apprehend and detain suspected terrorists without violating the principle of innocence until proven guilty and without provoking a backlash. In Iraq and Afghanistan in particular, the United States and its allies had to face the problem of weeding out persons who may be minor players, caught up in a sweep or victims of false or exaggerated charges leveled by their enemies or competitors for political, personal, or financial reasons.

Prosecution

Following *Hamdan* and the passage of the Military Commissions Act of 2006, the Department of Defense released further regulations to guide the military commission process and began using the system. The commissions were used to try and convict several individuals, including Salim Hamdan and Australian citizen David Hicks. In 2009, President Obama halted the commissions pending a review of their use and the individual cases of those still detained at Guantanamo Bay.

Later in 2009, the Department of Defense modified the Manual for Military Commissions, and the Senate passed the Military Commissions Act of 2009,[57] making reforms to the process including some proposed by President Obama. Also in 2009, President Obama's Detention Policy Task Force issued a preliminary report reaffirming that the White House considered military commissions to be an appropriate forum for trying suspected violations of the laws of the war, although civil courts would be the preferred forum.[58] The report also included guiding considerations for disposing of the cases still pending against detainees at Guantanamo Bay, including, in brief, efficiency, the nature and gravity of offenses or underlying conduct, and other prosecution considerations, such as the extent to which the forum permits a full presentation of the wrongful conduct and appropriate sentencing upon conviction. After review of the Guantanamo detainee's cases, approximately 110 were scheduled for release pending the identification of suitable host countries, 40 were to be tried using military commissions, and 50 were ordered to remain in detention without trial.

Obama administration officials, as mentioned above, clearly favored using civilian courts where possible, noting the wide variety of laws that could be used and their success rates in obtaining convictions. The incoming Trump administration indicated it intended to make more use of Guantanamo and military commissions. However nine months into the new administration, the acting Assistant Attorney General who heads the Justice Department's National Security Division, Dana Boente said the administration had not decided yet whether it will put more emphasis on the military commission route. "No options are off the table," he said in response to a question at an American Bar Association Luncheon.[59]

---

[57] Congress S. 3930. *Military Commission Act of 2006*. https://www.loc.gov/rr/frd/Military_Law/pdf/PL-109-366.pdf (accessed May 8, 2017).

[58] *Memorandum from the Detention Policy Task Force to the Attorney General and the Secretary of Defense*, July 20, 2009. http://www.nimj.com/display.aspx?base=MilitaryCommissions&ID=255 (accessed May 8, 2017).

[59] Question and answer period at luncheon of the American Bar association Standing committee on Law and National Security, September 15, 2017, attended by author Michael Kraft.

National Intelligence Reform Act of 2004[60]

Passed by both houses of Congress on December 8, 2004, this bill overhauls the U.S. intelligence organization. (Also see the accompanying conference report.[61]) The act creates a director of national intelligence with broad authority to unify intelligence gathering and operations. Additional provisions (1) require standards for state-issued identification, (2) authorize the Federal Bureau of Investigation to conduct surveillance of foreign nationals suspected of terrorism, (3) create a uniform security-clearance process, (4) allow federal prosecutors to share information from grand jury proceedings with law enforcement to prevent terrorist attacks, and (5) shift the burden of proof for (release/continued detention of) those detained for terrorist offenses from the government to the defense. In addition, the act increased security measures for airports, created national standards for drivers' licenses and other identification cards, increased incidents of mandatory sentencing for terrorist-related crimes, provided more border security agents and inspectors, and increased the number of detention spaces available for terrorists.

Foreign Intelligence Surveillance Act (FISA) Amendments Act of 2008[62]

The legislation provided retroactive immunity[63] to telecommunications providers that may have facilitated warrantless surveillance by the federal government under a terrorist surveillance program between 2001 and 2007.[64] Proponents of retroactive immunity argued that it was necessary to assure private cooperation with critical intelligence investigations. Opponents of retroactive immunity argued that the provision undermined the statutory penalties that were designed to deter unlawful intrusions into individual liberties.

60 P. L. 108–458 118 STAT. 3638 P. L. 108–458. Enacted December 17, 2004. http://www.nctc.gov/docs/pl108_458.pdf (accessed May 8, 2017).

61 Conference Report, *National Intelligence Reform Act of 2004*. https://www.congress.gov/bill/108th-congress/senate-bill/2845 (accessed May 8, 2017).

62 FISA Amendment Act of 2008. https://www.gpo.gov/fdsys/pkg/BILLS-110hr6304enr/pdf/BILLS-110hr6304enr.pdf (accessed May 8, 2017).

63 Liu, Edward. *Retroactive Immunity Provided by the FISA Amendments Act of 2008*. Congressional Research Service Issue Brief. July 25, 2008. http://www.fas.org/sgp/crs/intel/RL34600.pdf (accessed May 8, 2017), and Risen, James and Lightblau, Eric. Bush Lets U.S. Spy on Callers without Courts. *New York Times*, P. 1. December 16, 2005. http://www.nytimes.com/2005/12/16/politics/bush-lets-us-spy-on-callers-without-courts.html (accessed May 8, 2017).

64 Pub. L. No. 107–173 p. 116 Stat. 543. https://www.gpo.gov/fdsys/pkg/STATUTE-116/pdf/STATUTE-116-Pg543.pdf (accessed May 8, 2017).

Enhanced Border Security and Visa Entry Reform Act of 2002 (H.R. 3525, Public Law No. 107–173)

Signed into law on May 14, 2002, this act provides for increased numbers of Immigration and Naturalization Service (INS) investigators and inspectors; authorizes appropriations for INS, Border Patrol, and consular personnel, training, facilities, and security-related technology; and calls for information sharing among border security, law enforcement, and intelligence agencies (including technology standard and interoperability requirements), among other provisions. This law grew out of concern that terrorists might slip into the country to plan specific operations, such as the 9/11 attacks, or to become "sleepers" to be activated for later operations.

The Secure Fence Act of 2006, H.R. 6061, Public Law No. 109–367[65]

Enacted on October 26, 2006, this law directed the Secretary of Homeland Security to take appropriate actions within 18 months to achieve operational control over U.S. international land and maritime borders. It defines *operational control* as the prevention of all unlawful U.S. entries, including entries by terrorists, other unlawful aliens, narcotics, instruments of terrorism, and other contraband. A big factor in enactment of this legislation was the concerns raised, especially in southwestern states, about illegal immigrants crossing in from Mexico and the possibility that terrorists might sneak in with them. This later became an issue in the 2016 election campaign and candidate, then President Trump's proposal to build a high wall across the entire length of the U.S. Mexican border. However the proposal, estimated to cost over $20 billion, ran into opposition in Congress, even among Republicans, and funding was stalled in the early months of his administration.

International Emergency Economic Powers Act (U.S. Code Title 50, Chapter 35)[66]

It was amended in 2007 to codify sanctions against the Sudan, because of the bloodshed in Darfur, and against Iran. Both countries are also

---

[65] Pub. L. No. 107-173 p. 116 Stat. 543. https://www.gpo.gov/fdsys/pkg/STATUTE-116/pdf/STATUTE-116-Pg543.pdf (accessed May 8, 2017).

[66] House.gov. *IEPA Title 50*, Chapter 35. February 1, 2010. https://www.law.cornell.edu/uscode/text/50/chapter-35 (accessed May 8, 2017).

Pub. L. No. 110-96, Sec. 1, 121 Stat. 1011. Amending the Penalties in IEPA, October 16, 2007. https://www.congress.gov/110/plaws/publ96/PLAW-110publ96.pdf (accessed May 8, 2017). *Also see* Harold C. Relyea. *National Emergency Powers*. Congressional Research Service Issue Brief. August 30, 2007. http://www.fas.org/sgp/crs/natsec/98-505.pdf (accessed May 8, 2017).

on the State Department's terrorism list. IEEPA provides broad authority to the president to regulate foreign economic transactions when a national emergency is declared to deal with any unusual and extraordinary threat to the United States that has its source in whole or substantial part outside the United States. It has been used to freeze assets of terrorist organizations and individuals involved in terrorist activities. As amended after the September 11, 2001, terrorist attacks, it also provides the president with the authority to freeze assets in which any foreign country or national has an interest. The Treasury Department's OFAC published lists of designated persons and organizations.

Public Health Security and Bioterrorism Preparedness and Response Act of 2002 (H.R. 3448, Public Law 107–188)[67]

This act, signed into law on June 12, 2002, is intended to improve the ability of the United States to prevent, prepare for, and respond to bioterrorism and other public health emergencies. The Food and Drug Administration is charged with implementing this law and has prepared an online resource[68] to provide updates.

Project Bioshield Act of 2004 (Public Law 108–276)[69]

The FDA is responsible for carrying out certain provisions of the Bioterrorism Act, particularly Title III, Subtitle A (Protection of Food Supply) and Subtitle B (Protection of Drug Supply).

The Project Bioshield Act of 2004 permits the FDA Commissioner to authorize the use of an unapproved medical product or an unapproved use of an approved medical product during a declared emergency involving a heightened risk of attack on the public or U.S. military forces, or a significant potential to affect national security. It was signed into law on July 21, 2004.

---

[67] Library of Congress. http://thomas.loc.gov/cgi-bin/bdquery/z?d107:H.R.3448, also http://www.fda.gov/EmergencyPreparedness/Counterterrorism/BioterrorismAct/default.htm (accessed May 8, 2017).

[68] Food and Drug Administration. *Counterterrorism Legislation*. June 18, 2009. https://www.fda.gov/EmergencyPreparedness/Counterterrorism/MedicalCountermeasures/MCMLegalRegulatoryandPolicyFramework/ucm2007271.htm (accessed May 8, 2017).

[69] Project Bioshield Act of 2004. Enacted July 21, 2004. http://frwebgate.access.gpo.gov/cgi-bin/getdoc.cgi?dbname=108_cong_public_laws&docid=f:publ276.108 (accessed May 8, 2017).

SANCTIONS AND LEGISLATION

Resources (Partial) for Counterterrorism Laws

- Department of Justice. Counter-Terrorism. Training and Resources for Law Enforcement Legislation. http://www.counterterrorismtraining.gov/leg/index.html (accessed May 8, 2017).
- United Nations Office of Drugs and Crime. United States of America. Laws in Full Text. https://www.unodc.org/tldb/browse_country.html?cmd=add&node=USA1970232&&country=USA#folders (accessed May 8, 2017).
- University of Pittsburgh Law School. U.S. Counterterrorism Laws. http://jurist.law.pitt.edu/terrorism/terrorism3.htm (accessed May 8, 2017).
- Cornell University Law School. Title 18 U.S.C. 1203. Hostage Taking. http://www.law.cornell.edu/uscode/uscode18/usc_sec_18_00001203----000-.html (accessed May 8, 2017).
- Cornell University Law School. Title 18 U.S.C. 32 Destruction of Aircraft or Facilities. http://www.law.cornell.edu/uscode/uscode18/usc_sec_18_00000032----000-.html (accessed May 8, 2017).
- Cornell University Law School. Title 28 U.S.C., section 1605(a)(7). Terrorist Exception to Foreign Sovereignty Immunity. http://www.law.cornell.edu/uscode/28/usc_sec_28_00001605---A000-.html (accessed May 8, 2017).
- Cornell University Law School. Title 50 U.S.C. 2405, Foreign Policy Export Controls, Export Administration Act of 1979 subsection j as modified, http://www.law.cornell.edu/uscode/html/uscode50a/usc_sec_50a_00002405----000-.html (accessed May 8, 2017).

ADDITIONAL READINGS

- Abrams, Norman. *Anti-Terrorism and Criminal Enforcement.* Abridged Edition, 3rd Edition. St. Paul, MN: Thompson/West, 2008.
- Alexander, Yonah and Michael Kraft, eds. *The Evolution of U.S. Counterterrorism Policy*, Volume 1, Westport, Conn/London, England: Praeger Security/Greenwood publishing Group. 2008.

- Chesney, Robert. The Sleeper Scenario: Terrorism-Support Laws and the Demands of Prevention. *Harvard Journal on Legislation. Volume 42, No. 1 (2005)* http://ssrn.com/abstract¼587442 (accessed May 8, 2017).
- Doyle, Charles. Antiterrorism and Effective Death Penalty Act of 1996: A Summary. *American Law Division, Congressional Research Service.* June 3, 1996. http://www.fas.org/irp/crs/96-499.htm (accessed May 8, 2017).
- Doyle, Charles. Terrorism at Home: A Look at Applicable Federal and State Laws. *Library of Congress Issue Brief.* October 3, 2001. http://www.policyarchive.org/handle/10207/bitstreams/3517.pdf
- Elsea, Jennifer K. Suits against Terrorist States by Victims of Terrorism. *Congressional Research Service.* August 8, 2008. http://www.fas.org/sgp/crs/terror/RL31258.pdf (accessed May 8, 2017).
- Levitt, Matthew. 2003. *Targeting Terror: U.S. Policy Toward Middle Eastern State Sponsors and Terrorist Organizations, Post September 11.* Washington, D.C. Washington Institute for Near East Policy.
- McCormack, Wayne. 2008. *Legal Responses to Terrorism.* 2nd Edition. San Francisco, CA: LexisNexis, Mathew Bender and Co.
- Reagan, Ronald. *Radio Address to the Nation.* May 31, 1986. http://www.reagan.utexas.edu/archives/speeches/1986/53186a.htm (accessed May 8, 2017).
- Robert S. Mueller, III, Director Federal Bureau of Investigation, Statement before the House Judiciary Committee. March 16, 2011. http://www.fbi.gov/news/testimony/oversight-of-the-federal-bureau-of-investigation (accessed May 8, 2017).
- U.S. Department of Justice. Legal Attaché Offices, Federal Bureau of Investigation (FBI), International Operations. http://www2.fbi.gov/contact/legat/legat.htm (accessed May 8, 2017).
- U.S. Department of Justice. Omnibus Diplomatic Security and Anti-Terrorism Act of 1986, P.L. 99-399 and later modified as 18 USC 2332, Section 1202. http://www.usdoj.gov/usao/eousa/foia_reading_room/usam/title9/crm00012.htm (accessed May 8, 2017).
- U.S. Department of State. *Foreign Terrorist Organizations.* Office of the Coordinator for Counterterrorism, http://www.state.gov/s/ct/rls/other/des/123085.htm (accessed May 8, 2017).
- U.S. Department of State. *Rewards for Justice Program,* http://www.rewardsforjustice.net/ (accessed May 8, 2017).

- U.S. Department of State. *Anti-Terrorism Assistance Program,* Office of the Coordinator for Counterterrorism. http://www.state.gov/s/ct/about/c16885.htm (accessed May 8, 2017).
- Bjelopera, James and Mark A. Randol. April 24, 2011. The Federal Bureau of Investigation and *Congressional research Service Brief.* http://www.fas.org/sgp/crs/terror/R41780.pdf (accessed May 8, 2017).

CHAPTER 3

Background
Nixon to Clinton

Terrorism has been with us for all of recorded history, using knives and swords to more recently hijacked aircraft, car bombs, and vehicles driven deliberately into pedestrians. It has often attracted inordinate attention, but present-day terrorists have been employing a new level of brutality that threatens not only tens of thousands of people but also specific national governments and the stability of the international state system. The West in general and the United States, along with Iraq and Afghanistan and some other countries, are facing campaigns by organized groups using terrorism to further their political, ideological, and in some cases religious goals.

The motivations of individual terrorists vary, but many experts say the broad underlying motives appear to include opposition to an existing order, fueled by a mixture of social and political idealism, mass unemployment and hopelessness, social humiliation, national or ethnic affronted humiliation, and, more recently, religious fundamentalism and affronted nationalism. Some terrorists seem to be affected by personal alienation and other psychological and personal problems and often a desire to "be somebody" and part of a larger cause. This very largely personal motivation has become intertwined with various political movements and a recruiting tool for a number of insurgency movements.

Although many of the earlier terrorist groups had very specific nationalist goals, such as overthrowing the existing government in their country or obtaining territorial autonomy (for example, the Basques in Spain, Kurdish groups in Turkey, and the Tamils in Sri Lanka), some of the newer political movements and insurgencies (such as al-Qaeda and ISIS) have taken on a transnational character, adapting to the increasingly global character of contemporary society. Exacerbating this transnational political development is the intermingling of terrorist and insurgent activity with other types of transnational crime, including narcotrafficking, piracy, kidnapping, human and contraband smuggling, document fraud, money laundering, and old-style bank robberies. Criminal organizations as well as terrorist groups have gone global, presenting new challenges to governments, many of whose law enforcement agencies are overmatched and outgunned.

The result is a global transnational nexus of political and criminal threats. Another way of describing this development is to refer to the rise of network forms of organization, partially as the result of the ongoing information revolution. Even more or less stable nation-states now come under attack by persons representing self-proclaimed racial, ethnic, religious, or class entities. As borders have become more open in an increasingly globalized world, illegal trafficking of all kinds, illegal migration, and the opportunities for international terrorism increase exponentially.

RISE OF CONTEMPORARY TERRORISM

The modern terrorist challenge began with the so-called boutique terrorists of the 1970s, small groups of disaffected radical youth in developed countries in Europe and in Japan, but soon expanded in numbers and ambition.

The end of World War II was followed by two major changes in the international environment: the Cold War and decolonization. The post-1945 decolonization struggles produced a wave of insurgency campaigns affecting North and sub-Saharan Africa, South and Southeast Asia, and the Middle East. During the 1960s and 1970s, terrorism was largely viewed within an anticolonial and nationalist revolutionary context of insurgencies. Terrorist tactics had been practiced by insurgents in former colonial territories around the world and most notably in the Middle East much earlier in the twentieth century. Some of the Jewish and Arab movements in British-controlled Palestine, and anticolonial movements like the Mau Mau in Kenya, and insurgencies in other colonial territories such as Indonesia, Malaysia, and Yemen, have been accused of using terrorist tactics.

The Vietnam War stimulated another manifestation of terrorism in the 1960s as various left-wing political extremists in Europe, Latin America and the United States formed terrorist groups opposing U.S. intervention in Vietnam as well as their own governments for supporting the United States. Many participants showed an enormous ambivalence, if not outright opposition, to the values of the existing system and "the establishment." Many groups—such as the American Weather Underground, the West German Red Army Faction (RAF), the Italian Red Brigades, the Japanese Red Army, and the French *Action Directe*—saw themselves as vanguards for the masses of the third world. This was the era of "Boutique" or "New Left" terrorism that lasted into the 1980s.

Some groups, especially the RAF and the Red Brigades, opposed NATO and gloried in kidnapping prominent officials.

Although these various terrorist groups were essentially a nonstate phenomenon, some governments in the Soviet bloc and some of the self-proclaimed revolutionary states in the so-called third world (Libya, Syria, Iraq, Iran, Cuba, North Korea) encouraged the outbreaks and offered moral support and sometimes money, training, weapons, and sanctuary. However by the end of the 1980s, many of their leaders already had been captured and with the breakup of the Soviet Union, the European groups faded away.

With the end of the Vietnam War in 1975, the Palestinian nationalist movements replaced the Viet Cong as the "heroic" model for those who wished to glorify attacks on the "West" or the "Establishment." The Palestinian Liberation Organization (PLO), headed by Yasser Arafat, surfaced after the dramatic defeat of three Arab armies in the Six-Day War in 1967. The PLO soon moved from more classic guerrilla tactics to terrorism in the 1960s.

In addition to the PLO, various splinter groups emerged. In 1970, the Popular Front for the Liberation of Palestine hijacked four airliners and blew up three of them in front of television cameras at former RAF airbase Dawson Field in Jordan, ushering in the modern era of terrorism spectaculars. However, the PLO's prominence was strengthened and supported because of the strong support from Arab states across the political spectrum, the Soviet Union, and many third world nations in the United Nations.

Terrorist groups in the Middle East and South Asia have diverse origins and ideologies but can be roughly divided into two groups: those that arose in the 1960s and 1970s, which are essentially secular (Marxist and/or nationalist such as the Kurdish PKK or Tamil Tigers), and those that arose in the 1980s and 1990s, which base their ideology and goals on their interpretation of religion, mostly notably on Islam in the Muslim world, for example restoring a caliphate in areas of the Middle East and Northern Africa and even southern Spain that were controlled by Muslim leaders around the fifteenth century. However, at the same time radicalism and nationalism were often combined as long-standing conflicts were reinvigorated and groups such as the Basques, Armenians, Corsicans, Kurds, and Northern Irish Catholics became more active and more prominent.

There also was in this period a significant amount of right-wing terrorism as well. Although chaotic and internally divided, the so-called militia movement in the United States grew and then blossomed in the period 1980–1990. However shocking and outrageous, the terrorism of the extreme right, even the 1995 Oklahoma City bombing, which claimed the largest number of terrorism casualties in the United States until 9/11, did not become very important politically in any country, although Norway also suffered a mass attack in 2011 when a "lone wolf" killed sixty-nine persons with gunshots and another eight died in bombings outside the Prime Minister's office.

THE ERA OF TERRORISM AND RELIGION

Up to the 1980s political, insurgency, and terrorist movements in the Middle East were essentially secular in orientation and character, as described above. However, the rise of theological fundamentalism in religions around the world in the second half of the twentieth century soon produced a resurgence of radical religious movements.[1] In some cases this religious radicalism produced or transformed insurgencies, i.e. the nationalist movements in the Middle East, into religion-motivated organizations, such as the Muslim Brotherhood. The resurgence of religious-based terrorism is today largely identified with movements in the Muslim and Arab worlds, although there is also Hindu–Muslim violence in South Asia.

The reasons for this development were complex but underlying everything was the evident and increasing failure of the "secular" agenda. Arab secular political movements were not creating just and successful nations. Another obvious failure of these movements was their inability to achieve any of their anti-Israeli objectives and the collapse of pan-Arab movements promoted by the late Egyptian President Nasser. While anti-Israeli policies and positions were often adopted cynically by many (apart from the Palestinian movements), the remarkable success of Israel as a modern technologically advanced nation, combined with its continued occupation of the West Bank, was perceived as a rebuke to the Arab secular movements and the local governments, which struggled with high unemployment, a large youthful population, and poor economies.

However, two major and almost simultaneous developments may well have marked the beginning of this phase.

One was the Iranian Revolution against the American-backed Shah. The November 6, 1979, seizure of the American Embassy in Tehran marked a major turning point in Iranian–U.S. relations (Figure 3.1). Iranian-backed Lebanese were responsible for the bombings of the U.S. Marine barracks and embassy facilities in Beirut in 1983 and other attacks, including against the French. The suicide truck bomb against the barracks killed 241 U.S. servicemen. The victims of the embassy bombings included the CIA station chief, Robert Ames, and Agency for International Development officials working on health and economic programs for Lebanon.

---

[1] Almond, Appleby, and Sivan Strong. *Religion: The Rise of Fundamentalisms around the World* (University of Chicago Press, 2003).

FIGURE 3.1 During the Iran hostage crisis, Iranian students approach the U.S. embassy. (Public domain.)

The second development, perhaps with more widespread implications, was the reaction to the Russian invasion of Afghanistan, which brought thousands of Muslims to that isolated country to join the Mujadehin forces that were fighting to repel the "infidels." One of them was Usama bin Laden, a wealthy Saudi who went to Afghanistan in 1979 to help supply money, arms, and fighters to the Mujadehin. His efforts brought him considerable popularity and he later formed the al-Qaeda organization. Others also returned to their home countries with military experience.

The February 26, 1993, bombing of the World Trade Center (Figure 3.2) by al-Qaeda militant Islamic terrorists, the attempt by a militant radical to cross into the United States at Port Angels, Washington, into order to implement a "millennium plot," and then the well-planned 9/11 al-Qaeda attack brought this new version of the terrorist threat home to Americans.

HIJACKING, KIDNAPPINGS, AND OTHER TECHNIQUES

New "techniques" were developed as these nonstate movements pursued their objectives outside of colonial situations but in established countries. International hijacking of aircraft became almost common,

FIGURE 3.2 Underground damage after the February 26, 1993, bombing of the World Trade Center by al-Qaeda. (ATF 1993 Explosives Incident Report.)

hundreds occurring in the next several decades, including the hijacking of TWA 847 to Beirut in 1985 during which the terrorists managed to hold a news conference on live television, showing their new grasp of the use of modern communications.

Hijackings often were conducted to obtain hostages, which were used to make political claims against governments, including the release of jailed comrades. This was the goal of the hijacking of the Italian cruise ship *Achille Lauro*, in 1985, during which the Palestinian terrorists tossed overboard an elderly American, Leon Klinghoffer, while still in his wheelchair. Their initial plan was to disembark the ship in Israel and grab some hostages in order to trade for the release of their previously imprisoned colleagues. Instead, they were discovered with weapons by a crew member and the terrorists then hijacked the passenger liner.

Kidnappings themselves proliferated. Memorable incidents included the 1979 kidnapping and murder of the Italian Prime Minister Aldo Moro and the audacious act when the Sandinistas took Nicaragua's Congress hostage in 1978. Dozens of American and other Western hostages were seized by Hezbollah groups in Lebanon in the 1980s in an effort to force Washington and other capitals to pressure Kuwait to release Lebanese and other terrorists jailed for attacks on Kuwaiti facilities and the U.S. and French embassies in 1983. The kidnappings in Lebanon included the CIA station chief, William Buckley, who was later killed in 1985.

Efforts to free the American hostages led to the Iran–Contra scandal. The secret operation lead by Marine Lt. Col. Oliver North, who served on the NSC staff, traded antitank missiles to Iran, a backer of Hezbollah, in exchange for the release of hostages. Not only was the effort a violation of long-standing U.S. policy against making deals with hostage takers, but soon after one hostage was released another was captured. State Department counterterrorism officials at the time, who were kept in the dark about the North operation, said it was a setback to the efforts to persuade European governments to stop paying ransom for their captured citizens.

The abandoned practice of assassination was revived, as in the IRA assassination of the British ambassador to Ireland (1976), Lord Mountbatten (1979), and the Palestinian Black September killing of the Jordanian prime minister (1971). In 1973 Black September killed the American ambassador Leo A. Noel Jr., and George Curtis Moore, U.S. Deputy Chief of Mission to Sudan and several other diplomats in Khartoum, and the rising tide came home to the United States. This development, which had been brewing for some time, was an aspect of the increasing internationalization of terrorism. The revolutionary ethos created bonds between separate national groups, bonds that were developed and expanded as training facilities to groups were made available by Cuba, Libya, and the PLO. While many governments were targeted, the global role of the United States made it an inevitable target for groups whose primary target was elsewhere, for example, Saudi Arabia or Israel or Kuwait for its support of Iraq in the Iraq–Iranian war. One-third of international attacks in this period involved American targets.

Several Middle Eastern governments also were directly involved in terrorism. Syria used terrorism against Jordan in the 1980s. Libya gave weapons to various terrorist groups and conducted operations against the United States. Iran and Iraq used terrorism against each other as part of the Iraq–Iran war. North Korean agents fatally shot South Korean officials during a visit to Burma and blew up a South Korean airliner.

The era of largely secular terrorists began to ebb in the 1980s. So-called revolutionary terrorists were defeated in one country after another or they faded away after the breakup of the Soviet Union. The Israeli invasion of Lebanon in 1982 eliminated PLO training facilities in that country, and international counterterrorist cooperation became increasingly effective—including action in the United Nations and as many new states that had been colonies found that terrorism could now threaten their interests.

However during the same period, the age of "narcoterrorism" dawned. Although originally terrorists and guerrillas were ideological enemies of drug producers and trades, over the years the "distance between ideology and economic reality is shrinking."[2] The nexus between terrorists/insurgents and various criminal actors and activities became a common factor especially in Colombia, to a lesser extent in Lebanon, and more recently in Afghanistan and Mexico.

In the earlier period of modern terrorism, with the exception of the blowing up of airliners such as Pan Am 103 over Lockerbie, Scotland, the targets of secular groups were often relatively focused in their demands and goals. They typically sought publicity for their cause, publication of manifestoes, release of their imprisoned colleagues, or, in the case of the Spanish Basque and Turkish PKK Kurdish attacks or the IRA, attempts to achieve local autonomy or independence. Weapons were usually guns or hand grenades, although sometimes car bombs were used, especially in Lebanon.

However in the new century, a threshold was crossed with the emergence of attacks designed to cause high casualties, especially through the deployment of suicide terrorists. Although suicide has long been associated with terrorism—the zealots and the assassins of ancient Mideast times—it had receded from practice and memory. Then Hamas conducted suicide missions in Lebanon and later in Israel beginning in 1982 and then the Tamil Tigers of Sri Lanka—a secular, nationalist movement—picked up the technique beginning in the later 1980s. They developed the suicide belt and vest and used it extensively until their defeat in 2009. The technology was later adopted by Middle East terrorists. Various terrorist groups had been known to share information in the past, especially the European and Palestinian groups. Suicide belts were a favorite technique of Hamas against Israel, often recruiting young men who were later glorified as "martyrs."

However, the major impact suicide attacks have been those perpetuated by the militant Islamic radical group al-Qaeda in the decades of 1990 and 2000 and especially those against the United States and other Western countries: the Khobar Barracks, the *USS Cole* (Figure 3.3), the U.S. embassies in Nairobi and Dar es Salaam, and of course the 9/11 attacks on the World Trade Towers in New York and the Pentagon in Washington.

ISIS, an offshoot of al-Qaeda, emerged later in Iraq and Syria and took the level of brutality in new directions, including mass shootings of Shiite Muslims in areas it captured, raping women of minority groups, and beheading Western and other hostages and videotaping the deed for showing to local and Western audiences.

---

[2] Laquer, Walter. *The New Terrorism*, (Oxford University Press, 1999).

FIGURE 3.3 October 18, 2000: U.S. Navy and Marine Corps security personnel patrol past the damaged U.S. Navy destroyer *USS Cole* after the October 12, 2000, terrorist bombing attack on the ship. (Courtesy of U.S. Department of Defense, U.S. Navy photo by Senior Chief Engineman Lyle G. Becker.)

AT HOME: HOMELAND THREATS

While terrorism in various forms has been a part of U.S. history, the Ku Klux Klan for instance, terrorism in the United States took a jump in the 1960s, mostly on the left (the Weather Underground) although with a significant component of ethnic and nationalist groups (Puerto Rican Armed Forces). Although not very professional or effective, there were over 600 attacks in the 1970s. Still, the 1995 attack by Timothy McVeigh on the Murrah Federal Building in Oklahoma City, the activities of the "Unabomber"—"Ted" Kaczynski—and the anthrax attacks in 2001 that killed five persons raised the level of concern about domestic terrorism.

US GOVERNMENT RESPONSES

It was not until the 1970s that the United States began to develop a homeland counterterrorism approach, although it had begun earlier to think seriously about the international challenge. On the home front, the major radical and racial riots of the decade resulted in the creation of a

National Advisory Committee on Criminal Justice Standards and Goals, which issued a "Report on the Task Force on Disorders and Terrorism" in 1976. Still, while the focus on domestic terrorism remained limited it was not completely ignored, and an "Advisory Panel to Assess Domestic Capabilities for Terrorism Involving Weapons of Mass Destruction" was established in 1999.

Rising concern with the problem overseas and the increasingly dramatic character of attacks produced increasing activity by the USG, both by the executive branch and Congress.

Operational responsibility for dealing with terrorism was widely distributed throughout the U.S. government bureaucracy, and lines of jurisdiction tended to be blurred and overlapping. After Palestinian terrorists staged the 1972 Munich massacre, killing eleven Israeli Olympic athletes, President Nixon established a cabinet-level committee to coordinate counterterrorism efforts. That turned out to be impractical for day-to-day operations, and his administration then created a special counterterrorism office in the State Department to coordinate U.S. counterterrorism efforts and incident management overseas. It was named the Office of the Coordinator for Counterterrorism and the coordinator was given the rank of ambassador. (The counterterrorism office was upgraded to a bureau during the Obama administration). The FBI was designated the lead agency for domestic counterterrorism activities and the Federal Aviation Administration was made responsible for handling aircraft hijackings and safety.

An important change during the Reagan administration was the improved interagency and international coordination of the counterterrorism effort. Previously the counterterrorism office was buried in the State Department's management bureaucracy, but it was elevated to report directly to the Secretary, giving it more clout and visibility. Meanwhile, the United States led efforts to encourage other governments to coordinate better within their own governments and with each other. The United States began a program of regular bilateral meetings with some major allies, such as Britain and Canada, to exchange information and coordinate efforts to counter terrorism groups and countries that support them. In an early meeting with at least one European country, the heads of the different agencies involved in counterterrorism efforts were meeting each other for the first time.

The involvement of Libya, Syria, and other countries in terrorism activities themselves or supporting terrorist groups as proxies prompted Congress to enact legislation in 1979 that led to imposing economic sanctions against countries designated as repeated supporters of international terrorism. (See Chapter 2, "Sanctions.")

In 1983, Congress authorized an administration proposal to start a State Department Anti-terrorism Assistance (ATA) program for law enforcement officials of friendly countries. Following a series of aircraft hijackings, Congress enacted the Omnibus Diplomatic Security and Antiterrorism Act of 1986, which included measures to strengthen aircraft security. A task force led by then-Vice President George H.W. Bush developed a series of comprehensive recommendations for future counterterrorism policies and programs.[3] They included backing for an interagency counterterrorism research and development program to promote better equipment for deterring or coping with terrorist attacks. The programs have continued into the present, along with other "practical measures" that developed later. (See Chapter 4.)

Responding to increasing intelligence information on the trend by terrorist groups to use front companies and charities to raise funds instead of relying on state supporters, Congress adopted the Antiterrorism and Effective Death Penalty Act of 1996.[4] The measure included Clinton administration legislation to make it a criminal offense to provide funds or other forms of material support to designated foreign terrorist organizations or for specific terrorist attacks.

However, as the definition and the character of terrorism evolved from the 1960s on, jurisdictional matters became more complicated and new agencies became involved, such as the Department of Energy (for nuclear questions), Health and Human Services, and its Centers for Disease Control. The importance of terrorism was recognized by the establishment of the position in the NSC in 1998 of National Coordinator for Security, Infrastructure Protection, and Counter-terrorism. While at least in theory not having an executive role (at least not until 9/11), the CIA and the rest of the intelligence community took on additional responsibilities and roles. Providing intelligence for military operations against terrorists became one area of increasing importance.

U.S. BEGAN TO USE OVERT MILITARY ACTIONS

The Reagan administration launched an air strike against Libya in 1986 retaliation for the Gadaffi regime's bombing of a Berlin disco 9 days earlier (Figure 3.4a and b). Two U.S. soldiers and a Turkish woman were killed by the bomb placed near the dance floor. The terrorist attack was traced to Libya, reportedly through intercepts.

---

[3] Public Report of the Vice President's Task Force on Combatting Terrorism, February, 1986. http://www.population-security.org/bush_report_on_terrorism/bush_report_on_terrorism.htm (accessed May 8, 2017).

[4] The Antiterrorism and Effective Death Penalty Act of 1996, Pub. L. No. 104-132, 110 Stat. 1214, (also known as AEDPA), signed into law April 24, 1996. https://www.congress.gov/104/plaws/publ132/PLAW-104publ132.pdf (accessed May 8, 2017).

FIGURE 3.4 (a) April 14, 1986: President Ronald Reagan meeting with bipartisan members of the U.S. Congress to discuss the air strike on Libya (Operation El Dorado Canyon) in Room 208 of the Old Executive Office Building. (b) Ground crew prepares a 48th Tactical Fighter Wing F-111F aircraft for the air strike on Libya, conducted in response to Libya's bombing of a Berlin disco in which two U.S. soldiers were killed. (Courtesy of U.S. Executive Office of the President and U.S. Department of Defense.)

In August 1998, President Clinton ordered the firing of cruise missiles at an al-Qaeda training base at Khost, Afghanistan. The August 20, 1998, attack was in retaliation for al-Qaeda's car bombings of the U.S. embassies in Nairobi, Kenya, and Dar es Salaam, Tanzania, that killed 224 people, including 12 Americans, and wounded about 4,000 other persons. The missile attack caused damage and an unknown number of casualties, but bin Laden was not present.

Meanwhile the U.S. Navy fired cruise missiles against a pharmaceutical factory in Khartoum, Sudan, which was believed, from earlier covertly obtained soil samples, to be producing components chemical warfare materials for bin Laden's al-Qaeda organization. However, post attack investigations suggested the plant was not involved.

The Clinton administration had called off at least one cruise missile attack in Afghanistan because of the risk of hitting visiting foreign dignitaries. Cruise missiles have the disadvantage of the time lag, which can be hours for long flights, between launch and hitting the target. However, the administration sped up efforts to develop an armed drone, initially marrying a hellfire missile to existing reconnaissance drones. This set the stage for the first use of an armed drone to kill a top al-Qaeda commander, Mohammed Alef, in November 2001.[5]

This expanding activity had obvious impact on the federal government budget. By the time of the New York and Pentagon attacks in 2001, overall spending on terrorism by the federal government (in addition to military expenditure) was estimated to be approaching the $7 billion mark.[6]

---

[5] Micha, Zenco. *10 Things You Didn't Know About Drones.* Foreign Policy, February 27, 2012. http://foreignpolicy.com/2012/02/27/10-things-you-didnt-know-about-drones/ (accessed May 8, 2017).

[6] Howard, Russell D. Howard and Reid L. Sawyer. *Terrorism and Counterterrorism,* McGraw-Hill/Diskin, 2002), p. 451.

CHAPTER 4

Changes in Counterterrorism Policy in Bush Administration Following 9/11

The first attack on the World Trade Center in February 26, 1993, and then on the Twin Towers in New York on September 11, 2001, marked a significantly changed and much more dangerous terrorist threat. It revealed the evolution of the primary threat from secular organizations such as Abu Nidal, the Popular Front for the Liberation of Palestine, (PFLP) and ethnic-based groups (i.e., the Kurdish PKK, the Irish Republican Army, and Tamil Tigers) to more radical and more dangerous Islamist groups such as al-Qaeda, as well as the Taliban, and later ISIS plus their affiliates in Africa and Yemen. Then ISIS gained control of territories in Iraq and Syria that became bases for recruitment and training for terrorist attacks and raising funds.

Five days after the 9/11 attacks, U.S. Vice President Dick Cheney appeared on *Meet the Press* and promised that the United States would use "any means at its disposal" to fight terrorism.[1] Motivated by a desire for revenge, a felt need to mete out punishment, and fear of another major terrorist attack, the George W. Bush administration invaded Afghanistan to root out the al-Qaeda and the Taliban. Later the Bush administration invaded Iraq to overthrow Saddam Hussein, asserting that the dictator was developing nuclear weapons of mass destruction and had ties to al-Qaeda.

Fifteen years later, both those wars are still underway in one form or another. Prosecution of these counterterrorism wars involved the introduction of highly controversial policies and programs: "enhanced interrogation" of captured terrorist suspects, indefinite detention of

---

[1] Vice President Cheney. Interview. *Meet the Press*, September 16, 2001. https://georgewbush-whitehouse.archives.gov/vicepresident/news-speeches/speeches/vp20010916.html (accessed May 8, 2017).

"enemy combatants," and a major US Government detention facility in Guantanamo Bay, Cuba, warrantless domestic surveillance, and military commissions to conduct trials of detainees.

The first USG legislative reaction was the Authorization for the Use of Military Forces against Terrorists[2] (or AUMF), which was made law on September 14, 2001, to authorize the use of U.S. Armed Forces against those responsible for the attacks on September 11, 2001. It authorized the president to use all necessary and appropriate force against those nations, organizations, or persons he determined planned, authorized, committed, or aided the terrorist attacks that occurred on September 11, 2001, or harbored such organizations or persons, to prevent any future acts of international terrorism against the United States by such nations, organizations, or individuals. Congress declared this was intended to constitute specific statutory authorization within the meaning of Section 5(b) of the War Powers Resolution of 1973.

The direct attack on U.S. soil elevated public consciousness as well as redefining the threat, not only for the general public but also for the relatively new Bush administration. President George W. Bush set the tone with what amount to a declaration of war based on the AUMF. The War on Terror, also known as the GWOT, is a metaphor of war referring to the international military campaign that started after the September 11 attacks on the United States. President Bush and Vice President Cheney in effect portrayed terrorism as an existential threat against the United States.

President Bush first used the term *war on terror* on September 20, 2001, in a televised address to a joint session of Congress (Figure 4.1).[3] The Bush administration and the Western media have since used the term to argue a global military, political, legal, and conceptual struggle against both organizations designated terrorist and regimes accused of supporting them. It was originally used with a particular focus on countries associated with Islamic terrorist organizations including al-Qaeda and like-minded organizations. Later the overall title for the war (or wars) morphed into the more anodyne "Overseas Contingency Operations" and an effort was made to popularize the term "the long war." In any case, the effort would turn out to occupy two U.S. presidents throughout their terms and become a major item confronting President Donald Trump.

Al-Qaeda's increasingly sophisticated use of the Internet and social media to foster their propaganda and recruit activists and supporters created a new challenge to the United States and other countries. Radicalization efforts no longer depended largely on person-to-person

---

[2] Authorization for the Use of Military Forces against Terrorism. https://www.congress.gov/bill/107th-congress/senate-joint-resolution/23/ (accessed May 8, 2017).

[3] The White House. *President George Bush Speech to Joint Session of Congress*, September 20, 2001. https://georgewbush-whitehouse.archives.gov/news/releases/2001/09/20010920-8.html (accessed May 8, 2017).

FIGURE 4.1 September 20, 2011: In the immediate aftermath of the attacks on September 11, President Bush addresses a joint session of Congress and the nation to declare a war on terror.

recruitment efforts. The websites and chat rooms could reach disaffected persons, mainly young men, on their computers away from prying eyes and sometimes under the noses of their parents.

The Bush administration revived a public diplomacy effort, centered in the State Department, aimed at countering the messages of al-Qaeda. The early effort was ineffective and ridiculed, after the initial head, a former advertising executive, spent money on flashy brochures describing how well Muslims were treated and prospered in the United States. An earlier counterterrorism public diplomacy campaign was launched by Secretary of State George Shultz following the bombing of the Marine Barracks and U.S. embassy in Lebanon in 1983 but it later faded away under Secretary of State James Baker.

The new public diplomacy program later lead to the Countering Violence Extremism program, in which both the FBI and Department of Homeland Security work with local domestic agencies and organizations. The State Department and other agencies work to counter radicalization in the international arena, including helping other countries deal with their radicalized youth. At least a partial answer to bureaucratic issues of sharing information was provided in the USA PATRIOT Act passed by Congress on October 11, 2001. The Patriot Act gave federal officials greater authority to track and intercept communications, both for law enforcement and foreign intelligence gathering purposes and to share information between the CIA and FBI. As described in Chapter 2, it also gave the Treasury Department enhanced regulatory powers to combat financial transactions by terrorists.[4]

[4] The 2010 National Security Strategy for Terrorism. May 27, 2010. http://nssarchive.us/national-security-strategy-2010/ (accessed May 8, 2017).

REFORMS AND REORGANIZATION

The terrorism challenge after 9/11 also posed new problems in confronting terrorists and a fundamental management question for the Bush administration: how to manage the terrorist threat. This included the issue of who in the U.S. government has the responsibility to identify radicalization when it is occurring and to counter and interdict attempts at recruitment. Is this best done by federal law enforcement (e.g. the Federal Bureau of Investigation) or state and local jurisdictions working closely with federal authorities?

A partial answer to this question came with the establishment of the Office of Homeland Security by President George W. Bush to coordinate "homeland security" efforts. The initially temporary office was supplanted by the Department of Homeland Security (DHS) on November 25, 2002, by the Homeland Security Act of 2002. The concept, proposed by Senator Joseph Lieberman, then chairman of a key Senate committee, was originally opposed by the Bush administration but then suddenly adopted and expanded to incorporate 22 U.S. executive branch organizations related in some way to homeland security, including the Coast Guard, into a single cabinet agency.

The DHS was established as a cabinet department of the U.S. federal government with responsibilities in public security, roughly comparable to the interior or home ministries of other countries. Its stated missions involve antiterrorism, border security, immigration and customs, cybersecurity, and disaster prevention and management. With its various components deploying more than 240,000 employees, DHS became the third largest cabinet department, after the Departments of Defense and Veterans Affairs. Many observers have noted that DHS has undergone teething problems in trying to absorb so many agencies. Homeland security policy is coordinated at the White House by the Homeland Security Council. Nevertheless, other agencies retained significant homeland security responsibilities, including the Departments of Health and Human Services, Justice, and Energy.

Whereas the Department of Defense is charged with military actions abroad, the DHS works in the civilian sphere to protect the United States within, at, and outside its borders. Its stated goal is to prepare for, prevent, and respond to domestic emergencies, particularly terrorism. On March 1, 2003, DHS absorbed the Immigration and Naturalization Service (INS) and assumed its duties. In doing so, it divided the enforcement and services functions into two separate and new agencies: Immigration and Customs Enforcement, and Citizenship and Immigration Services. The investigative divisions and intelligence gathering units of the INS and Customs Service were merged, forming

Homeland Security Investigations. Additionally, the border enforcement functions of the INS, including the U.S. Border Patrol, the U.S. Customs Service, and the Animal and Plant Health Inspection Service, were consolidated into a new agency under the DHS: U.S. Customs and Border Protection. The Federal Protective Service falls under the National Protection and Programs Directorate.

The creation of DHS constituted the most significant government reorganization since the Cold War and the most substantial reorganization of federal agencies since the National Security Act of 1947, which placed the different military departments under a secretary of defense and created the National Security Council and Central Intelligence Agency.

The National Commission on Terrorist Attacks Upon the United States (also known as the *9/11 Commission*), was created in late 2002 to prepare a full and complete account of the circumstances surrounding the attack, including preparedness for and the immediate response to the attacks, and to provide recommendations designed to guard against future attacks. The 9/11 Commission, as well as other government and nongovernmental bodies, offered numerous recommendations on what the U.S. domestic as well as foreign security priorities should be, and what changes were necessary to meet them. The commission released its public report on July 22, 2004, noting first of all that:

> We learned of fault lines within our government—between foreign and domestic intelligence and between and within agencies. We learned of the pervasive problems of managing and sharing information across a large and unwieldy government that had been built in a different era to confront different dangers.

The underlying message of the 9/11 Commission recommendations (Figure 4.2) was that the existing bureaucratic cultures would need to change, to adapt. The required change was encapsulated in the comment that the traditional "need to know" criteria for intelligence and other information would need to be changed to "need to share." The terrorist attacks in the 1970s and then 9/11, however, opened an era in that the threats we face are diffuse, ambiguous, and express themselves in a multitude of potential forms.

What was now needed was a program to bring employees from departments and agencies (and allied governments) together in common program management courses and thereby to build a common culture, a sense of common interest, and analytical skills to bond the national security functions and agencies together. This became known as a "whole-of-government" approach to national security challenges with particular

FIGURE 4.2 The *9/11 Commission Report*. In short, it called for the existing bureaucratic cultures to change and adapt.

focus on partnership with the Department of State, the Department of Homeland Security, and the intelligence community.

The *9/11 Commission Report* set the stage for change and reform in the counterterrorism area. More focused on strategic views and recommendations were the Department of Defense Quadrennial Defense Review (QDR) of 2010 and the National Security Strategy of 2010.[5] The major recommendations implemented were:

- The establishment of a National Counterterrorism Center built on the foundation of the existing Terrorist Threat Integration Center.

[5] 2010 Quadrennial Defense Review Report full text. https://www.defense.gov/Portals/1/features/defenseReviews/QDR/QDR_as_of_29JAN10_1600.pdf (accessed May 8, 2017), and 2010 National Security Strategy. http://archive.defense.gov/home/features/2010/0510_nss/ (accessed May 8, 2017).

- The creation of a National Intelligence Director to manage the national intelligence program and oversee the agencies that contributes to it.

Implementing some of these recommendations was the Intelligence Reform and Terrorism Prevention Act of 2004 (IRTPA).[6] Enacted on December 17, 2004, the IRTPA established the position of Director of National Intelligence, the National Counterterrorism Center, and the Privacy and Civil Liberties Oversight Board. In addition, it requires the DHS to take over the conducting of preflight comparisons of airline passenger information to federal government watch lists for international and domestic flights.

Other major recommendations included calling on Congress to consolidate its many committees and subcommittees dealing with terrorism issues into a joint congressional committee or single committees in both the Senate and the House. But members of Congress are notoriously loath to give up their jurisdictional roles (and the political advantages that come with it). Those recommendations have not been implemented and probably never will be unless there is a major crisis and there are strong leaders in Congress of the same party as the White House.

While the *9/11 Commission Report* remains the fundamental reform document, the current QDR of the Department of Defense, dated February 1, 2010 also contains recommendations that relate to the military contribution to the overall CT effort. The QDR recognizes the expanded definition of national security that to some degree merges external and domestic concerns and, in addition to the traditional concern for defending the United States against foreign enemies, notes the obligation to "support civil authorities at home."

Pursuing the War on Terror, the Bush administration expanded diplomatic, intelligence, and especially military activity in the Middle East. The initial USG support for anti-Taliban government forces in Afghanistan eventually morphed into a large scale U.S. military effort (Operation Enduring Freedom—Afghanistan) that continues, albeit reduced, today. That effort was followed the next year by a U.S. military invasion of Iraq (Operation Iraqi Freedom) that overthrew the Saddam Hussein government. Here also, the lack of political stability and the sectarian infighting has resulted in a continuing USG military as well as political presence (Operation New Dawn). Under the general title of "Operation Enduring Freedom," activities were initiated in the Horn of Africa, the Red Sea, and the Trans-Sahara.

When a split in the ranks of al-Qaeda's organization resulted in the emergence of the Islamic State of Iraq and the Levant (ISIS/ISIL/Daesh),

---

6 Public Law No. 108-458. December 17, 2014. https://www.dni.gov/files/documents/IRTPA%202004.pdf

the United States reinitiated military involvement in Iraq and later began limited military involvement in Syria after ISIS took advantage of the Syrian civil war to take over territory. These activities continued, consisting largely of air support against ISIS but increasingly including training, liaison, and intelligence support by special operations forces for relatively moderate Syrian rebels and Kurdish allies.

The decade following the attack on 9/11 saw U.S. national security strategy rely increasingly on special operations to an unprecedented degree. Especially noteworthy has been the rise and expansion of U.S. military Special Forces to the forefront of U.S. military engagement. Special Operations units (SOF) have long been around formally in the U.S. military; the Army Special Forces or Green Berets were created in the 1950s and became well-known for their role in Vietnam. Similar units existed in the other services.

Special operations are military operations that are "special" or unconventional and carried out by dedicated, highly trained Special Forces and other special operations forces units using unconventional methods and resources. Special operations may be performed independently of, or in conjunction with, conventional military operations. These may be covert or clandestine missions and include direct action, special reconnaissance, counterterrorism, foreign internal defense, unconventional warfare, psychological warfare, civil affairs, and counter narcotics operations. The primary goal is to achieve a political or military objective where a conventional force requirement does not exist or might adversely affect the overall strategic outcome.

Beginning with the imaginative initial campaign in Afghanistan, identifying, hunting, and killing terrorists became a central task in the GWOT and the SOF, later paired with drones, were seen as the best instrument to achieve this goal.

USSOCOM is a global military synchronizer for the war on terrorism and responsible for coordinating planning, and as directed, executing operations against terrorist networks on a global basis in coordination with other combatant commands, the Services, appropriate USG agencies, and allied governments. The USSOCOM Center for Special Operations is the fusion point for Department of Defense (DoD) synchronization efforts, combining operations, intelligence, and long-range planning and strategy.

One aspect of this CT-focused mission is the authority to train friendly foreign forces. DoD has the authority—under Section 1206 of the Defense Authorization Act of 2006[7], with the concurrence of the

[7] Serafino, Nina M. *Security Assistance Reform: "Section 1206" Background and Issues for Congress*. Congressional Research Service, December 8, 2014. http://www.fas.org/sgp/crs/natsec/RS22855.pdf (accessed May 8, 2017).

Secretary of State—to quickly respond to bolster the ability of partner countries to confront urgent and emerging terrorism. Section 1208 authorities allow special operations forces to provide support (including training, funding, and equipment) to foreign forces, irregular forces, groups, and individuals supporting or facilitating military operations to combat terrorism. SOCOM also provides support for Treasury and other agencies involved in countering terrorism financing in areas such as Afghanistan and Iraq.

Although the general public reference to these activities refer to military SOF units and personnel forces, the Central Intelligence Agency has also created a serious "special forces" paramilitary capability. These military and CIA often work together with the specific identity fuzzed over in official commentary. One recommendation, to shift lead responsibility for directing and executing paramilitary operations, whether clandestine or covert, to the Defense Department, was never fully implemented but the expansion of Special Operations global combatant commend went a long way toward centralizing military special operations.

Finally, in the effort to deal with this expanding terrorism in various regions, the Bush administration initiated a wide range of intelligence as well as military programs that were continued by the Obama administration.

In the early years, especially, in Operation Iraqi Freedom, programs for the capture and control of suspected terrorist activists, which involved charges of the officially sanctioned use of torture and complicity of other governments, became very controversial. They were cancelled by the Bush administration and later formally prohibited by executive order and legislation under the Obama administration. However, questions concerning these activities remain both as political and operational concerns.

This range of expanded activities, especially the military, inevitably required significant increases in government spending and contributed to the growing government budget deficit. From 2001 to 2006, according to the Governmental Accounting Office, Congress had appropriated \$430 billion to cover the GWOT. (This figure does not include any estimated funds for longer term obligations such as equipment replacement, debt financing, and veterans' benefits.)[8]

[8] Government Accounting Office: *Global War On Terrorism: Observations on Funding, Costs, and Future Commitments.* GAO-06-885T: Published: July 18, 2006. www.gao.gov (accessed May 8, 2017).

CHAPTER 5

Obama Administration
Policy and Program Responses

BACKGROUND

Although there was a remarkable continuity in the counterterrorism issues from the Nixon administration to President Obama's, the evolution of the challenges and responses accelerated considerably during President Obama's 8 years. This was in large part not only because of changes in technology but also because of the political effects of the Arab Spring of 2011 and the increasing involvement of Iran and Russia.

The period was marked by increasingly sophisticated use of the Internet by terrorists to disseminate their propaganda, to gain new recruits and to organize and encourage attacks, and the emergence of cyber threats and hacking.

On the U.S. government's side, the Obama administration increased the use of intelligence gathering and armed drone missiles to attack individual terrorists as well as their facilities. It also expanded its programs to counter radicalization and lone wolves, to strengthen cybersecurity, and also to improve international cooperation. Beginning with the 9/11 attack, events created a very different terrorist threat environment, which continued to change over the ensuing years. U.S. government activities of the Bush administration contributed significantly to this change, as the GWOT reinforced old relationships, created new ones, and enhanced the role of some players while diminishing the influence of others. The most dramatic and obvious changes arose out of the U.S. invasion of Iraq. This resulted in a power vacuum and loss of governance in that country, due in part to the sectarian violence between the new Shiite-led government and the Sunni population.

The Arab Spring of 2011 dramatically exposed the weaknesses and then the collapse of the political system of much of the Arab Middle East, as governments from Tunisia to Syria imploded. As much of the Middle East became essentially "ungoverned space" with al-Qaeda and

ISIS moving in, international terrorism continued to grow. This evolving situation exacerbated the terrorist challenge for the United States and for the Obama administration as it came into office in January 2009:

> The great expanse of territory from the Eastern Mediterranean to the Hindu Kush is the contemporary world's worst geopolitical cauldron. ... The United States, as the world's remaining superpower, agonizes between the conflicting instincts of duty to intervene and of plunging in to something it cannot control.[1]

While US Government and allied efforts severely hurt and diminished the immediate threat from the Taliban and Al Qaeda, a new and more virulent organization arose. A self-defined Arab caliphate calling itself the Islamic State of Iraq and the Levant (ISIL), more commonly called ISIS (or Daesh), claimed territorial sovereignty over much of Syria and Iraq.

The challenge was both strategic and tactical as ISIL also proclaimed itself a worldwide caliphate, claiming religious, political, and military authority over all Muslims worldwide. ISIL originated as Jama'at al-Tawhid wal-Jihad in 1999, which originally pledged allegiance to al-Qaeda and participated in the Iraqi insurgency following the 2003 invasion of Iraq by Western forces. ISIL gained global notoriety in early 2014 when it drove Iraqi government forces out of key cities in its Western Iraq offensive, followed by its capture of Mosul. It also generated a great deal of publicity for itself with dramatic videos showing its executioners beheading Western hostages and its car and truck bombs exploding spectacularly during terrorist attacks.

By December 2015, the Islamic State covered a vast landlocked territory in western Iraq and eastern Syria. ISIL is now believed to be operational in 18 countries across the world, including Afghanistan and Pakistan, with "aspiring branches" in Mali, Egypt, Somalia, Bangladesh, Indonesia, and the Philippines. Along with the emergence of ISIS in Syria and Iraq, ISIS and AQ affiliates sprouted from Yemen to Africa. Terrorist attacks were now being conducted by so-called lone wolves or self-motivated terrorists, in places like Boston (Figure 5.1), San Bernardino, and Ottawa, as well as direct operatives, as had been the practice up to then. Other attacks hit subways and trains in London and Madrid, wedding parties in Jordan, night clubs and sports stadiums in Paris. And in a new type of attack first used by Palestinians against Israel, trucks and smaller vehicles were used to mow down pedestrians in Nice, France,

---

[1] Marks, Edward and Cox, Robert. *Trio of the Serious*. American Diplomacy, May, 2015. http://www.unc.edu/depts/diplomat/item/2015/0106/ca/markscox_trio.html (accessed May 8, 2017).

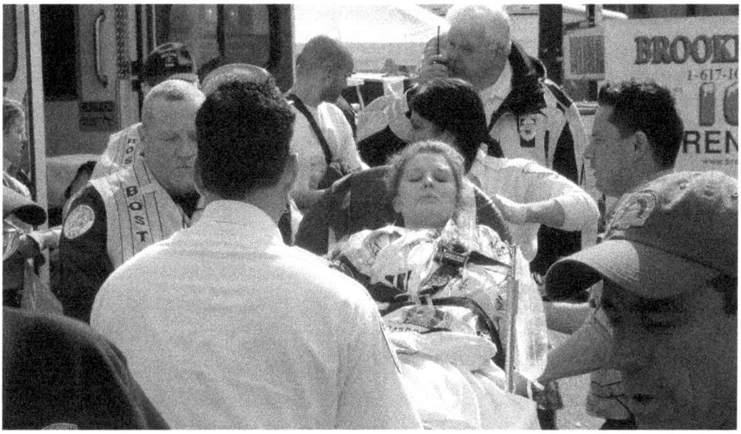

FIGURE 5.1 Medical teams assist those injured from the April 15, 2013, bombings at the Boston Marathon. (Courtesy of Federal Emergency Management Agency News. Available at: https://www.fema.gov/media-library/assets/images/70969)

Berlin, Germany, and, early in the Trump administration, in London near the House of Parliament and in Stockholm, Sweden.[2]

The sophisticated use of the Internet, including chat rooms as well as video displays, was an important element in radicalizing persons to become supporters and activists, sometimes under the noses of their families. Online publications tried to inspire disaffected young persons in Europe, North America, and even as far away as Australia, to make their way to ISIS-controlled territory in Iraq and Syria. Later, the emphasis shifted to radicalizing persons via the Internet to commit violent acts in cities where they lived, even providing instructions for making explosives or urging the use of vehicles to ram into pedestrians.

RESPONSES

The Obama administration's issues and responses essentially evolved from programs, policies, and legislation that had their origins during previous administrations. The USG legislation designed to deal with the overall terrorist threat in the aftermath of the attack on 9/11 remained the Authorization for the Use of Military Forces against Terrorists[3]

[2] Peritz, Aki. *Vehicle Attacks like Berlin's Are Nothing New and Likely to Continue.* NPR, December 12, 2016. http://www.npr.org/sections/parallels/2016/12/21/506354954/vehicle-attacks-like-berlins-are-nothing-new-and-are-likely-to-continue (accessed May 8, 2017).

[3] Authorization for the Use of Military Forces against Terrorists. https://www.congress.gov/107/plaws/publ40/PLAW-107publ40.pdf (accessed May 8, 2017).

(September 14, 2001), passed under the Bush administration. It remained in force during the Obama administration, although some tweaks were introduced to deal with state sponsors of terrorism and terrorist groups. The 2010 National Security Strategy (NSS)[4] by the Obama administration laid out the administration's strategic vision for U.S. security, one that drew from all elements of national power. The 2010 NSS also was the first to call for the full integration of homeland and national security intelligence.

In broad outline, the Obama administration pursued—albeit with some important shifts in emphasis—the path indicated by the Bush administration in its last 2 years. The Obama administration approach to the terrorist challenge was described by John Cassidy in the *New Yorker* as the "Obama doctrine:" "Constructed in response to the disaster that was the Iraq War, the Obama doctrine abjures direct U.S. military intervention in countries that don't represent a direct security threat to the United States, such as Syria. It favors working quietly through allies and proxies, such as Kurdish Peshmerga forces, and even, where necessary, Iranian militias, to attack America's enemies, and also through deploying U.S. military and technological assets that can be operated from afar, such as cyber-spying systems, reconnaissance planes, and drones."[5]

With the policy determination to shift from "GWOT" to "serious threat," President Barack Obama announced in 2013 that the United States was no longer pursuing a war on terror, as the military focus should be on specific enemies rather than a tactic. In effect, said Dan Benjamin, the State Department's Coordinator for Counterterrorism during much of the Obama administration, the United States moved out of the "war against terrorism" and into the phase of a war against al-Qaeda.[6] He stated, "We must define our effort not as a boundless 'Global War on Terror,' but rather as a series of persistent, targeted efforts to dismantle specific networks of violent extremists that threaten America." In essence, the policy was based on the conclusion that terrorism was a problem to be managed, like crime, not one that could be definitively resolved.

The new administration saw organizational integration as necessary in order to strengthen national capacity by adopting a "whole of

---

4 The 2010 National Security Strategy for Terrorism. May, 2010. http://nssarchive.us/national-security-strategy-2010/ (accessed May 8, 2017).

5 Cassidy, John. How Much of the Obama Doctrine Will Survive Trump? *The New Yorker*, December 8, 2016. http://www.newyorker.com/news/john-cassidy/how-much-of-the-obama-doctrine-will-survive-trump (accessed May 8, 2017).

6 Benjamin, Daniel. State Department Coordinator for Counterterrorism. *The State Department's Counterterrorism Office: Budget, Reorganization, Priorities*. Testimony before the Subcommittee on Terrorism, House Foreign Affairs Committee. April 14, 2011. https://2009-2017.state.gov/j/ct/rls/rm/2011/160853.htm (accessed May 8, 2017).

government" approach to the challenge of terrorism. The objective was to require programs to "update, balance, and integrate all of the tools of American power and work with our allies and partners to do the same."[7] Close cooperation with Congress and a deliberate and inclusive interagency process to achieve integration of the efforts to implement and monitor operations, policies, and strategies would also be required. To implement this effort, the White House merged the National Security Council and Homeland Security Council.

In implementing its conclusion that the Iraq War was a disaster and the United States could not effectively do more to resolve that country's internal political and religious divisions, the Obama administration drew down the number of U.S. military personnel in the region and shifted to an aggressive use of more selective instruments, such as armed drones and Special Forces. One factor was Iraq's refusal to renew the Status of Forces agreement that protected U.S. troops from being prosecuted in Iraqi courts if accused of crimes. The negotiations broke down during the Bush administration, but some Republican critics accused President Obama of not trying hard enough to renew the agreement.

The shift in policy and doctrine avoided direct U.S. military intervention in countries that were not seen as representing a direct security threat to the United States, such as Syria. It favored working quietly through allies and proxies, such as Kurdish Peshmerga forces to fight ISIS, and through deploying U.S. military and technological assets that can be operated from afar, such as cyber-spying systems, reconnaissance planes, armed aircraft, and armed drones. Accordingly, the Obama administration took the fight to ISIL in both Iraq and Syria—not with conventional U.S. army or marine battalions but with local forces backed by U.S. equipment and advisors, most importantly, Special Forces, which have grown to about 71,000 personnel.

The drone and conventional air campaigns have been the primary kinetic elements of U.S. activities in these countries.[8] The Obama admin istration conducted 10 times as many drone strikes as the Bush administration, according to one organization tracking the attacks. These U.S. assaults have been far deadlier than is generally recognized. U.S. military sources claim that drone strikes have killed between 20,000 and 25,000 Islamic State operatives in Iraq and Syria. Conventional U.S. attacks have killed about 30,000, for a claimed body count of

[7] The 2010 National Security Strategy for Terrorism. May, 2010. http://nssarchive.us/national-security-strategy-2010/ (accessed May 8, 2017).

[8] Bump, Philip. How many terrorists has President Obama actually 'taken out'? Probably more than 30,000. *Washington Post*, June 14, 2016. https://www.washingtonpost.com/news/the-fix/wp/2015/12/07/president-obama-likes-to-brag-about-the-terrorists-he-has-taken-out-how-many-is-that-exactly/ (accessed May 8, 2017).

more than 50,000.[9] The strikes continued into the final days of the administration. However, there also were reports by various monitoring organizations that large numbers of civilians have been killed during the strikes against terrorists.[10] It is impossible to verify exact numbers because accurate reporting is not possible, especially from remote areas.

The Obama administration's use of drones reflected a number of factors and went through phases. These included the improvement of intelligence gathering and the accelerated production of various models that began in the later stages of the Bush administration, according to Michael Sheehan, a counterterrorism expert who served as Assistant Secretary of Defense for Special Operations and Low Intensity Conflict from 2011 to 2013. Sheehan said that beginning in the later stages of the Bush administration and into the Obama administration there was a general consensus among top USG officials, including the Defense Department, to reduce the presence of conventional military forces in Afghanistan and Iraq and instead use drones, manned aircraft, and Special Forces to bolster government threatened by ISIS and al-Qaeda and their affiliates. Sheehan also said in an interview[11] that the Obama administration's use of drones went through phases, initially using them very heavily, and then reducing their use to targets that only directly threatened U.S. interests, such as al-Qaeda and ISIS elements in Yemen, rather than those also opposing President Abdrabbuh, who is opposed by a wider range of armed groups. The restrictions contributed to the continued weakness of the government when they resulted in the Saudi and UAE Air Forces' sometimes inaccurate bombing operations, which reportedly have caused many civilian casualties. Toward the end of his administration, President Obama then approved stepping up drone attacks.

Sheehan, who now teaches at West Point, says that the use of drones and other measures against the major terrorist organization, was a factor in the inability of ISIS and al-Qaeda to sustain a campaign of large-scale strategic terrorist attacks against the United States or other countries, although they conducted or inspired bombing or vehicle attacks in some major European cities.

"In those regions where we conduct these operations—not only do we kill off the most experienced, talented and dangerous terrorists—but those who come after them are principally concerned about staying

[9] The Bureau of Investigative Journalism. *Obama's Covert Drone War in Numbers: Ten Times More Strikes than Bush*. January 17, 2017. https://www.thebureauinvestigates.com/stories/2017-01-17/obamas-covert-drone-war-in-numbers-ten-times-more-strikes-than-bush (accessed May 8, 2017).

[10] Shane, Scott. Drone Strike Statistics Answer Few Questions, and Raise Many. *New York Times*, July 3, 2016. https://www.nytimes.com/2016/07/04/world/middleeast/drone-strike-statistics-answer-few-questions-and-raise-many.html (accessed May 8, 2017).

[11] Authors' interview with Michael Sheehan on May 3, 2017.

alive ... it is hard to run an international terrorist organization when your principal task is physical survival," he said in February 14 testimony to the House Armed Services committee.[12]

In another area, Bashar al-Assad's Syrian government meanwhile began bombing its own civilians after a civil war broke out following the regime's brutal repression of demonstrators, including children, in the wake of the Arab Spring in Tunisia and Egypt. The Obama administration considered establishing a no-fly zone to try to protect Syrian civilians from the attacks. Although Secretary of State Hillary Clinton supported the proposal, President Obama ultimately decided not to follow the course, concerned that it would result in the United States getting bogged down in another Middle East conflict and Muslim country.

The military situation in the Mideast underwent significant change during this period. The rapid defeat of the Iraqi regular forces in June 2014 by ISIL, during the early battle for Mosul, soon morphed into an insurgency war, with the United States and allies helping retrain the Iraqi army and providing some support. The Afghanistan operation, after its initial success as a largely Special Operations war, also became bogged down in an anti-insurgency and counterterrorism war. The Bush administration's invasion of Iraq had been a fairly classic all-arms effort, but the counterterrorism effort in the Middle East, and then later including Mali and Somalia, soon morphed into a combination of special operations programs, including training, logistics support, and air strikes.

However, during the same period, the Syrian government of Bashar al-Assad had obtained significant support from Iran and Russia. Russian President Vladimir Putin sent Russian air force planes to Syria as well as antiaircraft missiles. He even sent Russia's aging aircraft carrier to the Syrian coast in a relatively brief show of naval force. By then, it would have been much more complicated for the United States to establish a no-fly zone over parts of Syria. Fleeing the Syrian and Russian air force bombing campaigns and other military actions, hundreds of thousands of Syrians, about half the population, had become refugees, many of them sheltering in camps in Jordan and Turkey. Tens of thousands took flight to Europe, sometimes in dangerous crossings of the Mediterranean in small boats. The large numbers of refugees from not only Syria, but also Afghanistan and Africa, who reached Germany, Italy, and other countries prompted a backlash among citizens and added to political instability and the rise of nationalistic anti-refugee, anti-foreigner parties in some countries.

---

[12] Michael Sheehan. *The Evolving Threat and Effective Counter terrorism Strategies.* Testimony to the House Armed Services Committee, February 14, 2017. http://docs.house.gov/meetings/AS/AS00/20170214/105560/HHRG-115-AS00-Wstate-SheehanA-20170214.pdf

In Syria itself, Russia developed an equivocal relationship with Iran and its ally and client Hezbollah, which also supported the Assad regime and helped turn around the situation on the ground. The Syrian government appeared reestablished in the western part of the county, as the anti-Assad groups were weakened. The fight against ISIS continued, but the mix of combatants became more complex as an increasingly testy Turkish government insisted on the sidelining of Syrian Kurdish forces. Confusing the situation even further, U.S. support for the Saudi Arabian and UAE effort to support the Yemeni government of Abdrabbuh Mansur Hadi became problematic as that effort stalled; the Yemeni civil war continued without signs of an end and airstrikes by Saudi and UAE took a heavy civilian toll. U.S. involvement became confused in this murky situation and various shifts were under consideration as the Obama Administration came to an end.

Air power (including drones) seemed like the perfect middle ground between a large ground force invasion and inaction in these situations. The United States relied heavily on airpower to supplement Iraqi Security Forces, Peshmerga, Sunni tribal, and other militias to fight the Islamic State in Iraq and Syria. Over the course of Operation Inherent Resolve's 2-year life, coalition aircraft (with the United States by far the largest contributor) has flown an estimated 125,000 sorties and destroyed or degraded around 32,000 targets—a massive effort.[13] Air strikes also played an important role in Afghanistan, Somalia, Yemen, and other countries where the United States was fighting jihadist organizations. Airpower proved to have significant positive results tactically, causing serious damage to terrorist groups. President Obama said in a December 6, 2016, speech on counterterrorism: "ISIL has lost more than half its territory. ISIL has lost control of major population centers. Its morale is plummeting. Its recruitment is drying up. Its commanders and external plotters are being taken out, and local populations are turning against it."[14]

However, airpower has important limits. It requires bases near the combat zones and a relatively permissive operating environment with support from local governments. Most important, it does not contribute to the bolstering of effective local governments, which is required for a long-term solution to the terrorist challenge. And air strikes, even when

[13] Authorization for the Use of Military Forces against Terrorists. https://www.congress.gov/107/plaws/publ40/PLAW-107publ40.pdf (accessed May 8, 2017). *Also see* Department of Defense. *Statement on U.S. strike against al Qaeda*. January 20, 2017. https://www.defense.gov/News/News-Releases/News-Release-View/Article/1055821/statement-by-pentagon-spokesman-captain-jeff-davis-on-us-strike-against-al-qaid/ (accessed May 8, 2017).

[14] The White House. *Remarks by President Obama on the Administration's Approach to Counterterrorism*. MacDill Air Force Base, Tampa, Florida, December 6, 2016. https://obamawhitehouse.archives.gov/the-press-office/2016/12/06/remarks-president-administrations-approach-counterterrorism (accessed May 8, 2017).

well planned, sometimes inadvertently cause civilian casualties, creating political as well as humanitarian costs.

In addressing the issue, President Obama contended that overall, the use of drones can save lives by taking out of action terrorist leaders and operatives.[15] In his first major counterterrorism address of his second term, in May 2013, he outlined newly narrowed guidelines that called for deploying drones only against targets that pose a "continuing, imminent threat" to the United States and only in cases in which avoiding civilian casualties is a "near-certainty." Unfortunately, despite precautions and aborted missions, some of the strikes aimed at military targets also hit civilians and even friendly forces because of accidents stemming from undetected movements by civilians or inaccurate intelligence information.

Frank Taylor, the former head of DHS Intelligence and before that the State Department counterterrorism coordinator and a former Air Force General, noted that the effectiveness of the U.S. drones prompted the terrorists to adjust their operational security, causing them to be more careful with their communications, making it more difficult to track them than the situation with al-Qaeda 10–15 years ago.[16]

Although the role of special operations units in general and the Joint Special Operations Command (JSOC) in particular was only reluctantly discussed by official sources, the Special Operations Force (SOF) role soon became the centerpiece of media reporting. TV and films soon adopted the SOF operator and the Navy's SEAL Teams in particular as the American heroes of our age. Soon the central role of SOF was acknowledged, as in a statement by Defense Secretary Ashton at a news conference in Paris in October 2016: "We have put our Joint Special Operations Command in the lead of countering [the Islamic State's] external operations. And we have already achieved very significant results both in reducing the flow of foreign fighters and removing [Islamic State] leaders from the battlefield."[17] The most dramatic accomplishment was

[15] President Obama's speech on Drone Policy. National Defense University, Washington, May 23, 2013. http://www.nytimes.com/2013/05/24/us/politics/transcript-of-obamas-speech-on-drone-policy.html (accessed May 8, 2017). *Also see* Curry, Tom. *Obama reframes counterterrorism policy with new rules on drones.* http://nbcpolitics.nbcnews.com/_news/2013/05/23/18448515-obama-reframes-counterterrorism-policy-with-new-rules-on-drones?lite (accessed May 8, 2017).

[16] Authors' interview with Frank Taylor, a retired Air Force Brigadier General who later served as the State Department Coordinator for Counterterrorism and more recently the DHS Undersecretary for Intelligence and Analysis. March 31, 2015.

[17] Ignatius, David. Obama's tenure ends with a turf war over killing terrorists. *Washington Post*, December 8, 2016. https://www.washingtonpost.com/opinions/obamas-tenure-ends-with-a-turf-war-over-killing-terrorists/2016/12/08/b3c371d8-bd84-11e6-91ee-1adddfe36cbe_story.html (accessed May 8, 2017).

finding and fatally shooting bin Laden on May 2, 2011, in his Pakistan villa, thus lopping off the charismatic leader of al-Qaeda.

Others claimed that the emphasis on special operations precipitated a misconception that it was the solution to the problem of prolonged conflict. However, "... special operations (and by extension SOF) almost never achieve decisive strategic success on their own."[18] Indeed, special operations commanders themselves stated that grand strategy should include their "indirect approach," which meant working with non-U.S. partners to accomplish security objectives. Strategically, SOF troops were deployed in a training and coordination mission designed to both strengthen local forces in the short run and support local governance over the longer term. Special operations appropriations are costly—appropriations went from $2.3 billion in 2001 to $10.5 billion in 2012—but they appeared cost-effective compared with those required for the deployment of large numbers of regular units. At the same time, the small numbers of personnel involved in these operations somehow avoided the charge of placing large numbers of "boots on the ground," which had become a public affairs and political problem. In any case, some experts argued the investment

FIGURE 5.2 May 1, 2011: The U.S. national security team gathered in the White House Situation Room to monitor the progress of Operation Neptune Spear, the capture of Osama bin Laden from his hideout in Pakistan. (Courtesy of White House.)

[18] Long, Austin. *The Limits of Special Operations Forces*. PRISM, Vol. 6, No. 3, 2016. http://cco.ndu.edu/PRISM-6-3/Article/1020184/the-limits-of-special-operations-forces/ (accessed May 8, 2017).

was worthwhile, pointing to the raid in May 2011 that killed Osama bin Laden in Abbottabad, Pakistan (Figure 5.2).

Despite these efforts, the results were mixed. ISIS and al-Qaeda were clearly on the defensive but "jihadis," broadly defined, had gained more turf, more followers, and more money. As President Obama said in an end-of-term speech at MacDill Air Force Base on December 6, 2016[19]:

> We're still thinking through, until our last minutes here, the complex challenge of the Islamic State that we know will be around for a while. But we hope that the trajectory is now going in the right direction—on foreign fighters, funding, and fighting capacity. We want to make sure we pass along the most robust tool kit to the next Administration.

Nevertheless by the end of 2016, ISIS-controlled territory in Iraq had been cut in half and ISIS lost even more territory, including major cities, by mid-2017. Syria was a much more complex situation, as the United States attempted to cooperate with a mixed bag of local forces in a two-sided effort both to defeat ISIS and effect regime change in the Syrian government. U.S. troop levels were down to about 5,000 in Iraq and 500, mainly Special Forces, in Syria with the withdrawal of most troops from Afghanistan and Iraq and only limited ground support to the Syrian opposition. This became a feasible shift as new and improved technologies came on stream. The most obvious was the availability of increasingly more capable drone aircraft combined with more extensive deployment of SOF.

Other important elements of USG counterterrorism efforts continued, some being expanded, with varying degrees of success.

Meanwhile another form of security threats and conducting conflicts emerged in the cyber sphere.

CYBER ISSUES

As with many problems, cybersecurity issues, including terrorists' possible use of cyber tools and hacking, predate the Obama administration but the "bad guys" became more sophisticated and active during those 8 years.

Hackers of various types, ranging from youthful freelancers to those accused of working on behalf of such governments as Russia, North Korea, and China, have been increasingly active in recent years. Their targets have ranged from U.S. government military and civilian

[19] President Obama's speech on Drone Policy. National Defense University, Washington, May 23, 2013. http://www.nytimes.com/2013/05/24/us/politics/transcript-of-obamas-speech-on-drone-policy.html (accessed May 8, 2017).

websites, to the Democratic National Committee and its officials before the 2016 election. U.S. officials attributed it to a Russian government hacking operation and even issued a formal report, *GRIZZLY STEPPE: Russian Malicious Cyber Activity16*. Even before that, many companies and financial institutions and a major movie studio were hacked.[20]

The threats began emerging in the Clinton administration. President Clinton warned in a January 1999 speech that "we already are seeing the first wave of deliberate cyber-attacks, hackers break into Government and business computers."[21] After 9/11, the Bush administration stepped up efforts to counter the threat. President Bush created the Office of Cyberspace Security in the White House headed by Richard Clark, his former counterterrorism coordinator, who had been sounding the alarms about a possible major conventional terrorism attack during the summer of 2001, before the 9/11 attacks.

Earlier, the National Cyber Investigative Joint Task Force (NCIJTF) was officially established in 2008 to address this evolving cyber challenge. The NCIJTF is comprised of over 20 partnering agencies from across law enforcement, the intelligence community, and the Department of Defense. The NCIJTF has the primary responsibility to coordinate, integrate, and share information to support cyber threat investigations, supply and support intelligence analysis for community decision-makers, and assist other efforts against the cyber threat.[22]

The Obama administration reflected growing concerns about cyber threats and further strengthened the efforts to protect against cyber threats, bolstering programs in DHS, the FBI, DOJ, and other agencies to help counter the threat. And on February 9, 2016, the Obama administration issued a Cybersecurity National Action Plan that addressed "near-term actions and puts in place a long-term strategy to enhance cybersecurity awareness and protections, protect privacy, maintain public safety as well as economic and national security, and empower Americans to take better control of their digital security."[23] The plan called for greatly increased spending, $19 billion dollars—up one-third—to strengthen the

[20] Department of Homeland Security. *Executive Summary of findings on Russian hacking*. December 30, 2016. https://www.dhs.gov/news/2016/12/30/executive-summary-grizzly-steppe-findings-homeland-security-assistant-secretary (accessed May 8, 2017).

[21] President Clinton Speech to the National Academy of Sciences. Washington, DC, January 22, 1999. http://www.presidency.ucsb.edu/ws/index.php?pid=57688&st=&st1= (accessed May 8, 2017).

[22] FBI. *National Cyber Investigative Joint Task Force*. https://www.fbi.gov/investigate/cyber/national-cyber-investigative-joint-task-force (accessed May 8, 2017).

[23] White House archives: *Presidential Policy Directive—United States Cyber Incident Coordination*. https://obamawhitehouse.archives.gov/the-press-office/2016/02/09/fact-sheet-cybersecurity-national-action-plan.

government's IT program and also to help the private sector increase its security awareness and improve its electronic security.

To provide guidelines for the government and the public on the way the USG responds to a cyber-attack, whether criminal or terrorism related, the White House issued Presidential Policy Directive 41 in July 2016.[24] It said:

- ... [I]n view of the fact that significant cyber incidents will often involve at least the possibility of a nation-state actor or have some other national security nexus, the Department of Justice, acting through the Federal Bureau of Investigation and the National Cyber Investigative Joint Task Force, shall be the Federal lead agency for threat response activities.
- The Department of Homeland Security, acting through the National Cybersecurity and Communications Integration Center, shall be the Federal lead agency for assets and response activities.
- The Office of the Director of National Intelligence, through the Cyber Threat Intelligence Integration Center, shall be the Federal lead agency for intelligence support and related activities.

The DHS thus is the lead department in trying to protect the nation's critical infrastructure from cyber-attacks and working with state and local governments and the private sector.

Although there are numerous definitions of *cyberterrorism*, as there are with conventional terrorism, a key one is the definition used by the FBI, which is charged with investigating suspected terrorism-related crimes.[25] The FBI describes terrorism as any "premeditated, politically motivated attack against information, computer systems, computer programs, and data which results in violence against non-combatant targets by sub-national groups or clandestine agents." The definition is similar to the older State Department definition of *terrorism* (see Chapter 2), which describes terrorism as violence by subnational groups or clandestine agents, without specifying the form of attack.

---

[24] Fact Sheet, *Presidential Policy Directive—United States Cyber Incident Coordination*. The White House. July 26, 2016. https://obamawhitehouse.archives.gov/the-press-office/2016/07/26/presidential-policy-directive-united-states-cyber-incident (accessed May 8, 2017).

[25] Elmusharaf, Dr. Mudawi Mukhtar. *Cyber Terrorism: The New Kind of Terrorism*. Computer Crime Research Center, April 8, 2004. http://www.crime-research.org/articles/Cyber_Terrorism_new_kind_Terrorism (accessed May 8, 2017).

A huge breach of the federal government's Office of Personnel Management website took place when hackers broke into the records of about 21.5 million current and former government employees; it was disclosed in June 2015. Hackers have also broken into the FBI, State Department, and unclassified Defense Department websites.[26] Illustrating the scope of the attacks, the Office of Management and Budget reported to Congress in March 2017 that federal agencies had reported 30,899 cybersecurity incidents to the DHS Computer Emergency Readiness Team. Sixteen of the incidents were described as serious.[27]

Numerous U.S. companies and financial institutions also have been hijacked, apparently for criminal reasons, for example, to steal money, credit card numbers, or proprietary information. According to one survey released in 2016, about 90% of large U.S. businesses said they had been the target of hacking efforts the previous year.[28] In some cases, Chinese hackers are suspected by U.S. officials to be behind the breaches, including those into U.S. companies, in an electronic version of industrial espionage.

In one of the more bizarre attacks, which had elements of a terrorist attack, a group of hackers calling themselves "Guardians of Peace" in November 2014 leaked information they obtained by breaking into the Sony Pictures website. They threatened terrorist attacks against movie theaters unless the studio canceled plans to show its film *The Interview*, described as a comedy about a plot to assassinate North Korean leader Kim Jong-Un. After major U.S. cinema chains opted not to screen the film in response to these threats, Sony canceled the film's formal premiere but later, in December, released it to independent theaters and for digital distribution.

After examining the digital trails and other evidence, the FBI and other members of the intelligence community concluded that North Korea was behind the hijacking. The North Korean government denied it and some specialists raised doubt about the U.S. findings. Nonetheless, in January 2015, the U.S. government imposed additional sanctions against North Korea such as freezing any assets in the United States on top of already-existing sanctions for terrorism and nonproliferation reasons.

---

[26] Nakashima, Ellen. *Hacks of OPM Data Bases Compromised 22.1 Million People, Federal Authorities Say.* Washington Post, July 9, 2015. https://www.washingtonpost.com/news/federal-eye/wp/2015/07/09/hack-of-security-clearance-system-affected-21-5-million-people-federal-authorities-say/ (accessed May 8, 2017).

[27] Federal Information Security Modernization Act of 2014, *Annual Report to Congress.* 2016. https://www.whitehouse.gov/sites/whitehouse.gov/files/briefing-room/presidential-actions/related-omb-material/fy_2016_fisma_report%20to_congress_official_release_march_10_2017.pdf

[28] Brink Editorial Staff. *Survey: 90 Percent of U.S. Businesses Suffered Hacking Incident.* May 24, 2016. http://www.brinknews.com/survey-90-percent-of-u-s-businesses-suffered-hacking-incident/ (accessed May 8, 2017).

Earlier, on December 14, 2014, the Secretary for Homeland Security, Jeb Johnson, issued a statement saying:

> The cyber-attack against Sony Pictures Entertainment was not just an attack against a company and its employees. It was also an attack on our freedom of expression and way of life.
>
> This event underscores the importance of good cybersecurity practices to rapidly detect cyber intrusions and promote resilience throughout all of our networks. Every CEO should take this opportunity to assess their company's cybersecurity. Every business in this country should seek to employ best practices in cybersecurity.[29]

Johnson's statement reflected the concerns expressed publicly by DHS officials in a variety of forums that companies and banks were not taking enough precautions to secure their computer systems against hacking attacks.

Another form of cyberterrorism took place when hackers affiliated with ISIS publicly released the names, locations, phone numbers, and email addresses of more than 1,000 U.S. military and other government personnel for the purpose of encouraging terrorist attacks against them. A 20-year-old computer science student from Kosovo was arrested in Malaysia, extradited to the United States, and convicted in a U.S. federal court on September 24, 2016, to 20 years in prison for providing material support to a terrorist organization. The case was a good example of cyber and conventional detective work and international cooperation.

Yet another threat to U.S. institutions occurred in February 2016 when the Justice Department indicted a hacker, affiliated with the Iranian Islamic Revolutionary Guard Corps, for obtaining unauthorized access to the control systems of the Bowman Dam in New York, 25 miles north of New York City.[30] He was among seven Iranians indicted for launching denial of service attacks against the financial sector. The Justice Department said the actions cost the companies tens of millions of dollars to fix the problems and prevented hundreds of thousands of customers from accessing their accounts.

The U.S. Energy Department said the U.S. electricity system "faces imminent danger" from cyber-attacks, which are growing more frequent and sophisticated. In the department's landmark Quadrennial Energy Review,[31] it warned that a widespread power outage caused by

---

[29] DHS Secretary Jeb Johnson statement on Sony cyber attack. December 19, 2014. https://www.dhs.gov/news/2014/12/19/statement-secretary-johnson-cyber-attack-sony-pictures-entertainment (accessed May 8, 2017).

[30] Thompson, Mark. Iranian Cyber Attack on New York Dam Shows Future of War. *Time Magazine*, March 24, 2016. http://time.com/4270728/iran-cyber-attack-dam-fbi/ (accessed May 8, 2017).

[31] Department of Energy. *Quadrennial Review, 2nd Installment,* January, 2017. https://energy.gov/sites/prod/files/2017/01/f34/QER%20Transforming%20the%20Nations%20Electricity%20System%20Full%20Report.pdf (accessed May 8, 2017).

a cyber-attack could undermine "critical defense infrastructure" as well as much of the economy and place at risk the health and safety of millions of citizens. "Cyber threats to the electricity system are increasing in sophistication, magnitude, and frequency," it said in the 494-page report. "The current cybersecurity landscape is characterized by rapidly evolving threats and vulnerabilities, juxtaposed against the slower-moving deployment of defense measures." Grid operators, however, said they are coping with the problem, according to Bloomberg News.[32]

(As an example of the growing threat, in May and June, 2017, two separate waves of cyber-attacks hit various government offices and businesses around the world, affecting thousands of computer systems, especially in the Ukraine, but also other European countries, the United States, and even Australia. It was not immediately clear whether the unknown attackers were engaging in ransomware, in an effort to extort money, or whether they intended to cause disruption.)[33]

On the government front, the United States meanwhile reportedly has engaged in taking the cyber offensive, and the Pentagon established a U.S. cyber command. The Obama administration reportedly started a program to interfere with North Korea's testing of missiles that could threaten South Korea, Japan, and eventually the United States. The program may have been responsible for the failure of some of North Korea's missile launchings soon after blastoff.

Iran's nuclear program, much of which is hidden in deep underground facilities, also was targeted by a program called *Stuxnet*, developed with Israel, to speed up and destroy the centrifuges needed to develop nuclear weapons. The United States reportedly developed an even more extensive system to disrupt the Iranian infrastructure, but it was put aside when the nuclear deal with Iran was negotiated toward the end of the Obama administration.[34] In the case of both countries, the use of cyber weapons was perceived as a better alternative if needed than a kinetic strike, should either country succeed in building a nuclear device that could threaten neighboring nations or even U.S. facilities.

An overall picture of the cyber threat was presented by James Clapper, the director of national intelligence, in presenting an unclassified

---

[32] Ari Natter, Ari and Chediak, Mark. U.S. Grid in 'Imminent Danger' From Cyber-Attack, Study Says. *Bloomberg*, January 6, 2016. https://www.bloomberg.com/news/articles/2017-01-06/grid-in-imminent-danger-from-cyber-threats-energy-report-says (accessed May 8, 2017).

[33] Reuters. *New computer virus spreads from Ukraine to disrupt world business*. https://www.reuters.com/article/us-cyber-attack-idUSKBN19I1TD (accessed May 8, 2017).

[34] Sanger, David E. and Mazzetti, Mark.*U.S. Had Cyberattack Plan if Iran Nuclear Dispute Led to Conflict*. January 16, 2016. https://www.nytimes.com/2016/02/17/world/middleeast/us-had-cyberattack-planned-if-iran-nuclear-negotiations-failed.html?_r=0 http://www.telegraph.co.uk/news/2017/04/06/left-of-launch-attacks-may-bringing-north-korean-missiles/ (accessed May 8, 2017).

FIGURE 5.3 February 9, 2016: Director of National Intelligence James Clapper testifying before the Senate Armed Services Committee, providing an annual assessment of top global threats.

World Wide Intelligence assessment to Congress (Figure 5.3).[35] Among other things, he said in his February 9, 2016, testimony to the Senate Armed Services Committee, "Russia is assuming a more assertive cyber posture based on its willingness to target critical infrastructure systems and conduct espionage operations even when detected and under increased public scrutiny. Russian cyber operations are likely to target U.S. interests to support several strategic objectives: intelligence gathering to support Russian decision-making in the Ukraine and Syrian crises, influence operations to support military and political objectives, and continuing preparation of the cyber environment for future contingencies."

COUNTERING VIOLENT EXTREMISM AND LONE WOLVES

The traditional mission of American public diplomacy is to support the achievement of U.S. foreign policy goals and objectives, advance national interests, enhance national security by informing and influencing foreign

[35] Clapper, James. Director of National Intelligence. *Worldwide Threat Assessment of the US Intelligence Community*. Written statement to the Senate Armed Services Committee. February 9, 2016. https://www.armed-services.senate.gov/imo/media/doc/Clapper_02-09-16.pdf (accessed May 8, 2017).

publics and by expanding and strengthening the relationship between the people and government of the United States and citizens of the rest of the world.[36] Obviously, therefore, public diplomacy has a role to play in counterterrorism efforts. With the demise of the Soviet Union in the early 1990s, the USG's and especially the State Department's public diplomacy role shrank rapidly and the organizational capabilities, notably the United States Information Agency (USIA), were reduced significantly, largely by Congressional budget cuts and Executive Branch actions. United States Information Agency (USIA), government departments and agencies had little current experience with public diplomacy.

With the al-Qaeda attacks of September 11, 2001, the terrorist threat to America radically changed with the challenge from ideologically motivated extremists moving to the front of national security interests, both domestic and foreign. Of particular concern was the accelerated evolution of threats from the terrorists' use of the Internet for recruiting.

The terrorists' increasingly active and sophisticated use of the Internet presented a growing problem to the United States and other countries. Al-Qaeda and ISIS became adapt at producing and circulating slickly produced videos to gain new recruits. The videos of gruesome beheadings of kidnapped victims and footage of car bombs exploding appealed to many young men who seemed to have more testosterone than common sense. Thousands of persons, mainly young men but also some women, gravitated from other parts of the Middle East, Europe, North America, and even Australia, to ISIS-controlled territories to join in the "cause." They were motivated by a variety of reasons, to seek adventure, for personal and sometimes psychological reasons, for their interpretation of religious duty, and/or to become part of a bigger cause. "Many of them are searching for a meaning in their lives," said Ambassador Taylor, the former DHS Under-Secretary for Intelligence and Analysis.[37]

As John Carlin, the former Assistant Attorney General for the National Security Division, noted in an Interview, the terrorists made increasing use of the Internet to distribute "inspirational text" as well as guidance to operatives.[38] Carlin also said that the terrorists' "use of social media put a lot of pressure on the criminal justice system." Since late 2013, more

---

[36] Benjamin, Daniel. State Department Coordinator for Counterterrorism. *The State Department's Counterterrorism Office: Budget, Reorganization, Priorities*. Testimony before the Subcommittee on Terrorism, House Foreign Affairs Committee. April 14, 2011. https://2009-2017.state.gov/j/ct/rls/rm/2011/160853.htm (accessed May 8, 2017).

[37] Authors' interview with Frank Taylor, DHS Headquarters, March 31, 2015.

[38] Authors' telephone interview with John P. Carlin, former Assistant Attorney General, March 1, 2017.

than 110 persons have been charged for foreign fighter, homegrown violent extremism, and ISIL-related conduct, Carlin said in a September 2016 speech.[39]

Al-Qaeda and ISIS created websites and chat rooms to try to radicalize persons on by long distance, without having to meet face to face with local recruiters, although local recruiters also were used in some communities, especially overseas. Guidance to potential operatives, especially so-called lone wolves, was fostered by an online magazine, *Inspire*, produced by the terrorist group "Al-Qaeda in the Arabian Peninsula." Articles included instructions on how to make bomb devices. As authorities in European countries, the United States, and Turkey made it more difficult for ISIS recruits to make their way to Syria, ISIS turned its emphasis to encouraging its supporters to conduct attacks in the countries where they were living.

U.S. administrations had attempted to deal with this problem for years. For example, after the 1983 bombings of the U.S. embassy facilities and the Marine barracks in Beirut, the Reagan administration established an interagency public diplomacy program aimed at deglamorizing terrorism. The State Department, the USIA, and Defense Department were involved in promoting the basic message that terrorists were not glamorous freedom fighters but were criminals and should be arrested and prosecuted. The target audiences were primarily in Europe and the Middle East.

The effort later faded away during the first Bush administration in the early 1990s, but after 9/11 the George W. Bush administration started a new public diplomacy effort. Its efforts were much derided as an advertising campaign (it was started by a former Madison Avenue advertising executive). The initial product was a glossy brochure intended to show Muslims overseas how well Muslims were treated in the United States, in an attempt to show that the War on Terror was not anti-Muslim.

These efforts later evolved into the more focused CVE program during the latter part of the Bush administration. It was intended to counter the radicalization of susceptible youth who were responding to the Internet's siren calls or face-to-face contacts with recruiters. Public diplomacy was, therefore, adapted as a major program in the ideological struggle with those who practice and support terrorism and try to recruit others.

[39] John P. Carlin, Assistant Attorney General. *Opening remarks at the National Security Division 10 anniversary Conference.* Washington, D.C., September 14, 2006. https://www.justice.gov/opa/speech/assistant-attorney-general-john-p-carlin-delivers-opening-remarks-national-security (accessed May 8, 2017).

The Obama administration refined and expanded the effort, explaining toward the administration's end in 2016:

> In 2011, the United States adopted the Strategy for Empowering Local Partners to Prevent Violent Extremism in the United States (Strategy) and a corresponding Strategic Implementation Plan. Since publication, the mission to prevent violent extremism has progressed, and violent extremist threats have continued to evolve. The overall goal of the Strategy and United States Government efforts to implement it remains unchanged: to prevent violent extremists and their supporters from inspiring, radicalizing, financing, or recruiting individuals or groups in the United States to commit acts of violence. This updated Strategic Implementation Plan responds to the current dynamics of violent extremism and reflects experiences and knowledge acquired over the last five years.[40]

The CVE program itself was described by the USG this way: "CVE refers to proactive actions to counter efforts by violent extremists to radicalize, recruit, and mobilize followers to violence and to address specific factors that facilitate violent extremist recruitment and radicalization to violence. This includes both disrupting the tactics used by violent extremists to attract new recruits to violence and building specific alternatives, narratives, capabilities, and resiliencies in targeted."[41] As noted by one former State Department counterterrorism official who worked on the effort, the programs for working with people face-to-face at a local level are intended to reach susceptible youths before they start going online and running the risk of becoming radicalized.[42]

Implementing CVE, the USG developed what is in effect a three-track program aimed at countering violent extremism, including the recruitment of terrorists, foreign fighters, and radicalization of lone wolf terrorists who are not part of a terrorist cell and usually operate on their own. The CVE effort "focuses on three main lines of effort that will reduce terrorist recruitment: delegitimizing the violent extremist narrative in order to diminish its 'pull;' developing positive alternatives for youth vulnerable to radicalization to diminish the 'push' effect of

---

[40] DHS. *Strategic Implementation Plan for Empowering Local Partners to Prevent Violent Extremism in the United States*. October, 2016. https://www.dhs.gov/sites/default/files/publications/2016_strategic_implementation_plan_empowering_local_partners_prev.pdf (accessed May 8, 2017).

[41] Department of State & USAID *Joint Strategy on Countering Violent Extremism*. May 15, 2016. http://pdf.usaid.gov/pdf_docs/PBAAE503.pdf (accessed May 8, 2017).

[42] Eric Rosand, former senior advisor in the State Department Counterterrorism Office 2010–2014 during the Obama administration, interview with the authors, April 17, 2017.

grievances and unmet expectations; and building partner capacity to carry out these activities."[43]

One track works to counter the terrorists directly online. In 2011, the State Department set up the Center for Strategic Counterterrorism Communication. The operation was later modified and morphed into what is now called the Global Engagement Center (GEC), an interagency entity housed at the State Department, which is charged with coordinating U.S. counterterrorism messaging to foreign audiences.[44] The GEC was established pursuant to Executive Order 13721, signed on March 14, 2016, which states that the center "shall lead the coordination, integration, and synchronization of Government-wide communications activities directed at foreign audiences abroad in order to counter the messaging and diminish the influence of international terrorist organizations," such as ISIS.

This operation uses social media to try to counter the efforts by al-Qaeda and ISIS to radicalize and recruit persons online. This includes, according to various press reports, specialists going online into chat rooms, using Arabic or other appropriate languages to counter those who are trying to radicalize susceptible (usually young) persons. New communications hubs were set up in Dubai and Malaysia to be run by Muslims. State Department officials say 17 coalition members are producing content in five languages to counteract ISIS's propaganda and attack its online presence.

The second track is an overseas CVE program designed to help countries that face radicalization problems. The Obama administration began to devote considerable financial and human resources to help countries counter radicalization at the community level. The international aspect of the CVE effort aims to strengthen the capacity and engagement of partner nations in CVE work, propagating best practices and building an international consensus behind the effort to delegitimize extremists and their ideologies.

Key elements include helping other countries develop CVE programs, including strengthening CVE efforts by local and municipal groups, and programs that reach out to youths, women, and religious leaders. These include helping improve police engagement with local communities and juvenile justice systems and efforts to encourage youth programs to divert young people from possible criminal and radicalization activities.[45]

---

[43] Benjamin, Daniel. State Department Coordinator for Counterterrorism. *Al-Qa'ida and Its Affiliates*. New America Foundation Conference. April 27, 2011. https://2009-2017.state.gov/j/ct/rls/rm/2011/161895.htm (accessed May 8, 2017).

[44] State Department. *Global Engagement Center*. https://www.state.gov/r/gec/ (accessed May 8, 2017).

[45] State Department Counterterrorism Bureau website. https://www.state.gov/j/ct/programs/index.htm#CVE (accessed May 8, 2017).

- Enhancing civil society's role in CVE efforts, particularly among youth, women, and religious leaders
- Counter-messaging and promoting alternative narratives
- Addressing radicalization in and through the criminal justice sector, such as police community engagement, diversion programs, and juvenile justice

The overseas CVE effort is a Department of State and U.S. Agency for International Development (USAID) joint effort, with CVE having been institutionalized at State as part of the new Counterterrorism and CVE bureau that Secretary of State Hillary Clinton had elevated from the former Counterterrorism Coordinator's Office. (See below.) USAID has a CVE secretariat, which coordinates across USAID bureaus/missions. To share ideas and help develop a consensus, the Obama administration organized international conferences to promote the effort. The efforts drew from consultations with Britain and the Netherlands, which had begun some of the first programs in response to a perceived increase in radicalization among some of their Muslim citizens.

The third component is the domestic CVE program, which aims to deter U.S. residents from joining "violent extremist" groups by bringing community and religious leaders together with law enforcement, health professionals, teachers, and social service employees. As described in a 2016 strategy paper, the program also is intended to help people in local communities to spot someone who may be in the process of becoming a lone wolf terrorist or otherwise prone to committing violence.[46]

> There may be times when those closest to someone are concerned about whether the individual is at risk of being drawn into violent extremism. At that critical point, those concerned may search for resources on their own, or turn to respected members of their community for guidance. Sometimes these cases come to the attention of law enforcement personnel, who are also in need of response options in the event that a person is reasonably believed not to pose a threat or be immediately capable of committing a crime. The Federal Government will work with local communities and experts to develop models and resources for assisting these individuals. There may be times when those closest to someone are concerned about whether the individual is at risk of being drawn into violent extremism. At that critical point, those concerned may search for resources on their own or turn to respected members of their community for guidance.

[46] DHS. *Strategic Implementation Plan for Empowering Local Partners to Prevent Violent Extremism in the United States.* October, 2016. https://www.dhs.gov/sites/default/files/publications/2016_strategic_implementation_plan_empowering_local_partners_prev.pdf (accessed May 8, 2017).

The key goals of CVE programming are to counter the appeal of radicalization messages and reduce the effectiveness of terrorist propaganda, thus leading to lowered numbers in recruitment. Therefore, CVE involves more than messaging, and involves efforts by other various members of the interagency community. The DHS developed grant programs for local agencies and communities to develop programs that address the factors that make some people susceptible to extremism. These efforts include providing alternatives for at-risk youth, encouraging the use of social media to generate local initiatives, and enhancing the resilience of communities to counter extremism.

A domestic interagency task force was formed toward the end of 2015, with DHS, the FBI, and the National Counter Terrorism Center, to better coordinate efforts to counter radicalization inside the United States and minimize the previous problem of both DHS and the FBI trying to work separately with various religious and community groups.[47]

While attractive in theory, the CVE program came under criticism from different angles and remains a controversial approach. Some critics are concerned that the FBI might use the program for intelligence gathering. Some question whether radicalization on religious lines is the only reason someone becomes a terrorist but feel efforts still need to be made to prevent persons from turning to terrorism.[48] By contrast, an extensive study headed by former CIA and Defense Secretary Leon Panetta and former British Prime Minister Tony Blair recommended that CVE programs be expanded and funded at a $1 billion level to more vigorously counter radicalization threats worldwide.[49] This would be a big leap from the current funding; the State Department's Fiscal Year 2017 request, for example, was $59 million, and DHS sought $10 million for a grant program to assist local communities.

It is extremely difficult to quantify results. If a person is in one of the stages of becoming radicalized, either via the Internet or personal contacts, but draws back from the final step, he or she is hardly likely to go out of the way to report this to DHS, the FBI, or even a local nongovernment agency or their imam.

In February 2016, the State Department responded to criticism by the White House and Congress that more needed to be done to stop the spread of the extremists' ideology by changing the organizational structure of the State Department and tasking a single bureau at the State

---

[47] Ibid.

[48] Green, Emma. *What Lies Ahead for Obama's Counter Violent Extremism Program.* The Atlantic, March, 2017. https://www.theatlantic.com/politics/archive/2017/03/countering-violent-extremism/519822/ (accessed May 8, 2017).

[49] CSIS. *Turning Point, A New Comprehensive Strategy for Countering Violent Extremism study. Center for Strategic and International Studies*, November, 2016. https://www.csis.org/features/turning-point (accessed May 8, 2017).

Department with coordinating all counter-extremism efforts. The Office of the Coordinator for Counterterrorism, whose predecessor was originally established after the Munich 1972 Olympics attack, was renamed the Bureau of Counterterrorism and Countering Violent Extremism and given expanded responsibilities such as CVE. The renamed bureau was roughly tripled in size and allocated tens of millions of additional dollars in newly appropriated funds from Congress. The new bureau was also charged with becoming a hub for coordinating terror prevention efforts on everything from counterpropaganda, terrorist rehabilitation programs, aviation security, terrorist financing to antiterrorism training programs.

INTERNATIONAL COOPERATON

International cooperation has always been a key component in countering terrorism and the United States has close working bilateral relationships with many nations. To pursue this object, the Obama administration continued the series of annual bilateral meetings with close partners, such as Britain and Canada, and also programs to reach out and support legitimate local and regional partners that have a mutual and vested interest in combating terrorism. During the Clinton and Bush administrations the efforts engaged in multilateral efforts to encourage the development of regional organizations, such as those in Latin America, Africa, and Asia. In addition, the United Nations plays a role, including the development of international counterterrorism conventions and, after 9/11, programs to help assist other countries improve their legal mechanisms.

These approaches, however, have their limitations and the State Department helped created a new initiative in 2011, the Global Counterterrorism Forum.[50] The group of 29 nations, including a number of Muslim countries plus the European Union, cuts across regional lines and provides a way for senior counterterrorism officials of a variety of countries to meet regularly, usually twice a year.[51] The forum also has half a dozen working groups, such as those on foreign fighters and CVE, which meet more often for more detailed discussions and exchanges.

The program to limit and close down terrorist financing showed significant progress beginning during the Bush administration but also

[50] See Global Counterterrorism Forum summary, State Department website summary. https://www.state.gov/j/ct/gctf/, and the Global Counterterrorism Forum website. https://www.thegctf.org/ (accessed May 8, 2017).

[51] For an additional description see page 9, speech by State Department Counterterrorism Coordinator Daniel Benjamin to the Brookings Institute. December 18, 2012. https://www.brookings.edu/wp-content/uploads/2012/12/20121218_benjamin_remarks.pdf (accessed May 8, 2017).

evolved during the Obama period, with significant pressure especially on ISIS funding by the Treasury Department, the military, and the intelligence community. ISIS has run, in essence, a war economy and its ability to control significant territory enables it to tax and extort money from persons and businesses in areas it controls. Revenue from running oil operations in Iraq and Syria has been a major source of income for the group—taking advantage of the black market in oil and old Iraqi oil smuggling routes. Kidnapping for ransoms, especially of Westerners, also has been a source of funding.

Hostage Policy

The issue of whether the United States should pay ransom or otherwise make concessions to obtain the release of hostages captured by terrorist groups is a perennial one, coming up almost every time an American is taken hostage. The long-standing policy is no—that the United States should not pay ransom or make concessions, out of concern that it just encourages more hostage-taking. However, there have been departures (See the reference to the Iran–Contra deal in Chapter 2).

After several hostage situations early in his administration, President Obama ordered a study of the policy and basically reaffirmed it. He said in a June 24, 2015, statement[52]:

> ... I'm updating our hostage policy. I'm making it clear that our top priority is the safe and rapid recovery of American hostages. And to do so, we will use all elements of our national power. I am reaffirming that the United States government will not make concessions, such as paying ransom, to terrorist groups holding American hostages. And I know this can be a subject of significant public debate. It's a difficult and emotional issue, especially for the families. As I said to the families who are gathered here today, and as I've said to families in the past, I look at this not just as a President, but also as a husband and a father. And if my family were at risk, obviously I would move heaven and earth to get those loved ones back.
>
> As President, I also have to consider our larger national security. I firmly believe that the United States government paying ransom to terrorists risks endangering more Americans and funding the very terrorism that we're trying to stop. And so I firmly believe that our policy ultimately puts fewer Americans at risk.

[52] White House. *Statement by the President on the US Government's Hostage Policy Review.* June 24, 2015. https://obamawhitehouse.archives.gov/the-press-office/2015/06/24/statement-president-us-governments-hostage-policy-review (accessed May 8, 2015).

> He also said he was improving the efforts to provide information to families of hostages—many had complained they had not been receiving timely information.

Thus, economic disruption was a key element of the Obama administration war plan against ISIS. The United States accelerated its understanding of how ISIS was doing business and moving money within its territory and beyond. The U.S. and coalition airstrikes—including on cash distribution centers and eventually on oil facilities and tanker trucks—and pressure on the ground were intended to dislodge the Islamic State from some of its oil and gas supplies and infrastructure and cut its revenue. The successful military campaign to sharply reduce the territory controlled by ISIS also has cut into its ability to tax and extort money funds from the local population. Meanwhile, U.S. authorities have squeezed certain key chokepoints for the ISIS economy where it touches the regional and global financial system—including by isolating the financial institutions that sit in ISIS-controlled territory and sanctioning key financiers and brokers. Here too, international cooperation was key, and the Treasury Department played an increasingly active role. (See Chapter 2.)

> Ultimately though, we have had to recognize that a major enabling factor for financing is ISIS control of territory and resources—and therefore that the United States and its allies have to dislodge the group physically in order to fully cut off its financial lifeline. There is no magic button at Treasury to do this.

The effects were real, and the ISIS finances seem to be reduced significantly, with salaries being cut for some of the "fighters."[53]

Programs

The rest of the overall panoply of USG counterterrorism programs continued to evolve. A major tool to help other countries is the State Department's Antiterrorism Assistance Program, which was first authorized in 1983 and provides training to foreign law enforcement officials in such areas as strengthening law enforcement counterterrorism investigations, bomb detection and disposal, critical incident management, dignitary protection, airport and border security, hostage negotiation,

---

[53] Zarate, Juan. *Former Assistant Secretary of the Treasury, testimony to the Senate Foreign Relations Committee, for Terrorist Financing and Financial Crimes.* December 1, 2016. https://www.foreign.senate.gov/imo/media/doc/120116_%20 Zarate_Testimony.pdf (accessed May 8, 2017).

and cybersecurity. Funding for the program has fluctuated. When it began in 1983, the initial funding level was $5 million. After 9/11, funding rose and reached $215 million in FY 2010 for 7,000 participants from 64 countries. In later years, the program focused on fewer countries and the State Department budget request for FY 2017 from various accounts was $89.7 million.

Another State Department program was developed in the late 1990s after the 1998 al-Qaeda terrorist attacks on the U.S. embassies in Kenya and Tanzania. The Kenyan government asked for help in developing an investigative tool to help quickly identify persons who left the country just before or after a terrorist attack. The State Department counterterrorism office, working with other offices and agencies, developed a computerized database program that kept track of persons entering and leaving a country, called the Terrorist Interdiction Program/Personal Identification, Secure Comparison, and Evaluation System (TIP/PISCES) program. It provides state-of-the-art computerized screening systems that enable immigration and border control officials to quickly identify suspected persons attempting to enter or leave their countries, including foreign fighters who travel to Syria and Iraq and then try to return home. The State Department estimates that worldwide, more than 300,000 travelers are processed through PISCES-equipped airports and other border control sites every day in 22 high-counterterrorism-priority countries. The FY 2017 request is $30 million.

There are a variety of other programs in the counterterrorism arena; for example, both the State Department and FBI have rewards programs for information leading to the arrest and prosecution of terrorists or information that would foil a terrorist attack. The Defense Department and State Department co-chair an interagency counterterrorism research and development program that funds development of equipment to prevent terrorist attacks (such as improved airport and building scanner equipment), counter WMDs, and physical security improvements or to help counter an attack. The program, known as the Technical Support Working Group also conducts joint R&D programs with Britain, Canada, Israel, Australia, and Singapore. DHS also has a research and development program.

On the domestic front, the FBI and DHS have a number of training programs for law enforcement officials, including a DHS program for protecting infrastructure sites and an exercise program for dealing with a variety of threats, such as terrorism.

Meanwhile DHS, which was launched during the Bush administration, continued to refine its programs. For example, the Customs and Border Protection Program developed more sophisticated databases for people and cargo. For border crossings with Canada and Mexico where there are high volumes of people and goods, the trusted travelers and trusted trade programs were expanded. The database for the visa waiver for visitors from certain friendly countries was made more sophisticated. Meanwhile the Transportation Safety Administration (TSA) launched the Trusted Traveler program in 2011, which allows persons who fly frequently to sign up (for a fee) and undergo an advanced security check in order to go through a shorter airport security line.

Law enforcement actions against suspected terrorists also continued to be stepped up during the Obama era. Sharing information between the relevant federal agencies and also with state and local governments (as well as foreign allies) is an important part of the counterterrorism effort. A major factor was the lowering of the barrier to sharing sensitive investigative material between the intelligence community and the FBI, as described in Chapter 2 on counterterrorism legislation.

In 2006 during the Bush administration, the Justice Department consolidated several sections into the National Security Division (NSD), combining the Terrorism and Violent Crimes section and the Office of Intelligence and Review, bringing together prosecutors, law enforcement agencies and the intelligence community. Since the division was formed, 340 terrorists have been convicted. With the growth of the terrorism threat in the United States, the NSD became increasingly busy and since 2013, more than 110 individuals have been charged in more than 35 districts for foreign fighter, homegrown violent extremism, and ISIL-related conduct.[54]

There were some members of Congress and lawyers, mainly on the conservative side of the spectrum, who argued that more terrorist suspects, especially those with foreign connections, should be tried in military courts rather than civilian courts. However, the Obama administration and others contended that the civilian courts were actually more effective because a wider range of legal provisions could be used and they were perceived to be fairer, especially overseas where military courts were often misused. Overall, between 9/11 and 2016, more than 550 persons were convicted in civilian federal courts, as opposed to 8 in military commissions (see Chapter 2, the "Legislation" section).

Early on, the incoming Trump administration indicated it intended to make more use of Guantanamo and military commissions. However, nine months into the new administration, the acting Assistant Attorney General Dana Boente, who heads the Justice Department's National Security Division, said the administration had not decided yet whether it will put more emphasis on the military commission route. "No options are off the table," he said.

[54] Carlin, John P. Assistant Attorney General. *Opening remarks at the National Security Division 10 anniversary Conference*. Washington, D.C., September 14, 2006. https://www.justice.gov/opa/speech/assistant-attorney-general-john-p-carlin-delivers-opening-remarks-national-security (accessed May 8, 2017).

One tool used by the civilian sector was designed to facilitate the flow of information between the federal government and state and local law enforcement authorities, who were often on the front line of spotting and apprehending suspects. Fusion centers, which bring together local and state officials with DHS and FBI officials, have been established in each state to make sure that important information is shared. The exact composition varies from center to center, depending on local needs. Although there were teething problems in earlier years, during the Obama administration the level and intensity of information sharing became better than previously seen, said Ambassador Taylor, who headed the DHS Intelligence Unit.[55]

Government activity in the counterterrorism area has always raised numerous legal and civil liberties issues. Obama administration activity in the area of legal and civil liberties was both applauded and criticized. The FBI's use of "sting operations" to stop potential terrorists from actually committing an act was criticized by some of the suspects' lawyers as entrapment.[56] They suggested that the suspects were being led on by informers and undercover agents to turn their professed aspirations into an actual terrorist attack. Justice Department officials deny this and say the courts have upheld their cases. Initially more contentious was Obama's rejection, implemented in law and regulation, of the so-called enhanced interrogation methods by the CIA and the military, and the related use of "black" sites for detention (in some cases indefinite) and interrogation.

Another contentious area is that of domestic right-wing militia and related groups in the United States. Several years ago, DHS was forced by pressure from some members of Congress to withdraw a study on the subject. However, law enforcement officials, including the FBI, still have these groups on the radar screen. By some tallies, since 2002, there were 18 attacks by right-wing groups in the United States, resulting in 44 deaths, twice the number of attacks attributed to Islamists (9 attacks, with 45 deaths).[57]

Although President Obama made the closing of the Guantanamo Bay detention center a major commitment during his election campaign and reaffirmed it shortly after his inauguration, Congress took a firm stand against transferring to the United States any prisoners held in the

---

[55] Authors' interview with Frank Taylor, a retired Air Force General who later served as the State Department Coordinator for Counterterrorism and more recently the DHS Under Secretary for Intelligence and Analysis. March 31, 2015.

[56] Lichtblau, Eric. *F.B.I.* Steps Up Use of Stings in ISIS Cases. *The New York Times*. June 7, 2016. https://www.nytimes.com/2016/06/08/us/fbi-isis-terrorism-stings.html?_r=0 (accessed May 8, 2017).

[57] Swanson, Ana. San Bernardino would make 2015 the worst year for Islamist attacks in U.S. since 2001. *The Washington Post*. December 5, 2015. https://www.washingtonpost.com/news/wonk/wp/2015/12/05/san-bernandino-would-make-2015-the-worst-year-for-islamist-attacks-in-u-s-since-2001/?utm_term=.0a40b665cb72 (accessed May 8, 2017).

Guantanamo Bay prison, blocking his intention to close the controversial facility by January 2010. Congress repeatedly passed legislation that contained a ban in one form or another. For example, the 2011 National Defense Authorization Act, which was signed into law on January 7, 2011, prohibits any Defense Department funds from being used to transfer Guantanamo detainees into the United States for any purpose and also bars such funds from being used to assist in the transfer of such persons. The legislation also bars funding for constructing facilities in the United States to house transferred Guantanamo detainees and imposes restrictions on the transfer of detainees to certain foreign countries in order to prevent them from reengaging in hostilities against the United States (see Chapter 2, "the Legislative" section, for more details).[58]

Although the prison was not closed by the end of the Obama administration, the number of prisoners was reduced to 55 by January 5, 2016. In all, 779 prisoners had been brought to the prison facility since it was established in January 2012. All but 41 were released or paroled to other countries by the end of the Obama administration. President Trump has said he opposes future releases. Closely connected to the Guantanamo closure question was the administration's struggle to reform the role of military commissions as part of the effort to close Guantanamo.

These law enforcement actions and policies in the counterterrorism area raise hotly contested aspects of national security law. Among these are the extent of government surveillance and secrecy, the use of drones for targeted killings, the detention and interrogation of suspected terrorists, immigration and refugee policies, and the deployment of U.S. forces in various roles across the Middle East.

On the foreign policy side, the Obama administration was often criticized as the United States drawing back into itself and turning against military intervention. However, the record shows that the Obama administration launched, or helped enable, military strikes in more countries than the Bush administration did, extending the campaign against Islamist extremism to places like Mali and Libya (see also Chapter 1, "The Obama Administration").

In summation, the USG counterterrorism responses and programs evolved steadily over the years starting during the Nixon administration but at a more rapid pace during the Obama administration. This was not only because of refinements in earlier programs but largely because of the impact of more advanced technology and the terrorists' exploitation of the Internet.

---

[58] Committee on Armed Services, House of Representatives. *National Defense Authorization Act for Fiscal Year 2011*. https://www.gpo.gov/fdsys/pkg/CRPT-111hrpt491/pdf/CRPT-111hrpt491.pdf.

While specific programs were altered or modified, the basic continuation of policy was reflected in the counterterrorism "budget." Actually, there is no such budget, but overall expenses for the effort have been estimated. There were significant increased expenditures following 9/11, with the largest single category being the military. Estimates made in 2011 (see Chapter 3) figures the costs of the War on Terror had passed $1 trillion by 2011. By the end of the Obama administration, the Congressional Budget Office, while admitting that it was "impossible to determine precisely how much" the United States had spent on its efforts in "Afghanistan and Iraq and related activities," placed that price tag at just $1.5 trillion between 2001 and 2015, while a Brown University study[59] estimated that the country had spent approximately $4.79 trillion in Iraq, Afghanistan, Syria, Libya, and beyond. Of this, only a relatively small portion went for civilian programs by the State Department and USAID—about $123.2 billion, according to a report by the Center for Strategic and International Studies.[60]

The developments during the Obama administration provide a platform for the Trump administration and future ones, as a starting point to use as a base for their own responses and changes that they may feel necessary to make as the terrorism threat and responses continue to evolve.

[59] The Watson Institute of International and Public Affairs, Brown University. *Costs of War*. September 2016. http://watson.brown.edu/costsofwar/figures/2016/us-budgetary-costs-wars-through-2016-479-trillion-and-counting.

[60] Cordesman, Anthony. *The Uncertain Cost of Wars*. CSIS. May 10, 2016. https://www.csis.org/analysis/overseas-contingency-operations-oco-and-uncertain-cost-us-wars.

CHAPTER 6

The Policy Challenge for the Trump Administration

President John F. Kennedy once used a metaphor of an aircraft carrier to describe the U.S. government—a mammoth creature that only with difficulty and time can be moved into a very different direction. Its inertia is enormous. Almost every subject in the president's in-box, such as counterterrorism, involves a broad range of government responsibilities and authorities, all subject to the slowness of obtaining analysis, opinions, and decisions from different offices and agencies.

For years, the dominant issue in U.S. foreign policy was the Cold War. After it ended, the debate shifted to how America would interact with other countries in a globalizing world. In recent years, the liberal world order that has held sway over international affairs for the past seven decades has been fragmenting under the pressure of systemic economic stresses, growing tribalism and nationalism, and a general loss of confidence in established international and national institutions.

The newly elected Trump administration faced the question that all new administrations face, whether it wished to continue to uphold this relatively liberal order, which had helped to maintain a comparatively stable international system in the face of challenges from regional powers and other potential threats, or whether it will pursue a different role for the United States than as a guarantor of the system it helped to found and sustain.

The end of the Cold War obviously put a new light on this choice and the attack on 9/11 added a significant new complexity.

After 9/11 and up to the present, the terrorist challenge moved to the forefront of U.S. security concerns. There are both strategic and tactical considerations involved. At the strategic level, the primary question is whether contemporary terrorism with radical Islamic underpinnings is an existential threat or only one of the bundles of problems that face the United States. Even if not initially developed and fully articulated, this is eventually a necessary strategic judgment that inevitably affects U.S. foreign policy in today's world.

It is a key determinant of military policy, deployment, and tactics. International coordination, with allies, friends, and even others, must take account of the priority given to the various terrorism threats. The persistent question about if and when and how we should use military force around the world has taken on new complexity. Operational questions such as intelligence sharing, sanctions policy, and how to support friendly foreign forces will be formed with the terrorist challenge in mind in addition to more traditional considerations. And this judgment is challenge. The question about if and when and how we should military force and other tools is a key determinant for dealing with terrorist attacks and the longer-term allocation of resources and the budget.

As a result of the determination of the Bush administration following the attack on 9/11, the United States embarked on high-priority political and military involvement in the Middle East, encapsulated in the Global War on Terror. The introduction of large U.S. armies in Afghanistan and Iraq and prolonged occupation marked an escalation of U.S. policy in the area and reordering of U.S. global policy. The Bush administration moderated this view and pulled back in its last years, and the Obama administration consciously attempted to dial down the gravity of the threat and the resulting military involvement. Hence, the shift from "boots on the ground" to training local government and allied forces and also to special operations and drones.

The view of the terrorist challenge also influenced broader international relations as the US Government in 2011 organized a global alliance to deal with the threat, later renamed the Global Coalition to Defeat ISIS. Other countries joined us in the military effort on the ground, and a larger number expanded bilateral political and especially intelligence cooperation. Terrorism as a threat and counterterrorism as policy and operations moved up the priority scale for many countries, led by the United States.

This process can be seen clearly in the growth path for counterterrorism policy and programs and the effect on budgets. Civilian department budgets, including the new Department of Homeland Affairs but especially the intelligence organizations like the CIA and the FBI, were dramatically expanded. As of August 2016, the United States had already appropriated, spent, or taken on obligations to spend more than $3.6 trillion in current dollars on the wars in Iraq, Afghanistan, Pakistan, and Syria and on Homeland Security (2001 through fiscal year 2016). For the fiscal year 2017 budget sent to Congress, the Obama administration proposed $65 billion for the Defense and State Department spending, and $37 billion for DHS.

Nevertheless, those expenses were dwarfed by the costs of the military operations in the Middle East. The Defense Department's Overseas Contingency budget, that is annual operating expenses for Iraq, Afghanistan, Syria, and Yemen, was approximately $90 billion. That figure is "over budget," or additional, to DoD's formal annual budget of $560 billion, which finances the whole DoD establishment, much of which is now CT oriented.

The arrival of the Trump administration appeared to coincide with possible turning points in the long military campaign against ISIS. Long-standing air and ground operations using local forces against ISIS began to bear fruit and by mid-year the Islamic Caliphate had lost almost all its territory as well as its "capital city" of Raqqa in Syria and Mosul, Iraq's second largest city.

Nevertheless, many believe U.S. policy in Syria has failed, and there is widespread difference of opinion whether the Trump administration—or any administration—can make things better. Some of the options officials and other are considering might well make things worse. ISIS is likely to continue to exist in one form or another. As an article in *Foreign Policy* magazine suggested:

> The United States will soon reach a crossroads in its struggle against terrorism. The international coalition fighting the Islamic State (also known as ISIS) has driven the group out of much of the territory it once held and, sooner or later, will militarily defeat it by destroying its core in Iraq and Syria. But military victory over ISIS will not end the global war on terrorism that the United States has waged since 9/11. Some of ISIS' provinces may outlive its core. Remnants of the caliphate may morph into an insurgency. Al Qaeda and its affiliates will still pose a threat. Moreover, the conditions that breed jihadist organizations will likely persist across the greater Middle East. So the United States must decide what strategy to pursue in the next stage of the war on terrorism.[1]

Foreign policy in general and terrorism in particular were mentioned in the 2016 presidential campaign but not with much in the way of specifics. During the presidential campaign, candidate Donald Trump called for sweeping changes in U.S. counterterrorism strategy and promised to "defeat the ideology of radical Islamic terrorism."

For some time before the campaign, there had been a dispute over terminology. From the beginning of his presidential campaign,

---

[1] Feaver, Peter D. and Brands, Hal. *Trump and Terrorism*. Foreign Affairs, March-April, 2017. https://www.foreignaffairs.com/articles/2017-02-13/trump-and-terrorism (accessed May 8, 2017).

Mr. Trump repeatedly warned about "a major threat from radical Islamic terrorism." The question about how to identify the threat already had become a controversial issue in itself, with mainly conservative and vocally strong anti-Muslim critics arguing that the appropriate term was "radical Islamic terrorism" and implying that the Obama administration was weak or worse for not using it. The Obama administration used the much less specific term "violent extremism" out of concern that the radical Islamic phrase alienated millions of moderate peaceful Muslims.

In his "America First" inaugural speech, President Trump promised to "unite the civilized world against radical Islamic terrorism, which we will eradicate completely from the face of the Earth." An early action taken by the Trump administration was to implement the campaign promise to rename the terrorists as "radical Islamic terrorists," thereby replacing more general Obama administration terminology. This move, however, created a bit of confusion as the new National Security Advisor, General H.R. McMaster, was widely reported to have instructed the NSC staff that the term "radical Islamic terrorism" was not helpful and should not be used. However, only a few days later, President Trump deliberately used the term in public. Authoritative guidance on this question remained lacking, and the matter appeared to recede into the background as the days passed.

The idea that the conflict with "radical Islamic terrorism" is all-consuming and existential; the willingness to cut transactional deals with any actor with whom the United States shares even the most passing interests; the aspiration to get other countries to do more in the world, including Russia, all were concepts in candidate Trump's comments on the subject.

As the previously quoted *Foreign Affairs* article put it:

> He faces a broad range of choices. At one extreme, Washington could abandon its military commitments in the greater Middle East on the assumption that it is U.S. interference that provokes terrorism in the first place. At the other, it could adopt a heavy-footprint surge strategy that would involve using overwhelming military force to destroy globally capable terrorist organizations and attempt to politically transform the societies that produce them.[2]

"Fighting political Islam" is a theme that could imply making a significant change. There are a number of people, inside and outside the government, who favor a more aggressive approach to

[2] Ibid.

political Islam. Even here, however, Trump's response may differentiate between the foreign policy side, where so far there has been little in the way of clear ideas of what to do, and domestically, where the White House issued executive orders to impose much greater barriers for Muslim immigrants and refugees and even visitors from some Muslim countries.

Obviously there is a continuum between the three broad policy options: slimming down the Obama legacy, strengthening it in various and more robust ways, or devising and implementing radical new programs.

However, whether or not the Trump administration views terrorism as an existential threat in itself, it has become clear that it cannot be separated from other foreign policy concerns. The relationships with Russia and China —preceded by comments by candidate Trump—quickly became priority matters in themselves and were joined by North Korea and its nuclear activities. The complicated relationship with Iran continues. More pertinently these relationships became involved with counterterrorism policy in the Middle East, especially following a Syrian government poison gas attack in April 2016, followed by the launching of 59 Tomahawk cruise missiles against a Syrian air force base.

Earlier, Secretary of Defense Jim Mattis said at NATO Headquarters in Brussels on February 16, 2017:

> Terrorism emanating from the Middle East and North Africa is a direct and immediate threat to Europe and to us all. [...] We recognize as well that the imposition of stability has taken on new forms that we must now address, for example, in this cyber domain. In response to these threats, NATO is reinforcing deterrence and defense, and adapting to more directly address terrorist threats along our southern flank from the Mediterranean to Turkey.[3]

Gradual or evolutionary change in CT policy has been the norm to date in the four decades of CT effort. Policy evolved in the last years of the Bush administration and the Obama administration, demonstrating a fair degree of continuity. Some programs were expanded or intensified, but the only major change was the withdrawal—over a period of years—of the large American military forces from Iraq and Afghanistan, although significant forces from Iraq and air, remained

[3] Defense Department. *Press Conference by Secretary Jim Mattis*. NATO Headquarters, Brussels, Belgium, February 16, 2017. https://www.defense.gov/DesktopModules/ArticleCS/Print.aspx?PortalId=1&ModuleId=1144&Article=1085679 (accessed May 8, 2017).

FIGURE 6.1 April 12, 2017: President Donald J. Trump and NATO Secretary General Jens Stoltenberg hold a news conference following meetings at the White House. (Courtesy of Department of Defense, NATO.)

engaged in the region. President Trump reversed the trend somewhat in the summer of 2017 by sending several thousand more troops into Afghanistan to provide support and training for the Afghan Army, which has been losing men and ground to the Taliban.

As noted earlier, candidate and now President Trump has promised a more aggressive approach, to win the war against Islamic terrorism, to defeat—indeed smash—ISIS and the other movements (Figure 6.1). The details on how he intends to do this, not surprisingly, were not immediately available as the administration took office. However, there were three general areas identified where significant change was promised:

1. Identification and definition of the threat
2. Immigration and border policy
3. Role of the military

THE EARLY DAYS—STRATEGIC AND RHETORICAL

Upon assuming office President Trump clearly now "owned the problem" and quickly called for a new plan from his military advisors, while continuing for the moment with the range of policies and programs he inherited from Obama, especially in Iraq, Syria, and Afghanistan. With regard specifically to ISIS, President Trump issued a memorandum on January 28, 2017, outlining an aggressive plan:[4]

> Presidential Memorandum Plan to Defeat the Islamic State of Iraq and Syria
>
> ISIS, is not the only threat from radical Islamic terrorism that the United States faces, but it is among the most vicious and aggressive. [...] If ISIS is left in power, the threat that it poses will only grow. We know it has attempted to develop chemical weapons capability. It continues to radicalize our own citizens, and its attacks against our allies and partners continue to mount. The United States must take decisive action to defeat ISIS.
>
> 1. Development of a new plan to defeat ISIS (the Plan) shall commence immediately.
> 2. The Plan shall include:
>   a. a comprehensive strategy and plans for the defeat of ISIS;
>   b. recommended changes to any United States rules of engagement and other United States policy restrictions that exceed the requirements of international law regarding the use of force against ISIS;
>   c. public diplomacy, information operations, and cyber strategies to isolate and delegitimize ISIS and its radical Islamist ideology;
>   d. identification of new coalition partners in the fight against ISIS and policies to empower coalition partners to fight ISIS and its affiliates;
>   e. mechanisms to cut off or seize ISIS's financial support, including financial transfers, money laundering, oil revenue, human trafficking, sales of looted art and historical artifacts, and other revenue sources; and
>   f. a detailed strategy to robustly fund the Plan.

With regard to border and immigration matters, the administration moved quickly in a matter of days after the inauguration to issue an executive order closing down entry into the United States from seven Middle Eastern countries. This attempt ran into serious judicial and practical problems, was blocked in courts, and had to be withdrawn. It was replaced within a month by a revised version, but the process remained mired in judicial review, opposition, and bureaucratic complexities. The message here was that the Trump administration does intend to strengthen entry procedures as part of its CT program but will have to engage with the courts and Congress to achieve much change, much less a complete

[4] The White House. *Presidential Memorandum Plan to Defeat the Islamic State of Iraq and Syria*. January 28, 2017. https://www.whitehouse.gov/the-press-office/2017/01/28/plan-defeat-islamic-state-iraq (accessed May 8, 2017).

reversal of existing policy. The campaign promise to "build a wall on the Mexican border" was repeatedly expressed as a policy objective but little movement was noted and key members of Congress declined to approve the necessary funding in the Trump administration's first budget request.

The administration's intentions were expressed by DHS Secretary John F. Kelly for a House Committee on Homeland Security on February 7, 2017[5]:

> Within DHS and our Federal, State, local, and international partners, we must expand our vetting of those seeking to enter our country—particularly of those individuals from high-risk countries—including refugees. We currently lack a comprehensive strategy with uniform screening standards to prevent terrorists from entering the country. Unfortunately, our country has recently admitted some foreign nationals without an adequate understanding of their allegiances and intentions.

Others, including officials in the Obama administration who worked on the issue, however, said the screening of refugees takes up to 2 years, is very rigorous, and that no attacks had been conducted by immigrants from the banned countries.

Later, on April 20, Secretary Kelly gave a speech in which he painted a situation of serious, continuing threat, claiming that the United States is as vulnerable to an attack today as it was the morning of September 11, 2001. He said information in the press about national security is misleading or flat-out wrong, offering a false sense of security.[6]

The Trump administration will be making its own judgments about the desired long-term role of the military in its CT policy. However, indications were contained in President Trump's initial budget proposals released on March 16, 2017, which called for a $54 billion increase in the DoD budget—bringing it to $639 billion. Congress was poised to add even more. But this represents still an important increase in the budget for Homeland Security, much of it destined for border security.

When combined with a drastic cut of one-third in State Department funds for security and economic assistance, the shift in emphasis toward a more "hard power" approach to the challenge of terrorism appears

[5] DHS Secretary John F. Kelly. *Ending the Crisis: America's Borders and the Path to Security*. Written testimony to the House Committee on Homeland Security. February 7, 2017. https://www.dhs.gov/news/2017/02/07/written-testimony-dhs-secretary-john-f-kelly-house-committee-homeland-security (accessed May 8, 2017).

[6] DHS Secretary John F. Kelly. *Home and Away: DHS and the Threats to America*. Remarks delivered at George Washington University Center for Cyber and Homeland Security, Washington, DC. April 18, 2017. https://www.dhs.gov/news/2017/04/18/home-and-away-dhs-and-threats-america. *Also see New York Times*, April 21, 2017. https://www.nytimes.com/2017/04/21/opinion/fearmongering-at-homeland-security (accessed May 8, 2017).

likely. An expanded role for the military in counterterrorism was a reflection of the Trump administration's general intention to prioritize the role of the military in U.S. foreign policy in general.

Reflecting this perspective but using a platform created by previous administrations, the Trump administration convoked the Global Coalition Working to Defeat ISIS on March 22–23, 2017.[7] At the conference, the Trump administration reiterated its intended focus on defeating the Islamic State as its top priority at the 2-day strategy session. Initiated during the Obama administration, the 67 nation alliance was focused on military programs and created a network of subsidiary working groups. It was never very formal, however, and countries participated with greatly varying degrees of enthusiasm, although the number of participants grew.

The Trump administration used the conference to make one specific addition to the U.S. position: that other countries will be expected to contribute more to stabilize Iraq and Syria once the militants are expelled. (In addition to this coalition, the Obama administration created the Global Anti-Terrorist Coalition of 21 nations, plus the European Union, which is focused more on multilateral antiterrorism cooperation. It also has a system of committees and working groups that meet periodically.)

This position was emphasized by Secretary of State Rex W. Tillerson at the NATO Foreign Ministers' meeting in Brussels, Belgium, on March 31, 2017:

> On fighting terrorism, NATO can and should do more. Fighting terrorism is the top national security priority for the United States, as it should be for all of us.[8]

THE FIRST YEAR—TACTICAL AND OPERATIONAL

While the Department of Defense and presumably other agencies work to prepare a new strategic plan and the White House to officially promulgate it, the Trump White House began to expand the delegation of authority to the Pentagon, especially to the regional combatant commanders, to approve antiterrorist operations in order to step up the war on the so-called Islamic State. In his final days in office, President Obama sought to lock in procedures and rules governing targeted killings and drone strikes.

[7] *The Global Coalition against Daesh.* http://theglobalcoalition.org/en/mission-en/ (accessed May 8, 2017).

[8] State Department. Secretary of State Rex Tillison. *Remarks at NATO Ministerial Meeting*, Brussels, Belgium, March 31, 2017. https://www.state.gov/secretary/remarks/2017/03/269339.htm (accessed May 8, 2017).

Media reports in mid-March stated that President Trump was pushing to roll back some of these checks. Specifically, the objective is to make it easier for the Pentagon to launch counterterrorism strikes anywhere in the world by lowering the threshold on acceptance of civilian casualties and by authorizing designated military commanders to conduct such attacks without the need to obtain White House or NSC approval.

A dramatic product of this new policy was the dropping of the so-called 'Mother of All Bombs' in Afghanistan on April 13, 2017. The 21,600-pound bomb was dropped on an ISIS network of caves and tunnels in the eastern province of Afghanistan. The bomb is the largest nonnuclear bomb in the U.S. arsenal, but the decision to use it at this time and place was a tactical decision that, according to press reports, no longer required White House authorization—as had been the situation in the Obama administration—in accordance with the new Trump administration guidelines for military action.

In addition, expanded support for the U.S. military in Yemen and Somalia was announced. Whether these changes represent a modification in tactics rather than in strategy is yet to be made clear. As described in *Foreign Policy* magazine, President Trump signed off on "a new front:"

> ... President Trump has signed off on a Pentagon proposal to allow the head of the U.S. Africa Command to launch an offensive campaign against the al-Shabab militant group in Somalia, U.S. officials said on Thursday, clearing the way for more airstrikes, and potentially a more active presence of U.S. Special Operations Forces on the ground.

"It remains to be seen how active American forces will be in Somalia, where dozens of U.S. commandos already operate," *Foreign Policy Magazine's* Paul McLeary reported. But the order fits with an increasingly forward-leaning posture in Yemen, where Trump also recently signed an order allowing for more U.S. military action. Earlier, Africa Command head Gen. Thomas Waldhauser said, "I think the combatant commanders, myself included, are more than capable of making judgments and determinations on some of these targets." Giving his commanders the ability to launch offensive strikes would allow them "to prosecute targets in a more rapid fashion."[9]

In a parallel move to the granting of expanded operational authority to the military, President Donald Trump in mid-March, according to a news report, granted the CIA authority to conduct lethal drone strikes, rolling back the limits his predecessor Barack Obama imposed on the

---

[9] McLeary, Paul. Trump's promises to defeat ISIS Quickly Run into Syria Buzzsaw. *Foreign Policy*, March 3, 2017. http://foreignpolicy.com/2017/03/03/trumps-promises-to-defeat-isis-quickly-run-into-syria-buzzsaw-russia-terrorism/ (accessed May 8, 2017).

spy agency's paramilitary operations. This decision strengthens trends in CIA and other intelligence operations. According to press reports in September, the CIA was seeking to loosen restrictions on using drone strikes in Afghanistan.[10]

And as part of the bigger picture, the Trump administration's senior military advisors were reportedly proposing to dismantle key Obama-era limits on drone strikes and commando raids outside conventional battlefields. The proposed changes were described as laying the groundwork for possible counterterrorism missions in countries where Islamic militants are active but the United States has not previously tried to kill or capture them.[11]

Just as the U.S. military had shifted its strategy from "boots on the ground" to target-specific kills, the U.S. intelligence community, through both SOF raids and drone strikes, seems to have done likewise. Specifically, traditional resources once used to recruit and penetrate terrorist organizations, called "humint," seem to have been reduced, while targeting and drone killing have been significantly bolstered. As with the military, this seems to indicate some confusion regarding whether certain programs are tactical or strategic in regard to the terrorist target.

Traditional humint collection techniques would emphasize development and recruitment of individuals involved in terrorist organizations, usually in the support apparatus rather than front-line cadre. These individuals would be used to identify long-term planning, intentions, and funding and support channels. When intelligence agencies gain knowledge of the structural details of an organization, that organization becomes vulnerable and more susceptible to actions to destroy its capabilities to function effectively. That is a strategic use of human intelligence. Killing "leadership" is a tactical approach, as replacements can emerge. However, the structure of a terrorist organization is one of a kind and its destruction is strategic.

Other programs and questions will certainly surface as the Trump administration draws up and promulgates its CT policy. Two major areas are alliance arrangements and the Countering Violent Extremism program.

Since initiated in the Bush administration, Countering Violent Extremism (CVE) is not a soft alternative to counterterrorism but an essential toolkit to complement federal and state efforts to prevent

[10] Schmitt, Eric and Rosenthal, Matthew. C.I.A. Wants Authority to Conduct Drone Strikes in Afghanistan for the First Time. *New York Times*. https://www.nytimes.com/2017/09/15/us/politics/cia-drone-strike-authority-afghanistan.html (accessed September 16, 2017).

[11] Savage, Charles and Schmitt, Eric. Trump Likely to Ease Limits on Terror War: Broader Use of Drones and Comandos. *The New York Times*. https://www.nytimes.com/2017/09/21/us/politics/trump-drone-strikes-commando-raids-rules.html?hp&action=click&pgtype=Homepage&clickSource=story- (accessed September 22, 2016).

radicalization of individuals and their possible resulting violence. The CVE approach sees communities as the first line of defense against violent extremism; thus enabling and incentivizing them to become more active in the CVE space is in the local and national interest, as well as foreign allies' best interest. Results, not surprisingly, are hard to quantify and the Trump administration began a formal review in early March.

Similar evolutionary behavior was noted with respect to sanctions when on February 3, 2017, the Treasury Department said it was applying sanctions on 25 individuals and companies connected to Iran's mission program and those providing support to Iran's Islamic Revolutionary Guards Quds force as punishment for the country's launch of a ballistic missile.[12]

LOOKING AHEAD

However, whether terrorism is existential or "merely" serious, major problems of this magnitude and complexity are rarely, if ever, completely resolved or "solved." What governments generally do is manage them with varying degrees of success. Even the more concrete challenge of the USSR took 45 years to resolve, and the ongoing "Drug War" is now in

FIGURE 6.2 January 27, 2017: President Donald J. Trump swears in retired Marine Corps general James Mattis as the 26th Secretary of Defense during a ceremony in the Hall of Heroes at the Pentagon. (Courtesy of Department of Defense/Air Force Staff Sgt. Jette Carr.)

[12] Liptak, Kevin. *Treasury slaps sanctions on Iran after ballistic missile launch.* CNN. February 3, 2017. http://www.cnn.com/2017/02/03/politics/treasury-department-announcing-sanctions-against-iran-friday-morning/ (accessed May 8, 2017).

the its 30th year with absolutely no sign of "victory." It is at least possible that President Trump could end up preserving, or being forced by circumstances to preserve, major parts of the Obama approach, at least when it comes to using military force.

The outlines of the probable counterterrorism strategy under U.S. President Donald Trump have emerged. Judging from initial actions and statements—with due caution for rhetoric—a more intense campaign against the Islamic State and other terrorist groups could develop but the core of Washington's strategy, relying on local forces to do the brunt of the fighting, will likely remain unchanged. Early in the administration, on Monday, February 27, 2017, U.S. Defense Secretary James Mattis (Figure 6.2) briefed White House strategists on his 30-day strategic review of the fight against terrorism and signaled this approach. Based on Pentagon statements and leaked information, the options he outlined represent more an intensification of current efforts rather than a seismic shift in strategy. U.S. policy in Syria appears to be basically the same as under the Obama administration, although perhaps with more troops—focus on fighting ISIS while keeping Assad's Syrian regime at a distance and warily watching Iran and Syria. However, details had not been released as of the administration's first months and press leaks and President Trump's statements later in the year indicated that the White House wanted to take a more aggressive stance against Iran, especially regarding what President Trump considered a flawed nuclear treaty.[13]

The election of Donald Trump as president of the United States, of any new president in fact, raises a number of critically important issues about the future of U.S. government counterterrorism policy. Among these are hotly contested aspects of national security law, including the extent of government surveillance and secrecy, the use of drones for targeted killings, the detention and interrogation of suspected terrorists, immigration and refugee policies, and the deployment of U.S. forces in various roles across the Middle East. The stakes could not be higher: in the balance hang national security, democratic accountability, the rule of law, civil liberties, and the very nature of the republic.

There are a number of general "lessons learned" for fighting terrorism that are accepted by almost all counterterrorism practitioners and observers. These include the need for continuing strengthening international cooperation, intelligence gathering and sharing (both domestically and internationally), and continued use and refinement of the practical measures tool kit, such as the Antiterrorism

[13] DeYoung, Kevin. *Anti-ISIS strategy looks like Obama's*. Washington Post. June 29, 2017. https://www.washingtonpost.com/world/national-security/pentagon-plan-to-defeat-isis-looks-very-much-like-obamas-approach/2017/06/28/d43aa1b6-5c30-11e7-a9f6-7c3296387341_story.html?hpid=hp_rhp-top-table-main_ussyria-735pm%3Ahomepage%2Fstory (accessed May 8, 2017).

Assistance Program to help train foreign civilian law enforcement officials and domestic training programs for U.S. law enforcement. CVE outreach to local communities, especially Muslim communities, without alienating them by harsh rhetoric, was widely accepted as a necessary element of CT policy.

Other elements include Countering Terrorism Financing efforts, along with continuing improvement of aviation security equipment and procedures, maintaining export control and other sanctions, and strengthening immigration and visa entry programs. The general agreement on these programs within the executive branch, Congress, and our allies serves as the benchmark for existing policy responses and therefore the operational starting line for the Trump Administration.

However, the Trump administration assumed office with strong views about the terrorist challenge expressed during the presidential campaign but without a counterterrorism program in hand. There were two general theses: that Islamic terrorism must be absolutely defeated and that the Obama administration policy and programs have been insufficient. Since the inauguration some changes have been announced and some have been implemented, notably with respect to the activism of the military. Presumably more will be announced over time and eventually a coherent strategy will emerge—the Trump CT doctrine. As the Trump administration CT policy emerges, the old saying will apply, "God is in the details."

Key Documents

TRUMP ADMINISTRATION

1. *America First: A Budget Blueprint to Make America Great Again*, March 16, 2017

   Text of Trump Administration's FY2018 budget proposal that calls for a 28% cut in State Department and foreign assistance budgets and large increases for the Defense Department.

   https://www.whitehouse.gov/sites/whitehouse.gov/files/omb/budget/fy2018/2018_blueprint.pdf

2. Revised Executive Order, "Protecting The Nation From Foreign Terrorist Entry into the United States," March 6, 2017

   This revised the earlier EO 13769 (see below) issued on January 27, 2017, which was rejected by federal courts on the grounds that it discriminated against Muslims. The new EO also was challenged in court.

   https://www.whitehouse.gov/the-press-office/2017/03/06/executive-order-protecting-nation-foreign-terrorist-entry-united-states

3. "Presidential Memorandum Plan to Defeat the Islamic State of Iraq and Syria," January 28, 2017

   This National Security Presidential Memorandum called for "[...] development of a comprehensive strategy and plans for the defeat of ISIS; including public diplomacy, information operations, and cyber strategies to isolate and delegitimize ISIS and its radical Islamist ideology and to cut off its financial support."

   https://www.whitehouse.gov/the-press-office/2017/01/28/plan-defeat-islamic-state-iraq

4. Executive Order 13769, "Protecting The Nation From Foreign Terrorist Entry into the United States," January 27, 2017

   "Numerous foreign-born individuals have been convicted or implicated in terrorism-related crimes since September 11, 2001, including foreign nationals who entered the United States after receiving visitor, student, or employment visas, or who entered through the United States refugee resettlement program. ... The United States must be vigilant during the visa-issuance process to ensure that those approved for admission do not intend to harm Americans and that they have no ties to terrorism. ... The United States should not admit those who engage in acts of bigotry or hatred. [...]"

https://www.whitehouse.gov/the-press-office/2017/01/27/executive-order-protecting-nation-foreign-terrorist-entry-united-states

5. Executive Order, "Border Security and Immigration Enforcement Improvements," January 25, 2017

"The order directs executive departments and agencies (agencies) to deploy all lawful means to secure the Nation's southern border, to prevent further illegal immigration into the United States, and to repatriate illegal aliens swiftly, consistently, and humanely."

Also: "It is the policy of the executive branch to secure the southern border of the United States through the immediate construction of a physical wall on the southern border, monitored and supported by adequate personnel so as to prevent illegal immigration, drug and human trafficking, and acts of terrorism. [...]"

https://www.whitehouse.gov/the-press-office/2017/01/25/executive-order-border-security-and-immigration-enforcement-improvements

OBAMA ADMINISTRATION AND STRATEGY PAPERS

1. Letter to Congress, "Continuation of National Emergency with Respect to Terrorists Who Threaten to Disrupt the Middle East Peace Process," January 13, 2017

[...] the national emergency declared with respect to foreign terrorists who threaten to disrupt the Middle East peace process is to continue in effect beyond January 23, 2017. [...]

https://obamawhitehouse.archives.gov/the-press-office/2017/01/13/letter-continuation-national-emergency-respect-middle-east-peace

Original Executive Order 12947 by President William Clinton on January 23, 1995: https://www.treasury.gov/resource-center/sanctions/Documents/12947.pdf

2. Presidential Determination and Waiver—Pursuant to Section 2249a of Title 10, United States Code, and Sections 40 and 40A of the Arms Export Control Act to Support US Special Operations to Combat Terrorism in Syria, December 8, 2016

   https://obamawhitehouse.archives.gov/the-press-office/2016/12/08/presidential-determination-and-waiver-pursuant-section-2249a-title-10

3. Joint State Department-USAID Strategy to Counter Violent Extremism: http://pdf.usaid.gov/pdf_docs/PBAAE503.pdf

4. Presidential Policy Directive—United States Cyber Incident Coordination, July 26, 2016

   > "In responding to any cyber incident, Federal agencies shall undertake three concurrent lines of effort: threat response; asset response; and intelligence support and related activities. In addition, when a Federal agency is a target, it shall undertake a fourth concurrent line of effort to manage the effects of the cyber incident on its operations, customers, and workforce."

   https://obamawhitehouse.archives.gov/the-press-office/2016/07/26/presidential-policy-directive-united-states-cyber-incident

5. State Department Annual Country Report on Terrorism, 2015, June 2, 2016.

   Description of major terrorism events overseas, with country-by-country reports

   https://2009-2017.state.gov/j/ct/rls/crt/2015/index.htm

6. Nuclear Security Summit 2016 Action Plan in Support of the Global Initiative to Combat Nuclear Terrorism, April 1, 2016

   > "The Global Initiative to Combat Nuclear Terrorism (GICNT) supports the mission of the voluntary partnership of 86 countries and 5 official observer organizations to strengthen global capacity to prevent, detect, deter, and respond to nuclear terrorism by conducting multilateral activities that improve partner nations' plans, policies, operational procedures and capacity and the general concept of interoperability among partner nations."

   https://obamawhitehouse.archives.gov/the-press-office/2016/04/01/nuclear-security-summit-2016-action-plan-support-global-initiative

7. FACT SHEET: *The Nuclear Security Summits: Securing the World from Nuclear Terrorism*, March 29, 2016

   "*Progress Since Prague*

   "President Obama called for a worldwide effort to secure all vulnerable nuclear materials in four years. The Nuclear Security Summit process has been the centerpiece of these efforts."

   https://obamawhitehouse.archives.gov/the-press-office/2016/03/29/fact-sheet-nuclear-security-summits-securing-world-nuclear-terrorism

8. Certification – *Report to Congress with Respect to the Proposed Rescission of Cuba's Designation as a State Sponsor of Terrorism*, April 14, 2015

   The President certifies to Congress that Cuba has given assurances that it has not supported terrorist activities for the previous 6 months and has given assurances it will not support international terrorism in the future.

   https://obamawhitehouse.archives.gov/the-press-office/2015/04/14/certification-report-congress-respect-proposed-rescission-cubas-designat

9. The Defense department Cyber Strategy, April 2015

   "It focuses on building cyber capabilities and organizations for DoD's three cyber missions: defend DoD networks, systems, and information; defend the United States and its interests against cyberattacks of significant consequence; and provide integrated cyber capabilities to support military operations and contingency plans."

   https://www.defense.gov/Portals/1/features/2015/0415_cyber-strategy/Department_of_Defense_Cyber_Strategy_Fact_Sheet.pdf

10. Fact Sheet: *The 2015 National Security Strategy*, February 6, 2015

    The President's new National Security Strategy outlines a series of principles and goals to strengthen US security and strengthen international order.

    https://obamawhitehouse.archives.gov/the-press-office/2015/02/06/fact-sheet-2015-national-security-strategy

11. Fact Sheet: *The Administration's Strategy to Counter the Islamic State of Iraq and the Levant (ISIL) and the Updated FY 2015 Overseas Contingency Operations Request*, November 7, 2014

    "The President has set forward a comprehensive strategy featuring nine lines of effort to counter ISIL: (1) Supporting Effective Governance in Iraq; (2) Denying ISIL Safe-Haven; (3) Building

> Partner Capacity; (4) Enhancing Intelligence Collection on ISIL; (5) Disrupting ISIL's Finances; (6) Exposing ISIL's True Nature; (7) Disrupting the Flow of Foreign Fighters; (8) Protecting the Homeland; and (9) Humanitarian Support."

https://obamawhitehouse.archives.gov/the-press-office/2014/11/07/fact-sheet-administration-s-strategy-counter-islamic-state-iraq-and-leva

12. Department of Defense Strategy for Countering Weapons of Mass Destruction, June 2014

http://www.defenseinnovationmarketplace.mil/resources/DoD_Strategy_for_Countering_Weapons_of_Mass_Destruction_dated_June_2014.pdf

13. Fact Sheet: *U.S. Policy Standards and Procedures for the Use of Force in Counterterrorism Operations Outside the United States and Areas of Active Hostilities*, May 23, 2013

> "The President has approved, and senior members of the Executive Branch have briefed to the Congress, written policy standards and procedures that formalize and strengthen the Administration's rigorous process for reviewing and approving operations to capture or employ lethal force against terrorist targets outside the United States and outside areas of active hostilities."

https://obamawhitehouse.archives.gov/the-press-office/2013/05/23/fact-sheet-us-policy-standards-and-procedures-use-force-counterterrorism

14. National Infrastructure Protection Plan (NIPP 2013): *Partnering for Critical Infrastructure Security and Resilience*

> "The National Infrastructure Protection Plan (NIPP)—NIPP 2013: Partnering for Critical Infrastructure Security and Resilience—outlines how government and private sector participants in the critical infrastructure community work together to manage risks and achieve security and resilience outcomes. NIPP 2013 represents an evolution from concepts introduced in the initial version of the NIPP released in 2006. NIPP 2013 was issued in response to Presidential Policy Directive-21 on Critical Infrastructure Security and Resilience."

http://www.dhs.gov/sites/default/files/publications/NIPP-Fact-Sheet-508.pdf

Link to NIPP 2013:

http://www.dhs.gov/sites/default/files/publications/NIPP%202013_Partnering%20for%20Critical%20Infrastructure%20Security%20and%20Resilience_508_0.pdf

15. Executive Order 13584 – *Developing an Integrated Strategic Counterterrorism Communications Initiative*, September 9, 2011

This executive order sought to strengthen interagency public communications efforts to counter the propaganda and recruitment by al-Qaeda, its affiliates, and other international terrorist organizations and violent extremists overseas.

It also established in the Department of State a temporary organization to be known as the Counterterrorism Communications Support Office to support the interagency CVE effort.

https://obamawhitehouse.archives.gov/the-press-office/2011/09/09/executive-order-13584-developing-integrated-strategic-counterterrorism-c

16. National Strategy for Counterterrorism, June 29, 2011

The strategy document formalized the framework of the approach that President Obama and his administration had been taking to prevent terrorist attacks and to deliver blows against al-Qaeda, including the successful mission that captured and killed Usama bin Laden. The strategy included defeating al-Qaeda wherever it takes root and preventing terrorists from acquiring or developing weapons of mass destruction and eliminating the safe havens al-Qaeda needs to train, plot, and launch attacks.

https://obamawhitehouse.archives.gov/the-press-office/2011/06/29/fact-sheet-national-strategy-counterterrorism

17. Presidential Memorandum Regarding 12/25/2009 Attempted Terrorist Attack, January 7, 2010

"Following the attempt by the underwear bomber to blow up a plane over Detroit, the White House issued a Presidential memorandum to strengthen visa procedures and aviation screening and other agencies to take additional steps to counter terrorism threats."

https://obamawhitehouse.archives.gov/the-press-office/presidential-memorandum-regarding-12252009-attempted-terrorist-attack

18. President Obama Releases National Strategy for Countering Biological Threats, December 9, 2009

The National Strategy document outlined the Obama administration's strategy for countering the proliferation of biological weapons or their use by terrorists.

https://obamawhitehouse.archives.gov/the-press-office/president-obama-releases-national-strategy-countering-biological-threats

19. *The 9/11 Commission Report*, July 22, 2004

Report on the attacks on the World Trade Center and the Pentagon.

https://9-11commission.gov/report/

20. President Bush Releases National Strategy for Combating Terrorism, White House, Office of the Press Secretary, February 14, 2003

"[...] This strategy outlines the effort our nation is making to win the war against global terror. The strategy complements important elements of the National Security Strategy, as well as our National Strategies for: Homeland Security, to Combat Weapons of Mass Destruction, to Secure Cyberspace, for the Physical Protection of Critical Infrastructure and Key Assets, and the National Drug Control Strategy. Together these efforts establish critical goals for strengthening America's security against the threats of the 21st century. The United States' strategy for combating terrorism focuses on taking the fight to the terrorists themselves. We are using all elements of our national power and international influence to attack terror networks; reduce their ability to communicate and coordinate their plans; isolate them from potential allies and from each other; and identify and disrupt their plots before they attack."

http://2001-2009.state.gov/s/ct/rls/rm/2003/17798.htm

21. S. J. Res. 23—Authorization for Use of Military Force, introduced September 14, 2001

https://www.congress.gov/bill/107th-congress/senate-joint-resolution/23/text/enr

22. *Countering the changing threat of International Terrorism: Report of the National Commission on Terrorism*, June 7, 2000.

https://fas.org/irp/threat/commission.html

23. *The Five-Year Interagency Counter-Terrorism and Technology Crime Plan*, September, 1999

The 5-Year Plan is intended to serve as a baseline strategy for coordination of national policy and operational capabilities to combat terrorism in the United States and against American interests overseas. Although primarily a federal planning document, it has important implications for state and local governments.

https://www.justice.gov/sites/default/files/oip/legacy/2014/07/23/crime-plan.pdf

24. President Clinton Presidential Decision Directive (PDD)—39, "*U.S. Policy on Counterterrorism*," June 21, 1995

    http://www.fas.org/irp/offdocs/pdd39.htm

STATEMENTS AND TESTIMONIES

Trump Administration

1. Joint Press Conference with President Trump and German Chancellor Merkel, March 17, 2017

    "We also recognize that immigration security is national security. We must protect our citizens from those who seek to spread terrorism, extremism and violence inside our borders. Immigration is a privilege, not a right, and the safety of our citizens must always come first, without question."

    https://www.whitehouse.gov/the-press-office/2017/03/17/joint-press-conference-president-trump-and-german-chancellor-merkel

2. Readout of the President's Calls with Prime Minister Shinzo Abe of Japan and Acting President Hwang Kyo-Ahn of South Korea, March 6, 2017

    "President Trump emphasized that his Administration is taking steps to further enhance America's ability to deter and defend against North Korea's ballistic missiles using the full range of United States military capabilities."

    https://www.whitehouse.gov/the-press-office/2017/03/06/readout-presidents-calls-prime-minister-shinzo-abe-japan-and-acting

3. President Trump's address to joint session of Congress, February 28, 2017

    "We cannot allow a beachhead of terrorism to form inside America. We cannot allow our nation to become a sanctuary for extremists. That is why my administration has been working on improved vetting procedures, and we will shortly take new steps to keep our nation safe and to keep out those out who will do us harm. Our foreign policy calls for a direct, robust and meaningful engagement with the world. It is American leadership based on vital security interests that we share with our allies all across the globe. We strongly support NATO, an alliance forged through the bonds of two world wars that dethroned fascism, and a Cold War, and defeated communism. ... But our partners must meet their financial obligations. And now, based on our very strong and frank discussions, they are beginning to do just that."

https://www.whitehouse.gov/the-press-office/2017/02/28/remarks-president-trump-joint-address-congress

4. Joint Readout of Meeting between President Donald J. Trump and Israeli Prime Minister Benjamin Netanyahu, February 15, 2017

"The two leaders agreed that the Iran nuclear deal is a terrible deal for the United States, Israel, and the world. The President assured the Prime Minister that Iran must not, and will not, obtain nuclear weapons capability."

https://www.whitehouse.gov/the-press-office/2017/02/15/joint-readout-meeting-between-president-donald-j-trump-and-israeli-prime

5. President Trump's Weekly Address, February 10, 2017

"[...] The administration is committed to your security, which is why we will continue to fight to take all necessary and legal action to keep terrorists, radical and dangerous extremists from ever entering our country. We will not allow our generous system of immigration to be turned against us as a tool for terrorism and truly bad people. [...]"

https://www.whitehouse.gov/the-press-office/2017/02/10/president-trumps-weekly-address

6. Readout of the President's Call with President Recep Tayyip Erdoğan of Turkey, February 7, 2017

"President Donald J. Trump today spoke by phone with President Recep Tayyip Erdoğan of Turkey about the close, long-standing relationship between the United States and Turkey and their shared commitment to combating terrorism in all its forms. President Trump reiterated U.S. support to Turkey as a strategic partner and NATO ally, and welcomed Turkey's contributions to the counter-ISIS campaign."

https://www.whitehouse.gov/the-press-office/2017/02/07/readout-presidents-call-president-recep-tayyip-erdo%C4%9Fan-turkey

7. Remarks by President Trump to Coalition Representatives and Senior U.S. Commanders, MacDill Air Force Base, Tampa, Florida, February 6, 2017

> President Trump said, "All over Europe terrorist attacks are happening. It's gotten to a point where it's not even being reported and, in many cases, the very, very dishonest press doesn't want to report it. They have their reasons and you understand that. So today, we deliver a message in one very unified voice: To these forces of death and destruction, America and its allies will defeat you. We will defeat them. We will defeat radical Islamic terrorism, and we will not allow it to take root in our country. [...]"

https://www.whitehouse.gov/the-press-office/2017/02/06/remarks-president-trump-coalition-representatives-and-senior-us

8. Readout of the President's Call with King Salman bin Abdulaziz Al Saud of Saudi Arabia, January 29, 2017

> "They agreed on the importance of strengthening joint efforts to fight the spread of radical Islamic terrorism and also on the importance of working jointly to address challenges to regional peace and security, including the conflicts in Syria and Yemen. ... The two leaders also discussed an invitation from the King for President Trump to lead a Middle East effort to defeat terrorism and to help build a new future, economically and socially, for the people of the Kingdom of Saudi Arabia and the region."

https://www.whitehouse.gov/the-press-office/2017/01/29/readout-presidents-call-king-salman-bin-abd-al-aziz-al-saud-saudi-arabia

9. Readout of the President's Call with Chancellor Angela Merkel of Germany, January 28, 2017

> "The President and Chancellor also agreed on the NATO Alliance's fundamental importance to the broader transatlantic relationship and its role in ensuring the peace and stability of our North Atlantic community. The leaders agreed on the need to strengthen already robust cooperation in the fight against terrorism and violent extremism, and to work to stabilize conflict areas in the Middle East and North Africa."

https://www.whitehouse.gov/the-press-office/2017/01/28/readout-presidents-call-chancellor-angela-merkel-germany

10. President Trump and Prime Minister May's Opening Remarks, Office of the Press Secretary, January 27, 2017

Prime Minister Theresa May said, "We're discussing how we can work even more closely together in order to take on and defeat Daesh and the ideology of Islamist extremism wherever it's found. ... On defense and security cooperation, we are united in our recognition of NATO as the bulwark of our collective defense ... we're also discussing the importance of NATO continuing to ensure it is as equipped to fight terrorism and cyber warfare as it is to fight more conventional forms of war."

https://www.whitehouse.gov/the-press-office/2017/01/27/president-trump-and-prime-minister-mays-opening-remarks

11. Remarks by President Trump and Vice President Pence at CIA Headquarters, Langley, Virginia. January 21, 2017

"We have to get rid of ISIS. Have to get rid of ISIS. We have no choice ... it has to be eradicated just off the face of the Earth. Discussing Iraq, President Trump said 'if we kept the oil you probably wouldn't have ISIS because that's where they made their money in the first place. So we should have kept the oil. But okay. (Laughter.) Maybe you'll have another chance. But the fact is, should have kept the oil.'"

https://www.whitehouse.gov/the-press-office/2017/01/21/remarks-president-trump-and-vice-president-pence-cia-headquarters

12. Remarks of President Trump—As Prepared for Delivery at the Inaugural Address, January 20, 2017

"[We will] unite the civilized world against Radical Islamic Terrorism, which we will eradicate completely from the face of the Earth."

https://www.whitehouse.gov/inaugural-address

Trump Cabinet Members

1. DHS Secretary John F. Kelly, *Home and Away: DHS and the Threats to America*, Remarks at George Washington University Center for Cyber and Homeland Security, Washington, DC, April 18, 2017

"[...] Recently, based on intelligence, I banned electronics bigger than a cell phone on some commercial flights to the United States. This program will likely expand given the sophisticated threats aviation faces...That ban, and the intelligence that drove it, demonstrates that commercial aviation continues to be a prime target for terrorists."

https://www.dhs.gov/news/2017/04/18/home-and-away-dhs-and-threats-america

Also see "DHS Secretary Kelly says congressional critics should 'shut up' or change laws," Devlin Barrett, *Washington Post*, April 19, 2017. https://www.washingtonpost.com/world/national-security/dhs-secretary-kelly-says-congressional-critics-should-shut-up-or-change-laws/2017/04/18/8a2a92b6-2454-11e7-b503-9d616bd5a305_story.html

2. Secretary of State Rex W. Tillerson, *NATO Foreign Ministerial Intervention Remarks* Brussels, Belgium, March 31, 2017

"On fighting terrorism, NATO can and should do more. Fighting terrorism is the top national security priority for the United States, as it should be for all of us ... NATO has a number of unique capabilities it can bring to this fight. At the Warsaw Summit last year, NATO members recognized cyberspace as an operational domain, alongside land, air, and sea. ... As ISIS increasingly leverages the internet as a powerful tool for recruitment and propaganda, we must consider how we can disrupt and aggressively counter their online operations."

https://www.state.gov/secretary/remarks/2017/03/269339

3. Press Availability Secretary of State Rex W. Tillerson with Turkish Foreign Minister Mevlut Cavusoglu, Ankara, Turkey, March 30, 2017

"SECRETARY TILLERSON: Our discussions today reaffirmed that we will prevent the resurgence of Daesh in previously held territory, and aggressively stop the emergence of new terrorist threats on the ground as well as the recruitment of terrorists online. Over the past 18 months, the U.S. Military's ability to operate from Turkish bases has enabled us to increase operations against ISIS by 25 percent without the utilization of any additional aircraft required. The Turkish Government has stopped the influx of foreign fighters into Iraq and Syria. Turkish troops have permanently pushed ISIS off the Turkish-Syria border. [...]"

Asked by a reporter if President Assad of Syria should stay or go, Secretary Tillison said: "I think the status and the longer-term status of President Assad will be decided by the Syrian people."

https://www.state.gov/secretary/remarks/2017/03/269318.htm

4. Remarks at the Ministerial Plenary for the Global Coalition Working to Defeat ISIS, Secretary of State Rex W. Tillerson, the Department of State, March 22, 2017

"[...] Degradation of ISIS is not the end goal. We must defeat ISIS. I recognize there are many pressing challenges in the Middle East, but defeating ISIS is the United States' number one goal in the region. Our end goal is the regional elimination of ISIS through military force. Soon, our efforts in Iraq and Syria will enter a new phase defined by transition from major military operations to stabilization. We will pursue regional diplomatic solutions for the underlying political and sectarian disputes that helped ISIS to flourish. [...]"

On stabilization, Tillison said: "As a coalition, we are not in the business of nation-building or reconstruction. We must ensure that our respective nations' precious and limited resources are devoted to preventing the resurgence of ISIS and equipping the war-torn communities to take the lead in rebuilding their institutions and returning to stability. A successful stabilization phase will set the stage for a successful normalization phase. [...]"

"In order to stay ahead of a global outbreak, we must all adopt the following countermeasures: First, continue to persist with in-country counterterrorism and law enforcement operations. Second, we need greater intelligence and information sharing within our own domestic intelligence agencies and among our nations. Lastly, in tandem with our aggressive push-back on the ground in multiple countries, we must break ISIS's ability to spread its message and recruit new followers online. A 'digital caliphate' must not flourish in the place of a physical one. [...]"

https://www.state.gov/secretary/remarks/2017/03/269039.htm

5. FBI Director James Comey CNN: *Comey: There is no such thing as absolute privacy in America*. Mary Kay Mallonee and Eugene Scott, CNN, March 9, 2017

"There is no such thing as absolute privacy in America; there is no place outside of judicial reach," Comey said at a Boston College conference on cybersecurity.

In the last 4 months of 2016, the FBI lawfully gained access to 2,800 devices recovered in criminal, terrorism, and counterintelligence investigations and the FBI was unable to open 43% of those devices, Comey said.

http://www.cnn.com/2017/03/08/politics/james-comey-privacy-cybersecurity/

https://www.c-span.org/video/?424885-1/james-comey-says-hell-serve-full-term-fbi-director Also see: FBI website: https://www.fbi.gov/news/stories/fbi-director-addresses-cyber-security-gathering

6. Press Briefing by Press Secretary Sean Spicer: Comments on ISIS, White House press briefing room, February 9, 2017

> "There's no question that the spread of it [radical Islamic terrorism] ... in the last eight years has proliferated. And I think that the resources that we have to spend—this isn't a traditional war where you're just looking at the other enemy with a uniform and saying, here's the country we're fighting. The proliferation of ISIS throughout this country has made it so that we have to focus a lot more in a lot more places and expend a lot more resources because it's more of a disparate approach that we have to employ, as opposed to having one country that you're facing at one time."

https://www.whitehouse.gov/the-press-office/2017/02/09/press-briefing-press-secretary-sean-spicer-292017-11

7. DHS Secretary John F. Kelly, *Ending the Crisis: America's Borders and the Path to Security,* Written testimony for a House Committee on Homeland Security hearing, February 7, 2017

> "Within DHS and our Federal, State, local, and international partners, we must expand our vetting of those seeking to enter our country—particularly of those individuals from high-risk countries—including refugees. We currently lack a comprehensive strategy with uniform screening standards to prevent terrorists from entering the country. Unfortunately, our country has recently admitted some foreign nationals without an adequate understanding of their allegiances and intentions."

https://www.dhs.gov/news/2017/02/07/written-testimony-dhs-secretary-john-f-kelly-house-committee-homeland-security

Obama Administration

1. President Obama's ISIL Strategy. A group of statements and videos following the March 22, 2016 terrorist bombing in Brussels that killed 32 civilians and wounded another 300.

https://obamawhitehouse.archives.gov/isil-strategy

2. President Obama's Farewell Address, January 10, 2017

In his farewell speech marking the end of his presidency, President Obama said he tried to keep the fight against terrorism "on a firmer legal footing. That's why we've ended torture, worked to close Gitmo, reformed our laws governing surveillance to protect privacy and civil liberties."

https://obamawhitehouse.archives.gov/the-press-office/2017/01/10/remarks-president-farewell-address

3. President Obama's Remarks on the Administration's Approach to Counterterrorism, MacDill Air Force Base, Tampa, Florida, December 6, 2016

"The campaign against ISIL has been relentless. It has been sustainable. It has been multilateral ... Instead of pushing all of the burden onto American ground troops, instead of trying to mount invasions wherever terrorists appear, we've built a network of partners. Today's terrorists can kill innocent people, but they don't pose an existential threat to our nation, and we must not make the mistake of elevating them as if they do. ... We have to fight terrorists in a way that does not create more terrorists. And that means the best option for us to get those terrorists becomes a targeted strike. We do have to be careful to make sure that when we take actions, we're not alienating local populations, because that will serve as recruitment for new terrorists. [...]"

https://obamawhitehouse.archives.gov/the-press-office/2016/12/06/remarks-president-administrations-approach-counterterrorism

4. Remarks by the President on Plan to Close the Prison at Guantanamo Bay, February 23, 2016

"[...] the detention facility at Guantanamo Bay does not advance our national security—it undermines it. This is not just my opinion. This is the opinion of experts; this is the opinion of many in our military. It's counterproductive to our fight against terrorists, because they use it as propaganda in their efforts to recruit. It drains military resources, with nearly $450 million spent last year alone to keep it running, and more than $200 million in additional costs needed to keep it open going forward for less than 100 detainees. Guantanamo harms our partnerships with allies and other countries whose cooperation we need against terrorism."

https://obamawhitehouse.archives.gov/the-press-office/2016/02/23/remarks-president-plan-close-prison-guantanamo-bay

5. Remarks by the President on the Cybersecurity National Action Plan, February 9, 2016

    "The President is directing his Administration to implement a Cybersecurity National Action Plan (CNAP) that takes near-term actions and puts in place a long-term strategy to enhance cybersecurity awareness and protections, protect privacy, maintain public safety as well as economic and national security. [...]"

    https://obamawhitehouse.archives.gov/the-press-office/2016/02/09/fact-sheet-cybersecurity-national-action-plan

6. Remarks by the President at Islamic Society of Baltimore, February 3, 2016

    President Obamas's first speech at an American Mosque called for tolerance towards Muslims. He said, "Muslim political leaders have to push back on the lie that the West oppresses Muslims, and against conspiracy theories that says America is the cause of every ill in the Middle East."

    https://obamawhitehouse.archives.gov/the-press-office/2016/02/03/remarks-president-islamic-society-baltimore

7. President Obama's State of the Union Address, January 12, 2016

    "[...] For more than a year, America has led a coalition of more than 60 countries to cut off ISIL's financing, disrupt their plots, stop the flow of terrorist fighters, and stamp out their vicious ideology. With nearly 10,000 air strikes, we are taking out their leadership, their oil, their training camps, and their weapons. We are training, arming, and supporting forces who are steadily reclaiming territory in Iraq and Syria. [...]"

    https://medium.com/@WhiteHouse/president-obama-s-2016-state-of-the-union-address-7c06300f9726#.6ym253xp8

8. President Obama's Press Conference, December 18, 2015

    Speaking after the San Bernardino attack, President Obama discussed lone wolf terrorism, noting that that the difficulty in anticipating and preventing isolated terror attacks is not all that different than detecting mass shootings before they happen—something that the United States has not had much success in doing. "[...] This is a different kind of challenge than (countering) organizations like al Qaeda that involve highly trained operatives who are working as cells or as a network."

    https://obamawhitehouse.archives.gov/the-press-office/2015/12/18/press-conference-president-121815

9. Statement by the President after Briefing at the National Counterterrorism Center, McLean, Virginia, December 17, 2015

> "[...] the mission to protect our homeland goes on, on three main fronts. ... First, we're going after terrorists over there, where they plot and plan and spew their propaganda. ... Second, we continue to do everything in our power to prevent terrorists from getting into the United States. ... Third, we're stepping up our efforts to prevent attacks here at home."

https://obamawhitehouse.archives.gov/the-press-office/2015/12/17/statement-president-after-briefing-national-counterterrorism-center

10. President Obama's Pentagon Speech on the Military Campaign to Destroy ISIL, December 14, 2015

> "[...] our strategy is moving forward with a great sense of urgency on four fronts—hunting down and taking out these terrorists; training and equipping Iraqi and Syrian forces to fight ISIL on the ground; stopping ISIL's operations by disrupting their recruiting, financing and propaganda; and, finally, persistent diplomacy to end the Syrian civil war so that everyone can focus on destroying ISIL."

https://obamawhitehouse.archives.gov/the-press-office/2015/12/14/remarks-president-military-campaign-destroy-isil

11. President Obama's Weekly Address, on terrorism, December 12, 2015

> "[...] In recent weeks, our strikes have taken out the ISIL finance chief, a terrorist leader in Somalia and the ISIL leader in Libya. Our message to these killers is simple—we will find you, and justice will be done."

https://obamawhitehouse.archives.gov/the-press-office/2015/12/12/weekly-address-standing-strong-face-terrorism

12. President Obama Oval Office Speech to the Nation on Terrorism following the San Bernardino Attack, December 6, 2015

> "Over the last few years ... the terrorist threat has evolved into a new phase. As we've become better at preventing complex, multifaceted attacks like 9/11, terrorists turned to less complicated acts of violence like the mass shootings that are all too common in our society."

https://obamawhitehouse.archives.gov/the-press-office/2015/12/06/address-nation-president

13. President Obama's Weekly Address: *We Will Not Be Terrorized*, December 5, 2015

> "[...] people on the No-Fly list can walk into a store and buy a gun. That is insane. If you're too dangerous to board a plane, you're too dangerous, by definition, to buy a gun. And so I'm calling on Congress to close this loophole, now. We may not be able to prevent every tragedy, but—at a bare minimum—we shouldn't be making it so easy for potential terrorists or criminals to get their hands on a gun that they could use against Americans."

https://obamawhitehouse.archives.gov/the-press-office/2015/12/05/weekly-address-we-will-not-be-terrorized

14. President Obama Press Conference on Terrorism Issues, at Antalya, Turkey, November 16, 2015

> "[...] the attacks in Paris remind us that it will not be enough to defeat ISIL in Syria and Iraq alone. Here in Antalya, our nations, therefore, committed to strengthening border controls, sharing more information, and stepping up our efforts to prevent the flow of foreign fighters in and out of Syria and Iraq."

https://obamawhitehouse.archives.gov/the-press-office/2015/11/16/press-conference-president-obama-antalya-turkey

15. Leaders' Summit on Countering ISIL and Violent Extremism, September 29, 2015

> "Leaders from more than 100 countries, 20 multilateral bodies, and 120 civil society and private sector organizations met today in New York City to review progress in countering ISIL, addressing the threat posed by foreign terrorist fighters (FTFs), and countering and preventing violent extremism. ... Coalition members outlined efforts to help counter the FTF threat, to include strengthening counterterrorism legislation in their own countries and expanding information sharing on terrorist identities."

https://obamawhitehouse.archives.gov/the-press-office/2015/09/29/leaders-summit-countering-isil-and-violent-extremism

16. Fact Sheet: *Leaders' Summit to Counter ISIL and Violent Extremism*, September 29, 2015

> President Obama hosted a summit highlighting the international community's efforts to counter ISIL, address foreign terrorist fighters (FTFs), and counter violent extremism. The State Department's

Center for Strategic Counterterrorism Communications operationalized an Interagency Counterterrorism Communications cell to improve cross-government collaboration on countering ISIL's online messaging.

https://obamawhitehouse.archives.gov/the-press-office/2015/09/29/fact-sheet-leaders-summit-counter-isil-and-violent-extremism

17. Fact Sheet: *U.S. Support for Peace, Security, and Countering Violent Extremism in Africa*, July 27, 2015

Obama administration announced Counterterrorism Partnerships Fund, to provide approximately $465 million in new training, equipment, capacity building, and other assistances to help African countries counter terrorism.

https://obamawhitehouse.archives.gov/the-press-office/2015/07/27/fact-sheet-us-support-peace-security-and-countering-violent-extremism

18. Remarks by the President on Progress in the Fight against Terrorism, July 6, 2015

"Increased numbers of fighters are emerging in the fight against ISIS, and the U.S. continues its campaign to train the moderate Syrian opposition. The efforts against large scale terror attacks are being handled with more and more expertise, while lone wolf attacks become a larger and more significant threat than ever before."

https://obamawhitehouse.archives.gov/the-press-office/2015/07/06/remarks-president-progress-fight-against-isil

19. President Obama's Statement on the U.S. Government's Hostage Policy Review, June 24, 2015

"[...] I'm updating our hostage policy. I'm making it clear that our top priority is the safe and rapid recovery of American hostages. And to do so, we will use all elements of our national power. I am reaffirming that the United States government will not make concessions, such as paying ransom, to terrorist groups holding American hostages. ... As President, I also have to consider our larger national security. I firmly believe that the United States government paying ransom to terrorists risks endangering more Americans and funding the very terrorism that we're trying to stop."

https://obamawhitehouse.archives.gov/the-press-office/2015/06/24/statement-president-us-governments-hostage-policy-review

20. Fact Sheet: *The White House Summit on Countering Violent Extremism*, The White House Press Office, February 18, 2015

> "This week, the White House is convening a three-day summit on Countering Violent Extremism (CVE). ... Violent extremist threats can come from a range of groups and individuals, including domestic terrorists and homegrown violent extremists in the United States, as well as terrorist groups like al-Qaeda and ISIL."

https://obamawhitehouse.archives.gov/the-press-office/2015/02/18/fact-sheet-white-house-summit-countering-violent-extremism

21. Remarks by the President in Closing of the Summit on Countering Violent Extremism. *US at war with those who have perverted Islam*. White House Press Office. February 18, 2015

> "[...] countering violent extremism ... is not just a matter of military affairs. By 'violent extremism,' we don't just mean the terrorists who are killing innocent people. We also mean the ideologies, the infrastructure of extremists—the propagandists, the recruiters, the funders who radicalize and recruit or incite people to violence. We all know there is no one profile of a violent extremist or terrorist, so there's no way to predict who will become radicalized."
>
> "But we are here at this summit because of the urgent threat from groups like al Qaeda and ISIL ... we are focused on prevention—preventing these groups from radicalizing, recruiting or inspiring others to violence in the first place."

https://obamawhitehouse.archives.gov/the-press-office/2015/02/18/remarks-president-closing-summit-countering-violent-extremism

22. White House statement on the 3-day international summit to counter violent extremism, February 18, 2015

> "The underlying premise of the approach to countering violent extremism in the United States is that (1) communities provide the solution to violent extremism; and (2) CVE efforts are best pursued at the local level, tailored to local dynamics, where local officials continue to build relationships within their communities through established community policing and community outreach mechanisms." [...]
>
> "*U.S. Government Policy to Counter Violent Extremism Globally*: ... At the United Nations in September 2014,

President Obama called on member nations to do more to address violent extremism within their regions."

https://obamawhitehouse.archives.gov/the-press-office/2015/02/18/fact-sheet-white-house-summit-countering-violent-extremism

23. Remarks by the President on Afghanistan, at Joint Base McGuire-Dix-Lakehurst, New Jersey, December 15, 2014

"Afghans will take full responsibility for their security. This month, after more than 13 years, our combat mission in Afghanistan will be over. ... Even as our combat mission ends, our commitment to Afghanistan endures. We'll continue to have a limited military presence there because we've got to keep training and equipping Afghan forces, and we've got to conduct counterterrorism missions because there are still remnants of al Qaeda there. ... The time of deploying large ground forces with big military footprints to engage in nation-building overseas, that's coming to an end."

https://obamawhitehouse.archives.gov/the-press-office/2014/12/15/remarks-president-military-and-civilian-personnel-joint-base-mcguire-dix

24. Fact Sheet: *Comprehensive U.S. Government Approach to Foreign Terrorist Fighters in Syria and the Broader Region*, Office of the Press Secretary, September 24, 2014

"[...] we take seriously the terrorist threat posed by fighters in Iraq, Syria, and the broader region, including foreign terrorist fighters. More than 15,000 foreign terrorist fighters from more than 80 countries have traveled to Syria to fight alongside terrorist groups including dozens of Americans from a variety of backgrounds. The White House is leading an interagency effort to address this threat. Our approach brings together homeland security, law enforcement, intelligence, diplomatic, military, capacity building, and information sharing efforts."

https://obamawhitehouse.archives.gov/the-press-office/2014/09/24/fact-sheet-comprehensive-us-government-approach-foreign-terrorist-fighte

25. Statement by the President on ISIL, September 10, 2014

"Over the last several years, we have consistently taken the fight to terrorists who threaten our country. We took out Osama bin Laden and much of al Qaeda's leadership in Afghanistan and Pakistan. We've targeted al Qaeda's affiliate in Yemen, and recently eliminated the top commander of its affiliate in Somalia. We've done so while bringing more than 140,000 American troops home from Iraq, and drawing down our forces in Afghanistan, where our combat mission will end later this year. Thanks to our military and counterterrorism professionals, America is safer."

https://obamawhitehouse.archives.gov/the-press-office/2014/09/10/statement-president-isil-1

26. Also see Fact Sheet: *Strategy to Counter the Islamic State of Iraq and the Levant (ISIL)*, September 10, 2014

"That strategy harnesses all elements of national power and features the following core elements: 1) Supporting Effective Governance in Iraq; 2) Denying ISIL Safe-Haven; and 3) Building Partner Capacity."

"The growing and evolving nature of the ISIL threat underscores the importance of the Counterterrorism Partnerships Fund (CTPF): Enhancing Intelligence Collection on ISIL; Disrupting ISIL's Finances; Exposing ISIL's True Nature; Disrupting the Flow of Foreign Fighters; Protecting the Homeland; and Humanitarian Support."

https://obamawhitehouse.archives.gov/the-press-office/2014/09/10/fact-sheet-strategy-counter-islamic-state-iraq-and-levant-isil

27. Also see President Obama, *How We're Responding to the ISIL Threat*, September 10, 2014

"Let's be clear: While this group may call itself the 'Islamic State,' it is not 'Islamic.' No religion condones the killing of innocents, and the vast majority of ISIL's victims have been Muslim. Nor is it a 'state.' It is not recognized by any government, nor by the people it subjugates. This is nothing but a terrorist organization with no vision or goal other than to slaughter all who stand in its way … these terrorists have threatened America and our allies. And the United States will meet this threat with strength and resolve."

https://obamawhitehouse.archives.gov/blog/2014/09/10/president-obama-how-were-responding-isil-threat

28. Fact Sheet: *Partnering to Counter Terrorism in Africa*, August 6, 2014

"The United States and African partners committed to counterterrorism partnerships that draw on all the tools: military, diplomacy, financial action, intelligence, law enforcement, and development alike. […]"

https://obamawhitehouse.archives.gov/the-press-office/2014/08/06/fact-sheet-partnering-counter-terrorism-africa

29. Fact Sheet: *U.S.–E.U. Counterterrorism Cooperation*, March 26, 2014

    Description of U.S. and European Union efforts to strengthen the international capacity to counter terrorism, including public-private sector programs to counter violent extremism.

    https://obamawhitehouse.archives.gov/the-press-office/2014/03/26/fact-sheet-us-eu-counterterrorism-cooperation

30. Joint Statement of the Presidents of the United States of America and the Russian Federation on Cooperation in Countering Terrorism, June 17, 2013

    The two countries agree to cooperate to prevent weapons of mass destruction from falling into the hands of terrorists and to work to halting terrorist funding, recruitment, and training activities.

    https://obamawhitehouse.archives.gov/the-press-office/2013/06/17/joint-statement-presidents-united-states-america-and-russian-federation-

    Also see the statement *following the May 26, 2011* meeting of the Presidents of the United States and Russia that included a discussion of improving aviation security.

    https://obamawhitehouse.archives.gov/the-press-office/2011/05/26/joint-statement-presidents-united-states-america-and-russian-federation-

31. Remarks by the President on bin Laden's death, National Defense University, Fort McNair, Washington, May 23, 2013

    "[...] Today, Osama bin Laden is dead, and so are most of his top lieutenants. There have been no large-scale attacks on the United States, and our homeland is more secure. Fewer of our troops are in harm's way, and over the next 19 months they will continue to come home. Our alliances are strong, and so is our standing in the world. In sum, we are safer because of our efforts. ... Now, make no mistake, our nation is still threatened by terrorists ... But we have to recognize that the threat has shifted and evolved from the one that came to our shores on 9/11."

    https://obamawhitehouse.archives.gov/the-press-office/2013/05/23/remarks-president-national-defense-university

32. Fact Sheet: *U.S. Policy Standards and Procedures for the Use of Force in Counterterrorism Operations Outside the United States and Areas of Active Hostilities*, May 23, 2013

    "The President has approved, and senior members of the Executive Branch have briefed to the Congress, written policy standards and procedures that formalize and strengthen the Administration's rigorous process for reviewing and approving operations to capture or employ lethal force against terrorist targets outside the United States and outside areas of active hostilities."

https://obamawhitehouse.archives.gov/the-press-office/2013/05/23/fact-sheet-us-policy-standards-and-procedures-use-force-counterterrorism

33. Joint Statement on Nuclear Terrorism, March 27, 2012

"The governments of the United States, United Kingdom, and French Republic each understand the threat of nuclear terrorism and share the collective responsibility to inform and strengthen international measures designed to secure sensitive information, technology or nuclear material from access by terrorists, and to develop emergency response measures. In recognition of these shared principles, consistent with our rights and obligations under the Non-Proliferation Treaty, our three governments are taking the following initial steps."

https://obamawhitehouse.archives.gov/the-press-office/2012/03/27/joint-statement-nuclear-terrorism

34. President Obama addresses the nation to announce that the United States has killed Osama bin Laden, May 2, 2011

"For over two decades, bin Laden has been al Qaeda's leader and symbol, and has continued to plot attacks against our country and our friends and allies. The death of bin Laden marks the most significant achievement to date in our nation's effort to defeat al Qaeda."

"Yet his death does not mark the end of our effort. There's no doubt that al Qaeda will continue to pursue attacks against us. We must—and we will—remain vigilant at home and abroad."

"... The cause of securing our country is not complete. But tonight, we are once again reminded that America can do whatever we set our mind to."

https://obamawhitehouse.archives.gov/blog/2011/05/02/osama-bin-laden-dead

35. Statement by the President on the U.S.–European Union Agreement on the Terrorist Finance Tracking Program, July 8, 2010

"The United States welcomes today's decision by the European Parliament to join the Council and Commission of the European Union in approving a revised agreement between the United States and the European Union on the processing and transfer of financial messaging data for the Terrorist Finance Tracking Program (TFTP). ... This new, legally binding agreement reflects significant additional data privacy safeguards but still retains the effectiveness and integrity of this indispensable counterterrorism program."

https://obamawhitehouse.archives.gov/the-press-office/statement-president-us-european-union-agreement-terrorist-finance-tracking-program-

ORIGINAL: https://www.treasury.gov/resource-center/terrorist-illicit-finance/Terrorist-Finance-Tracking/Documents/Final-TFTP-Agreement-Signed.pdf

https://www.treasury.gov/resource-center/terrorist-illicit-finance/Terrorist-Finance-Tracking/Pages/tftp.aspx

https://ec.europa.eu/home-affairs/what-we-do/policies/crisis-and-terrorism/tftp_en

Obama Cabinet Members

1. John Kerry: *What We Got Right*, *New York Times* Op-Ed article, January 19, 2017

"[…] President Obama has restored assertive diplomacy as our foreign policy tool of first resort and deployed it time and again to advance our security and prosperity. … This is evident, first of all, in our campaign to defeat the Islamic State, also known by its Arabic acronym, Daesh. […]"

https://www.nytimes.com/2017/01/19/opinion/john-kerry-what-we-got-right.html?action=click&pgtype=Homepage&clickSource=story-heading&module=span-abc-region&region=span-abc-region&WT.nav=span-abc-region&_r=0

2. Secretary Kerry at Sabin conference, Washington, DC, December 4, 2016

"[…] the strategy we put together two years ago or a year and a half ago now to go after Daesh has worked. We have taken back 55 percent of the territory that Daesh took in Iraq; we're— we've liberated Fallujah, Tikrit, Ramadi; we're moving on Mosul now, we're pressing in on al-Raqqa—that's the heart of the so-called caliphate. We've eliminated almost every top Daesh/ISIL leader … We're putting enormous pressure on their financing; we've taken their 1,000 a day recruits down to 500 last year and now down to a dribble. And so we're drying up their capacity to wage this war and I believe we're going to be turning over to the next administration a situation that is moving absolutely in the right direction."

https://2009-2017.state.gov/secretary/remarks/2016/12/264824.htm

3. Remarks of Acting Under Secretary Adam Szubin on Countering the Financing of Terrorism at The Paul H. Nitze School of Advanced International Studies, October 20, 2016

> "[…] Success is not measured by the false goal of 'turning off a spigot.' Active terror groups will always be able to get their hands on some level of funds. A more accurate way to look at success is: can we constrain a group's ability to earn and move money to an extent that its activities are impeded? If a group is used to operating on a certain budget, and it faces a 20 percent shortfall in its funding, that presents immediate challenges. Do the group's leaders cut their fighters' salaries? Do they pull back on media or recruitment? Do they stop supporting social welfare programs that are used to shore up their popularity and support? Any of these trade-offs will impede a group and will also often generate useful information about a group's vulnerabilities."

https://www.treasury.gov/press-center/press-releases/Pages/jl0590.aspx

4. Brett McGurk, Special Presidential Envoy for the Global Coalition to Counter ISIL, Office of the Special Presidential Envoy for the Global Coalition to Counter ISIL, October 7, 2016

> "Coalition airstrikes targeted ISIL's energy infrastructure, modular refineries, petroleum storage tanks, and crude oil collection points, as well as bulk cache storage sites. These airstrikes degraded ISIL's ability to generate revenue."
>
> "Confronting Iran's destabilizing activities and its support for terrorism was a key element of our expanded dialogue with the countries of the Gulf Cooperation Council, following the leaders' summit at Camp David in May of last year. We've also expanded our cooperation with partners in Europe, South America, and West Africa to develop and implement strategies to counter the activities of Iranian-allied and sponsored groups, such as Hezbollah."

https://2009-2017.state.gov/r/pa/prs/ps/2016/10/262934.htm

5. Strategic Implementation Plan for Empowering Local Partners to Prevent Violent Extremism in the United States, October 2016

> *For the domestic CVE program.* This updated Strategic Implementation Plan responds to the current dynamics of violent extremism and reflects experiences and knowledge acquired over the last five years. It replaces the 2011 Strategic Implementation

Plan for Empowering Local Partners to Prevent Violent Extremism in the United States.

https://www.dhs.gov/sites/default/files/publications/2016_strategic_implementation_plan_empowering_local_partners_prev.pdf

6. Remarks at the Global Counterterrorism Forum Ministerial, by Antony J. Blinken, Deputy Secretary of State, Roosevelt Hotel, New York City, September 21, 2016

"As we collapse the foundation of the so-called caliphate in Iraq and Syria, Daesh will continue—and indeed emphasize—these kinds of indiscriminate terror attacks in all of our countries as the foreign fighters who have traveled to Iraq and Syria will try to go home to perpetrate those attacks. That means … information sharing and collective action among our police and intelligence services is even more important than ever."

"We also know that we cannot react to these attacks in ways that silence political dissent or censor speech in the name of countering violent extremism—online or offline. We stress this point not solely to defend the fundamental freedoms we all believe in, but also because terrorists are quick to exploit evidence of discrimination in trying to rationalize their actions and attract new members. Whatever the intent, repression tends to fuel terrorism, not stop it."

http://2009-2917.state.gov/s/d/2016d/262233.htm

7. Written testimony of I&A Under Secretary Francis Taylor, USCIS Director León Rodriguez, TSA Deputy Administrator Huban Gowadia, ICE Deputy Director Daniel Ragsdale, and CBP Deputy Commissioner Kevin McAleenan for a House Committee on Homeland Security hearing titled *Shutting Down Terrorist Pathways into America*, September 14, 2016

"In the 15 years since the tragic attacks on September 11, 2001, DHS, with critical support from our interagency partners, has implemented comprehensive measures to enhance our immigration and border management systems and prevent the travel of terrorists to and within the United States, including:

- "Implementing robust, continuous, and timely screening and vetting capabilities;
- "Preventing and disrupting illicit migration of Special Interest Aliens to and across U.S. borders;

- "Expanding information sharing with our federal, State, local, and international partners;
- "Enhancing DHS aviation security efforts; and
- "Building community partnerships to Counter Violent Extremism."

https://www.dhs.gov/news/2016/09/14/written-testimony-ia-uscis-tsa-ice-and-cbp-house-committee-homeland-security-hearing

8. Assistant Attorney General John P. Carlin Delivers Opening Remarks at the National Security Division 10 Year Anniversary Conference, September 14, 2016

"In the next decade, the threats will certainly change again. In addition to continuing efforts by terrorists to undermine our way of life, we foresee risks posed by data theft, ransomware and other extortion efforts and the increased vulnerabilities of the so-called "Internet of Things." What is more, already, we are seeing how cyber attacks can blend and blur with real-world terrorist attacks in unexpected ways."

https://www.justice.gov/opa/speech/assistant-attorney-general-john-p-carlin-delivers-opening-remarks-national-security

9. Attorney General Loretta E. Lynch, Remarks at National Security Division 10-Year Anniversary Event, Washington, DC, September 14, 2016

"[...] the emergence of ISIL, which uses social media to spread hateful propaganda and encourage lone-wolf attacks, requires us to adapt to a more diffuse brand of terrorism. Meanwhile, rival nations continue to seek a military advantage by stealing our assets; others flout international norms by attempting to increase their nuclear capabilities or develop weapons of mass destruction. ... We must confront increasing threats in cyber space—from the theft of security and trade secrets by state-sponsored actors, to destructive attacks by terrorists and rogue states. These are among the most pressing national security concerns of our time. They are complex and fast-moving and they require quick thinking and nimble action."

https://www.justice.gov/opa/speech/attorney-general-loretta-e-lynch-delivers-remarks-national-security-division-10-year

10. Sarah Sewall, Under Secretary for Civilian Security, Democracy, and Human Rights. Remarks on the CVE Program, at 9/11+15 Conference: *A Strategic Review of the Fight against Terrorism*,

National Defense University,Fort McNair, Washington, DC, September 8, 2016

"[...] Countering Violent Extremism, or CVE, and U.S. efforts have anchored a parallel international effort which the U.N. often refers to as PVE or Preventing Violent Extremism. These terms are often used interchangeably.

"CVE and PVE seek to prevent the next generation of terrorist threats by inoculating the most vulnerable people and places from terrorist recruitment and expansion by addressing issues of rights and governance and community resilience. In doing so, it seeks to convert our military gains against terrorist groups into lasting reductions in terrorist violence."

https://2009-2017.state.gov/j/remarks/261765.htm

11. *Special Briefing on the Annual State Department Country Report* by Justin Siberell, Acting Coordinator for Counterterrorism, Press Briefing Room, Washington, DC, June 2, 2016

"A key element of that strategy is to empower and amplify locally credible voices that can challenge the terrorist narrative and thereby weaken terrorists' ability to radicalize and recruit new members. This will be the focus of a newly established—of the newly established Global Engagement Center under the leadership of Michael Lumpkin."

https://2009-2017.state.gov/r/pa/prs/ps/2016/06/258013.htm

12. Justin Siberell, Acting Coordinator for Counterterrorism, *Protecting America from the Threat of ISIL*. Testimony to Senate Committee on Homeland Security, Washington, DC, May 26, 2016

Testimony describes international cooperation and discusses the Visa Waiver Program (VWP), which "... helps reinforce some of our strongest counterterrorism partnerships and serves as an incentive to other governments to adhere to the strongest possible security standards. ...We attribute the reduction in FTF flows to a range of factors, including military gains by the Counter-ISIL Coalition and proactive steps by governments to strengthen and enforce border security, counter-facilitation, and counter-recruitment efforts."

http://2009-2017.state.gov/j/ct/rls/rm/257777.htm

13. State Department Bureau of Counterterrorism. FY 2017 Request: Testimony by Justin Siberell, Acting Coordinator for

Counterterrorism to the House Foreign Affairs Subcommittee: Terrorism, Nonproliferation & Trade, Washington, DC, May 17, 2016

> The testimony provides a broad overview of the State Department's counterterrorism efforts, including specific programs. "[...] the success of U.S. counterterrorism efforts increasingly depends upon capable civilian partners. Police, investigators, and prosecutors are on frontlines of preventing and responding to asymmetric attacks by terrorist groups, especially attacks on so-called soft targets. Border and aviation security officials are working to stop foreign terrorist travelers, transfer of materiel, and terrorist threats. Moreover, local law enforcement, prison officials, and community leaders are on the frontlines in preventing and countering radicalization and recruitment to violence in their communities. [...]"

http://2009-2017.state.gov/j/ct/rls/rm/257307.htm

14. Statement by NSC Spokesperson Ned Price on Assistant to the President for Homeland Security and Counterterrorism Lisa O. Monaco's Visit to Belgium, May 11, 2016

> "Ms. Monaco and Belgian officials agreed to advance a foreign terrorist fighter work plan the U.S. Foreign Fighter Surge Team developed with its Belgian counterparts immediately following the attacks, to disrupt the recruitment and flow of foreign terrorist fighters to Syria and Iraq. [...]"

https://obamawhitehouse.archives.gov/the-press-office/2016/05/11/statement-nsc-spokesperson-ned-price-assistant-president-homeland

15. John Kerry, Secretary of State, *Remarks at Northeastern University Commencement*, TD Garden, Boston, MA, May 6, 2016

> "[...] in Syria and Iraq, we have degraded the leadership of the terrorist group known as ISIL or Daesh, and we and our partners have liberated a third of the land that it once occupied, and we are continuing to move. They have not taken one piece of territory and held it since May of last year, but we're not going to be successful in the long run—(applause)—we're not going to be successful in the long run if the world continues to turn away from other kinds of problems and allows the production of terrorists at such an alarming rate. And that is why it is critical that we expand our commitment to taking on violent extremism at the roots."

http://2009-2017.state.gov/secretary/remarks/2016/05/256963.htm

16. Secretary of State John Kerry, Testimony before the Senate Foreign Relations Committee, *Fiscal Year 2017 Budget Request for State Department and Related Agencies,* February 23, 2016

> "This year's budget seeks resources to enhance our nation's leadership of the 65 member global coalition to degrade and destroy the terrorist group Daesh. Our strategy is to combine our power and the power of our partners—to degrade Daesh's command structure, shrink the territory under its control, curb its financing, hammer its economic assets, discredit its lies, slow its recruitment, and block any attempt to expand its networks."

http://www.foreign.senate.gov/imo/media/doc/022316_Kerry_Testimony.pdf

17. Press Briefing by Press Secretary Josh Earnest and Special Presidential Envoy for the Global Coalition to Counter ISIL Brett McGurk, February 23, 2016

> "[...] we have to defeat them (ISIL) in the core and show that this is not an expanding movement; it's actually a shrinking movement. And so to defeat them in the core is how you actually begin to unravel the entire global network, and we've begun to see that now in some concrete ways."

https://obamawhitehouse.archives.gov/the-press-office/2016/02/24/press-briefing-press-secretary-josh-earnest-and-special-presidential

18. James Capper, Director of National Intelligence, *Worldwide Threat Assessment of the US Intelligence Community*, testimony to Senate Armed Services Committee, February 9, 2016

> Homegrown extremists probably will "continue to pose the most significant Sunni terrorist threat to the U.S. homeland in 2016" ... Iran remains "the foremost state sponsor of terrorism." The Islamic Republic and its "terrorist partner" Hezbollah "remain a continuing terrorist threat to U.S. interests and partners worldwide."

http://www.dni.gov/files/documents/SASC_Unclassified_2016_ATA_SFR_FINAL.pdf

19. Tina S. Kaidanow, Coordinator for Counterterrorism, *Countering the Spread of ISIL and Other Threats,* Remarks to the Center for Strategic and International Studies, Washington, DC, February 3, 2016
http://2009-2017.state.gov/j/ct/rls/rm/252082.htm

20. Defense Secretary Ash Carter, Remarks on Counter ISIL Campaign at the Ecole Militaire, Paris, France, January 21, 2016

> "[...] ISIL is a cancer that's threatening to spread. And like all cancers, you can't cure the disease just by cutting out the tumor. You have to eliminate it wherever it has spread, and stop it from coming back. [...]"

http://www.defense.gov/News/Speeches/Speech-View/Article/643904/counter-isil-campaign-remarks-at-the-ecole-militaire-paris

21. *United States Begins Implementation of Changes to the Visa Waiver Program*, DHS Release, January 21, 2016

> "Under the new law, the Secretary of Homeland Security may waive these restrictions if he determines that such a waiver is in the law enforcement or national security interests of the United States. Such waivers will be granted only on a case-by-case basis. As a general matter, categories of travelers who may be eligible for a waiver include:
>
> - "Individuals who traveled to Iran, Iraq, Sudan or Syria on behalf of international organizations, regional organizations, and sub-national governments on official duty;
> - "Individuals who traveled to Iran, Iraq, Sudan or Syria on behalf of a humanitarian NGO on official duty;
> - "Individuals who traveled to Iran, Iraq, Sudan or Syria as a journalist for reporting purposes;
> - "Individuals who traveled to Iran for legitimate business-related purposes following the conclusion of the Joint Comprehensive Plan of Action (July 14, 2015); and
> - "Individuals who have traveled to Iraq for legitimate business-related purposes."

https://www.dhs.gov/news/2016/01/21/united-states-begins-implementation-changes-visa-waiver-program

22. Defense Secretary Ash Carter, Fort Campbell, KY, January 13, 2016

> "[...] Our military campaign accordingly focuses on three military objectives: One, destroy the ISIL parent tumor in Iraq and Syria by collapsing its two power centers in Mosul and Raqqah. Two, combat the emerging metastases of the ISIL tumor worldwide, and three, protect the homeland. ... And to do it, we're going to enable local, motivated forces and an international coalition with a clear campaign plan, with American leadership, and with all of our awesome capabilities—ranging from air strikes, special forces, cyber tools, intelligence, equipment,

mobility and logistics, to training, advice, and assistance from those on the ground—including you. […]"

http://www.defense.gov/News/Speeches/Speech-View/Article/642995/remarks-to-the-101st-airborne-division-on-the-counter-isil-campaign-plan

23. FBI Director James Comey, *Testimony on terrorism threat*, Senate Judiciary Committee, December 9, 2015

FBI Director James Comey describes the FBI counterterrorism role and said that the United States is at its greatest threat level from terrorist groups since 9/11. He also expressed concern about terrorists' use of encryption.

https://www.fbi.gov/news/testimony/oversight-of-the-federal-bureau-of-investigation-8

Also see: http://www.cnn.com/2015/12/09/politics/terrorist-threats-fbi-director-9-11/

24. DHS/TSA. *Examining TSA's Global Efforts to Protect the Homeland from Aviation Threats and Enhance Security at Last Point of Departure Airports*. Testimony by TSA Office of Global Strategies Deputy Assistant Administrator Joe Terrell for a House Committee on Homeland Security, Subcommittee on Transportation Security Hearing, December 8, 2015

"[…] OGS coordinates with foreign governments, air carriers, and international organizations to implement responses that will effectively mitigate the likelihood of a successful attack. This involves a spectrum of activities to identify risk in terms of threat, vulnerability, and consequence. Once a threat is identified, OGS analyzes the underlying factors and develops mitigation plans."

http://www.dhs.gov/news/2015/12/08/written-testimony-tsa-house-homeland-security-subcommittee-transportation-security

25. Vice President Joe Biden, Weekly Address, The White House, November 21, 2015

"There is no possibility of being overwhelmed by a flood of refugees landing on our doorstep tomorrow. Right now, refugees wait 18 to 24 months while the screening process is completed. And unlike in Europe, refugees don't set foot in the United States until they are thoroughly vetted."

https://obamawhitehouse.archives.gov/the-press-office/2015/11/21/weekly-address-face-terror-we-stand-one

26. Fact Sheet: *Visa Waiver Program*, White House Press Office, November 11, 2015

"DHS will immediately take steps to modify its Electronic System for Travel Authorization (ESTA) applications to capture information from VWP travelers regarding any past travel to countries constituting a terrorist safe haven. The Director of National Intelligence, in coordination with the Secretary of Homeland Security, will identify and regularly review these countries so that traveler risk assessments can be made on the most up-to-date information."

https://obamawhitehouse.archives.gov/the-press-office/2015/11/30/fact-sheet-visa-waiver-program-enhancements

27. DHS Secretary Jeh Johnson. *Worldwide Threats and Homeland Security Challenges*. Testimony to the House Committee on Homeland Security, October 21, 2015

Counterterrorism overview, including dealing with foreign fighter concerns and cybersecurity.

http://www.dhs.gov/news/2015/10/08/written-testimony-dhs-secretary-jeh-johnson-senate-committee-homeland-security-and

28. FBI Director Comey, Testimony to Senate Homeland Security Committee, October 8, 2015.

"Counterterrorism remains the FBI's top priority; however, the threat has changed in two significant ways. First, the core al Qaeda tumor has been reduced, but the cancer has metastasized. The progeny of al Qaeda—including AQAP, al Qaeda in the Islamic Maghreb, and the Islamic State of Iraq and the Levant (ISIL)—have become our focus.

"Secondly, we are confronting the explosion of terrorist propaganda and training on the Internet. It is no longer necessary to get a terrorist operative into the United States to recruit. Terrorists, in ungoverned spaces, disseminate poisonous propaganda and training materials to attract troubled souls around the world to their cause. They encourage these individuals to travel, but if they can't travel, they motivate them to act at home. This is a significant change from a decade ago."

https://www.fbi.gov/news/testimony/threats-to-the-homeland

29. Secretary Kerry, *Remarks at a Meeting on International Peace and Security and Countering Terrorism*, United Nations, September 30, 2015

Discussion of the need for a comprehensive approach to counter terrorism, ISIL, and Syrian–Russian situation.

http://2009-2017.state.gov/secretary/remarks/2015/09/247639.htm

30. Assistant Attorney General for National Security John P. Carlin, *Update on U.S. Government Counterterrorism Efforts,* New York, September 28, 2015

Discussion of DOJ's efforts, including a number of criminal cases involving ISIS.

http://www.justice.gov/opa/pr/transcript-assistant-attorney-general-john-p-carlin-s-briefing-foreign-press-center-foreign-0

31. NSC Spokesperson Ned Price, *Statement on U.S. Support for the Countries Fighting Boko Haram*, September 24, 2015

"The President today delegated authority to the Secretary of State to direct the drawdown of up to $45 million in defense articles and services, as well as military education and training, to support Benin, Cameroon, Chad, Niger, and Nigeria's efforts to defeat Boko Haram. This will enable the Secretary to authorize the provision of critical airlift support and other assistance, including to help the Lake Chad Basin countries move troops and equipment to the border region from which Boko Haram terrorists continue to launch brutal attacks on civilians. The United States also continues to provide advisors and share information with our regional partners to enhance counter–Boko Haram operations, as well as victim support and counter-violent extremism programming. [...]"

https://obamawhitehouse.archives.gov/the-press-office/2015/09/24/statement-nsc-spokesperson-ned-price-us-support-countries-fighting-boko

32. Ambassador Tina S. Kaidanow, State Department Assistant Secretary for Counterterrorism, *Al-Qaida, the Islamic State, and the Future of the Global Jihadi Movement,* Remarks at the Brookings Institute, Washington, DC, September 16, 2015

Overview of the threats from these groups and the countermeasures and cooperation with other countries to counter the threat.

http://2009-2017.state.gov/j/ct/rls/rm/246983.htm

33. *Press Conference Call on Additional Steps to Counter ISIL* by Ben Rhodes, the Deputy National Security Advisor for Strategic Communications, June 10, 2015

> "We've been pursuing a strategy since last year to degrade and ultimately destroy ISIL, focusing on efforts within Iraq and Syria ... to push it out of areas that it had claimed, and also, importantly, to strengthen the capacity of partners on the ground in that effort ... The President is authorizing the deployment of additional U.S. military personnel to train and advise and assist Iraqi security forces at Taqaddum military base in eastern Anbar Province ... These advisors will give us a greater capacity to strengthen Iraqi forces, including, importantly, working with the local tribal fighters who are going to be essential to our efforts to conduct operations against ISIL. [...]"

https://obamawhitehouse.archives.gov/the-press-office/2015/06/10/press-conference-call-additional-steps-counter-isil

34. Justin Siberell, Principal Deputy Coordinator for Counterterrorism, Testimony to the House Foreign Affairs Committee Subcommittee on Terrorism, Nonproliferation, and Trade, June 2, 2015

> "As the U.S. military expands its efforts with foreign militaries, it is equally critical that we strengthen the capacity of civilian security agencies to ensure effective, whole-of-government approaches to terrorism challenges. It is also critical that we expand our partnerships with non-governmental actors who can help counter violent extremist recruitment and messaging in key regions around the world. Lastly, with governments and non-governmental actors alike, we must do more to address the drivers that fuel the spread of violent extremism."

http://2009-2017.state.gov/j/ct/rls/rm/243114.htm

35. DOJ/OPDAT Counterterrorism Programs, *Overview of Justice Department programs to help strengthen the legal systems of friendly countries*, May 26, 2015

http://www.justice.gov/criminal/opdat/worldact-programs/ctu.html

36. Statement by NSC Spokesperson Bernadette Meehan on Counter-ISIL Operation in Syria May 16, 2015

> "Last night, at the President's direction, U.S. personnel based out of Iraq conducted an operation in al-Amr in eastern Syria

to capture an ISIL senior leader known as Abu Sayyaf and his wife Umm Sayyaf. During the course of the operation, Abu Sayyaf was killed when he engaged U.S. forces. Abu Sayyaf was a senior ISIL leader who, among other things, had a senior role in overseeing ISIL's illicit oil and gas operations—a key source of revenue."

https://obamawhitehouse.archives.gov/the-press-office/2015/05/16/statement-nsc-spokesperson-bernadette-meehan-counter-isil-operation-sy-1

37. Remarks by Secretary of Homeland Security Jeh Johnson: *DHS 2015: The Secretary's Progress Report*—As Delivered, December 29, 2014

"We are restructuring the whole manner in which we make decisions within the Department of Homeland Security. In April I directed a 'Unity of Effort' initiative, which has brought about a more centralized and integrated process for making decisions concerning budget requests, acquisition, strategy and other department functions. We are moving away from decisions made in stove pipes. As part of this initiative, we have created a Joint Requirements Council consisting of senior leaders from the DHS components, to identify and recommend investments to maximize efficiency. We have also realigned seven major DHS headquarters functions, to consolidate like functions and promote efficiency."

http://www.dhs.gov/news/2015/01/29/remarks-secretary-johnson-dhs-2015-secretarys-progress-

38. Director of National Intelligence (DNI) Clapper Establishes the National Counterintelligence and Security Center, December 1, 2014

"[...] The establishment of the National Counterintelligence and Security Center supports our effort to ensure counterintelligence and security are addressed as interdependent and mutually supportive disciplines," said Director Clapper. "These disciplines have shared objectives and responsibilities associated with the protection of information, sources and methods."

https://www.dni.gov/index.php/newsroom/press-releases/198-press-releases-2014/1142-dni-clapper-establishes-the-national-counterintelligence-and-security-center

39. Fact Sheet: *Prosecuting and Detaining Terror Suspects in the U.S. Criminal Justice System*, September 14, 2014
http://www.justice.gov/opa/pr/2009/June/09-ag-564.html

40. *2014 Quadrennial Homeland Security Review* (QHSR), June 14, 2014

Outlines five basic homeland security missions revised to address threats and hazards: (1) prevent terrorism and enhance security; (2) secure and manage our borders; (3) enforce and administer our immigration laws; (4) safeguard and secure cyberspace; and (5) strengthen national preparedness and resilience.

http://www.dhs.gov/sites/default/files/publications/2014-qhsr-final-508.pdf

41. Statement by Assistant to the President for Homeland Security and Counterterrorism John Brennan on Bulgaria's Announcement of Hizballah's Role in the 2012 Burgas Terrorist Attack, February 5, 2013

"Bulgaria's implication of Hizballah underscores the importance of international cooperation in disrupting terrorist threats. We call on our European partners as well as other members of the international community to take proactive action to uncover Hizballah's infrastructure and disrupt the group's financing schemes and operational networks in order to prevent future attacks."

https://obamawhitehouse.archives.gov/the-press-office/2013/02/05/statement-assistant-president-homeland-security-and-counterterrorism-joh

42. Reese, Shawn, *Defining Homeland Security: Analysis and Congressional Considerations*, Congressional Research Service Issue Brief, January 8, 2013

This report discusses the evolution of national and DHS-specific homeland security strategic documents and their homeland security definitions and missions and analyzes the policy question of how varied homeland security definitions and missions may affect the development of national homeland security strategy.

http://fas.org/sgp/crs/homesec/R42462.pdf

43. Judge William H. Webster, *The Final Report of the William H. Webster Commission on The Federal Bureau of Investigation, Counterterrorism Intelligence, and the Events at Fort Hood,*

Texas, on November 5, 2009, FBI National Press Office, July 19, 2012

https://archives.fbi.gov/archives/news/pressrel/press-releases/judge-webster-delivers-webster-commission-report-on-fort-hood

44. CIA Director John Brennan, *The Efficacy and Ethics of U.S. Counterterrorism Strategy*, Remarks at the Wilson Center, Washington, DC, April 30, 2012

Discussion of the use of armed drones

CIA Director John Brennan discusses the use of armed drones and the considerations and justifications in using them.

https://www.wilsoncenter.org/event/the-efficacy-and-ethics-us-counterterrorism-strategy?utm_source=newsletter&utm_medium=email&utm_campaign=ww_05_03_12d

45. Attorney General Eric Holder Speech at the American Constitution Society Convention, June 16, 2011

The Attorney General reaffirmed commitment to try terror suspect in civilian federal court system. "Every single suspected terrorist captured on American soil—before and after the September 11th attacks—has first been taken into custody by law enforcement—not the United States military. Our criminal justice system has proven—time and again—that it provides all the authority and flexibility we need to effectively combat terrorist threats. Since 9/11, hundreds of individuals have been convicted of terrorism or terrorism-related offenses in civilian courts.

Not one of these individuals has escaped custody. Not one of the judicial districts involved has suffered retaliatory attacks. [...]"

Even though excellent work has been done to improve and reform the military commissions, these tribunals are largely untested.

http://www.justice.gov/iso/opa/ag/speeches/2011/ag-speech-1106161.html

46. John Brennan Assistant to the President for Homeland Security and Counterterrorism, *Securing the Homeland by Renewing American Strength, Resilience and Values, address to CSIS, May 26, 2010*

"Our enemy is not 'terrorism' because terrorism is but a tactic. Our enemy is not 'terror' because terror is a state of mind and as Americans we refuse to live in fear. Nor do we describe our enemy as 'jihadists' or 'Islamists' because jihad is a holy struggle, a legitimate tenant of Islam, meaning to purify oneself or one's community, and there is nothing holy or legitimate or Islamic about murdering innocent men, women and children. ... Our enemy is al Qaeda and its terrorist affiliates. ... And the president's strategy outlines how we will achieve this mission and keep Americans safe."

https://obamawhitehouse.archives.gov/the-press-office/remarks-assistant-president-homeland-security-and-counterterrorism-john-brennan-csi

47. Statement by U.S. Department of Homeland Security Secretary Janet Napolitano on the Threat of Right-Wing Extremism, April 15, 2009

"Let me be very clear: we monitor the risks of violent extremism taking root here in the United States. We don't have the luxury of focusing our efforts on one group; we must protect the country from terrorism whether foreign or homegrown, and regardless of the ideology that motivates its violence."

https://www.dhs.gov/news/2009/04/15/secretary-napolitanos-statement-right-wing-extremism-threat (accessed April 27, 2017).

Subject Matter: CVE

1. *Updating Our Plan to Counter Violent Extremism at Home*, The White House, October 19, 2016

"Today, the Administration issued new strategic guidance on federal efforts to counter violent extremism at home. This plan incorporates the many lessons we have learned over the years from working hand-in-hand with local communities and lays the groundwork for the years to come. The Strategic Implementation Plan to Empower Local Partners to Prevent Violent Extremism in the United States (*PDF, 18 pages, 322 KB*) will help ensure our Nation remains vigilant in preventing terrorists from recruiting and radicalizing Americans to violence."

https://www.dhs.gov/blog/2016/10/19/updating-our-plan-counter-violent-extremism-home

2. *Department of State & USAID Joint Strategy on Countering Violent Extremism*, May 2016

Secretary of State Kerry's introduction: "[...] The Department of State and USAID have produced a proactive international strategy recognizing immediate needs, utilizing our strengths, and demonstrating our will to comprehensively address the challenge of violent extremism, including the root causes. Together, we are building organizational structures needed to pursue a more aggressive and integrated approach to this challenge. This is a generational struggle, but we must begin now.

"Carrying forth the work of the White House CVE Summit agenda, this strategy recognizes the need to foster and empower a broad-based coalition of government and non-governmental actors to address this scourge and project a positive vision."

http://2009-2017.state.gov/documents/organization/257913.pdf

3. Acting Coordinator for Counterterrorism Justin Siberell, *Assessing the State Department's Efforts to Counter Violent Extremism*, address to the Program on Extremism at George Washington University, Washington, DC, May 15, 2016

   https://2009-2017.state.gov/j/ct/rls/rm/257726.htm

4. Statement by NSC Spokesperson Ned Price on Updates to U.S. Government Efforts to Counter Violent Extremism, January 8, 2016

"The Department of Homeland Security and the Department of Justice will announce the establishment of the Countering Violent Extremism Task Force, a new organization that will integrate and harmonize domestic CVE efforts here at home. The State Department will establish the Global Engagement Center, which will allow us to place an intensified focus on empowering and enabling the voices of international partners, governmental and non-governmental, and shift away from direct messaging. Additionally, today some of the most senior officials from the White House and across the President's national security team are meeting in Silicon Valley with representatives from a number of leading technology companies, to follow up on the President's call in his address on December 6 for the government and private sector to work together to combat terrorism and counter violent extremism online."

https://obamawhitehouse.archives.gov/the-press-office/2016/01/08/statement-nsc-spokesperson-ned-price-updates-us-government-efforts

5. Also see DHS Statement: *Countering Violent Extremism Task Force*, January 8, 2016

> "The CVE Task Force will be a permanent interagency task force hosted by the Department of Homeland Security (DHS) with overall leadership provided by DHS and the Department of Justice ... The task force will be administratively housed at DHS. The CVE Task Force will address the gaps identified in the review by (1) synchronizing and integrating whole-of-government CVE programs and activities; (2) leveraging new CVE efforts, for example those of the DHS Office for Community Partnerships; (3) conducting ongoing strategic planning; and (4) assessing and evaluating CVE programs and activities."

   http://www.dhs.gov/news/2016/01/08/countering-violent-extremism-task-force

6. *Countering the Islamic State's Message*, article by Alberto M. Fernandez, former State Department's Coordinator for Strategic Counterterrorism Communication, The Journal of International Security Affairs, Winter 2016

> "All too often, ISIS has found our doors unlocked and our voices silenced. It is our lack of care and attention that gave its toxic message the opportunity to flourish. Even a qualitative improvement in what we are already trying to do could yield very positive results in a relatively short period of time."

   http://www.securityaffairs.org/issues/number-30/countering-islamic-states-message#sthash.tKrOc1ZI.dpuf

7. *Mobilizing against a Preeminent Challenge of the 21st Century: Countering Violent Extremism, presentation by Sarah Sewall, Under Secretary for Civilian Security, Democracy, and Human Rights*, Washington Institute for Near East Policy, Washington, DC, November 20, 2015

   http://2009-2017.state.gov/j/remarks/249839.htm

   CVE Source from Brenna Center for Justice: https://www.brennancenter.org/analysis/cve-programs-resource-page

8. Background Conference Call by Senior Administration Officials Previewing the White House Summit on Countering Violent Extremism, February 16, 2015

> "CVE efforts are premised on the central goal of preventing violent extremism and the extremists themselves and their supporters from inspiring, radicalizing, financing or recruiting individuals or groups in the United States from committing acts of violence."

"Our approach empowers communities to push back against violent extremists. Really at the core of our approach is that the government does not have all the answers in combatting violent extremism. It is, at its core, a bottom-up approach. [...] The goal there [of the panel of strategic communications and social media] is to highlight the effective techniques and strategies to counter violent extremism, and the violent extremist narrative, including online spaces, and how to effectively and rapidly scale up effective models and assess their effectiveness."

https://obamawhitehouse.archives.gov/the-press-office/2015/02/16/background-conference-call-senior-administration-officials-previewing-wh

9. FBI Director Comey on Countering Violent Extremists, October 7, 2014
   http://leb.fbi.gov/2014/october/a-new-approach-to-countering-violent-extremism-sharing-expertise-and-empowering-local-communities

Subject Matter: WMD

1. Department of Defense Strategy for Countering Weapons of Mass Destruction, June 2014
   http://www.defenseinnovationmarketplace.mil/resources/DoD_Strategy_for_Countering_Weapons_of_Mass_Destruction_dated_June_2014.pdf

2. *Majidi, Vahid. Assistant Director, Weapons of Mass Destruction Directorate, Federal Bureau of Investigation. Testimony before the Senate Committee on Homeland Security and Governmental Affairs. *Ten Years After 9/11 and the Anthrax Attacks: Protecting against Biological Threats.* Washington, DC, October 18, 2011
   http://www.fbi.gov/news/testimony/ten-years-after-9-11-and-the-anthrax-attacks-protecting-against-biological-threats

3. Federal Efforts to Address the Threat of Bioterrorism, Congressional Research Services Issue Brief by Frank Gorton and Dana Shea, February 8, 2011

   "This report focuses on four areas under congressional consideration deemed critical to the success of the biodefense enterprise: strategic planning; risk assessment; surveillance; and the development, procurement, and distribution of medical countermeasures."

   https://fas.org/sgp/crs/terror/R41123.pdf

4. KD Testimony of Jane Holl Lute, Deputy Secretary, "*Nuclear Terrorism: Strengthening Our Domestic Defenses, Part II*" before the United States Senate Committee on Homeland Security and Governmental Affairs, September 15, 2010
   http://www.dhs.gov/ynews/testimony/testimony_1286544936791.shtm

5. *Anne M. Harrington, Deputy Administrator for Defense Nuclear Nonproliferation, Testimony to the Senate Armed Services Sub Committee on Emerging Threats and Capabilities, May 10, 2010

   > "Investing in the future of the scientific and technical underpinnings of our program is critical to implementing the President's nuclear security agenda."

   http://www.nnsa.energy.gov/mediaroom/congressional testimony/harringtonsenateremarks51011

6. KD National Strategy for Countering Biological Threats, November 23, 2009
   https://obamawhitehouse.archives.gov/sites/default/files/National_Strategy_for_Countering_BioThreats.pdf

7. Fact Sheet on the United Nations Security Council Summit on Nuclear Nonproliferation and Nuclear Disarmament UNSC Resolution 1887, September 24, 2009

   > "UNSC Resolution 1887 ... expresses the Council's grave concern about the threat of nuclear proliferation and the need for international action to prevent it. It reaffirms that the proliferation of weapons of mass destruction and their means of delivery are threats to international peace and security and shows agreement on a broad range of actions to address nuclear proliferation and disarmament and the threat of nuclear terrorism."

   https://obamawhitehouse.archives.gov/the-press-office/fact-sheet-united-nations-security-council-summit-nuclear-nonproliferation-and-nucl

8. National Counterproliferation Center, Office of the Director for National Intelligence
   https://www.dni.gov/index.php/about/organization/national-counterproliferation-center-who-we-are

Subject Matter: CYBER

1. Executive Summary of Grizzly Steppe Findings from Homeland Security Assistant Secretary for Public Affairs Todd Breasseale, December 30, 2016

"Russia's civilian and military intelligence services engaged in aggressive and sophisticated cyber-enabled operations targeting the U.S. government and its citizens. The U.S. Government refers to this activity as GRIZZLY STEPPE. These cyber operations included spearphishing campaigns targeting government organizations, critical infrastructure entities, think tanks, universities, political organizations, and corporations, and theft of information from these organizations. This stolen information was later publicly released by third parties."

https://www.dhs.gov/news/2016/12/30/executive-summary-grizzly-steppe-findings-homeland-security-assistant-secretary

2. Joint Statement from the Department of Homeland Security and Office of the Director of National Intelligence on Election Security, October 7, 2016

"The U.S. Intelligence Community (USIC) is confident that the Russian Government directed the recent compromises of e-mails from US persons and institutions, including from US political organizations. The recent disclosures of alleged hacked e-mails on sites like DCLeaks.com and WikiLeaks and by the Guccifer 2.0 online persona are consistent with the methods and motivations of Russian-directed efforts. These thefts and disclosures are intended to interfere with the US election process. Such activity is not new to Moscow—the Russians have used similar tactics and techniques across Europe and Eurasia, for example, to influence public opinion there. We believe, based on the scope and sensitivity of these efforts, that only Russia's senior-most officials could have authorized these activities. [...]"

https://www.dhs.gov/news/2016/10/07/joint-statement-department-homeland-security-and-office-director-national

3. The State of Homeland Security, Remarks by Secretary of Homeland Security Jeh C. Johnson, Wilson Center, Washington, February 11, 2016

Overview of a variety of efforts to increase homeland security. "While counterterrorism remains a cornerstone of our Department's mission, I have concluded that cybersecurity must be another. Making tangible improvements to our nation's cybersecurity is a top priority for me and President Obama before we leave office."

https://www.dhs.gov/news/2016/02/11/remarks-secretary-homeland-security-jeh-c-johnson-state-homeland-security

4. *Waging a Digital Counterinsurgency*, Remarks by Richard Stengel Under Secretary for Public Diplomacy and Public Affairs, Chatham House, London, United Kingdom, January 18, 2016

"[...] ISIL messaging is not all about social media. Social media is in some ways the tip of the iceberg. There's a very fancy term in sociology called the availability heuristic, which means that thing that you see assumes gigantic proportions, much bigger proportion than it actually is. Because we see the few things they do on social media in English, we think everything they do is on social media. In Iraq and Syria, they're on billboards, they have kiosks, they do flyers, and they have imams preaching sermons. [...]"

http://2009-2017.state.gov/r/remarks/2016/252253.htm

5. Drell Lecture: *Rewiring the Pentagon: Charting a New Path on Innovation and Cybersecurity*, Stanford University, April 23, 2015.

Secretary of Defense Ash Carter emphasized the importance of relationships between the government, as well as the private sector, placing particular importance on these relationships having to do with cyber and technical support. He inferred how much there is to be learned by the government from the private sector, especially having to do with cyber technology and security. The Secretary of Defense reiterated, "We want to partner with businesses on everything from autonomy to robotics to biomedical engineering; from power, energy, and propulsion to distributed systems, data science, and the Internet of things. Because if we're going to leverage these technologies to defend our country and help make a better world, the Department of Defense cannot do everything in all these areas alone. We have to work with those outside."

http://www.defense.gov/Speeches/Speech.aspx?SpeechID=1935

6. Statement by Assistant to the President for Homeland Security and Counterterrorism Lisa Monaco: *Update on Implementation of Signals Intelligence Reform and Issuance of PPD-28*, February 3, 2015

"As the President indicated in PPD-28, our signals intelligence activities must take into account that all persons have legitimate privacy interests in the handling of their personal information. At the same time, we must ensure that our Intelligence

Community has the resources and authorities necessary for the United States to advance its national security and foreign policy interests and to protect its citizens and the citizens of its allies and partners from harm. As we continue to face threats from terrorism, proliferation, and cyber-attacks, we must use our intelligence capabilities in a way that optimally protects our national security and supports our foreign policy while keeping the public trust and respecting privacy and civil liberties."

https://obamawhitehouse.archives.gov/the-press-office/2015/02/03/statement-assistant-president-homeland-security-and-counterterrorism-lis

7. National Security Strategy February 2015.

In the counterterrorism portion of the 2015 National security Strategy, President Obama said, "In all our efforts, we aim to draw a stark contrast between what we stand for and the heinous deeds of terrorists. We reject the lie that America and its allies are at war with Islam. We will continue to act lawfully. Outside of areas of active hostilities, we endeavor to detain, interrogate, and prosecute terrorists through law enforcement. However, when there is a continuing, imminent threat, and when capture or other actions to disrupt the threat are not feasible, we will not hesitate to take decisive action. We will always do so legally, discriminately, proportionally, and bound by strict accountability and strong oversight. The United States—not our adversaries—will define the nature and scope of this struggle, lest it define us.

https://obamawhitehouse.archives.gov/sites/default/files/docs/2015_national_security_strategy_2.pdf

8. Written testimony of S&T Under Secretary Dr. Reginald Brothers for a House Committee on Homeland Security, Subcommittee on Cybersecurity, Infrastructure Protection, and Security Technologies, and House Committee on Science, Space, and Technology, Subcommittee on Research and Technology hearing titled "*Strategy and Mission of the DHS Science and Technology Directorate*", September 9, 2014

The Presidential Policy Directive (PPD) on Critical Infrastructure Security and Resilience advances a national unity of effort to strengthen and maintain secure, functioning, and resilient critical infrastructure.

http://www.dhs.gov/news/2014/09/09/written-testimony-st-under-secretary-joint-subcommittee-hearing-house-committee

STATEMENTS AND SPEECHES OF PRESIDENTS AND CABINETS (NIXON TO BUSH)

The Presidents

Bush Post-9/11

1. President Bush Visits National Defense University, Discusses Global War on Terror, October 23, 2007

> "[...] in this new war, the enemy conspires in secret—and often the only source of information on what the terrorists are planning is the terrorists themselves. So we established a program at the Central Intelligence Agency to question key terrorist leaders and operatives captured in the war on terror. This program has produced critical intelligence that has helped us stop a number of attacks ... in London. ... Despite the record of success, and despite the fact that our professionals use lawful techniques, the CIA program has come under renewed criticism in recent weeks. Those who oppose this vital tool in the war on terror need to answer a simple question: Which of the attacks ... would they prefer we had not stopped? Without this program, our intelligence community believes that al Qaeda and its allies would have succeeded in launching another attack against the American homeland. This CIA program has saved lives—it is vital to the security of the American people. [...]"

http://2001-2009.state.gov/r/pa/ei/wh/94059.htm

2. President Bush Discusses War on Terror, Charleston AFB, Charleston, South Carolina, July 24, 2007

The President presented a detailed discussion of the history of al-Qaeda and al-Qaeda in Iraq.

http://2001-2009.state.gov/r/pa/ei/wh/rem/89039.htm

3. President Bush Discusses the Global War on Terror, Tipp City, Ohio, April 19, 2007

> "I've chosen a path that says we will go overseas and defeat them there. I also know full well that it's important for us if we're facing an ideology, if we're facing ideologues, if we're confronting people who believe something, that we have got to defeat their belief system with a better belief system. Forms of government matter, in my opinion. It matters how—the nature of the government in which people live. And therefore, I have

put as part of our foreign policy not only an aggressive plan to find extremists and radicals and bring them to justice before they hurt us, but also to help people live in liberty—free societies, as the great alternative to people living under a tyrant, for example.

"And so my decision making was based upon those principles. And now we're involved in—I call it a global war against terror. You can't [sic] call it a global war against extremists, a global war against radicals, a global war against people who want to hurt America; you can call it whatever you want, but it is a global effort. [...]"

http://2001-2009.state.gov/r/pa/ei/wh/83261.htm

4. President Bush Discusses Progress in Afghanistan, Global War on Terror, American Enterprise Institute, Washington, DC, February 15, 2007

"[...] one of the lessons of that September the 11th day is that we cannot allow terrorists to gain sanctuary anywhere, and we must not allow them to reestablish the safe haven they lost in Afghanistan.

"Our goal in Afghanistan is to help the people of that country to defeat the terrorists and establish a stable, moderate, and democratic state that respects the rights of its citizens, governs its territory effectively, and is a reliable ally in this war against extremists and terrorists. [...]"

http://2001-2009.state.gov/p/sca/rls/rm/2007/80548.htm

5. Press Conference by the President, Indian Treaty Room, December 20, 2006

"[...] I haven't questioned whether or not it was right to take Saddam Hussein out, nor have I questioned the necessity for the American people ... I've come to the conclusion it's the right decision. But I also know it's the right decision for America to stay engaged, and to take the lead, and to deal with these radicals and extremists, and to help support young democracies. It's the calling of our time. And I firmly believe it is necessary. ... And I believe the next President, whoever the person is, will have the same charge, the same obligations to deal with terrorists so they don't hurt us, and to help young democracies survive the threats of radicalism and extremism. [...]"

http://2001-2009.state.gov/r/pa/ei/wh/rem/78120.htm

6. President Bush Meets with British Prime Minister Tony Blair, The White House, December 7, 2006

   "The increase in sectarian attacks we're seeing in and around Baghdad are unsettling. It has led to much debate in both our countries about the nature of the war that is taking place in Iraq. And it is true that Sunni and Shia extremists are targeting each other's innocent civilians and engaging in brutal reprisals. It's also true that forces beyond Iraq's borders contribute to this violence. And the Prime Minister put it this way, he said, 'The violence is not an accident or a result of faulty planning. It is a deliberate strategy. It is the direct result of outside extremists teaming up with internal extremists—al Qaeda with the Sunni insurgents, and Iran with the Shia militia—to foment hatred and to throttle, at birth, the possibility of a non-sectarian democracy."

   http://georgewbush-whitehouse.archives.gov/news/releases/2006/12/images/20061207-1_d-0263-2-515h.html

7. President George W. Bush's Radio Address on National Intelligence Estimate and Iraq, September 30, 2006

   "[...] The NIE is a classified document that analyzes the threat we face from terrorists and extremists. Parts of this classified document were recently leaked to the press. That has created a heated debate in our Nation's capital, and a lot of misimpressions about the document's conclusions. ... The National Intelligence Estimate confirms that we are up against a determined and capable enemy. The NIE lists four underlying factors that are fueling the extremist movement: first, long-standing grievances such as corruption, injustice, and a fear of Western domination; second, the jihad in Iraq; third, the slow pace of reform in Muslim nations; and fourth, pervasive anti-Americanism. It concludes that terrorists are exploiting all these factors to further their movement. [...]"

   http://www.presidency.ucsb.edu/ws/?pid=23955

8. President Bush Discusses Progress in the Global War on Terror, Cobb Galleria Centre, Atlanta, Georgia, September 7, 2006

   "[...] Another top priority after 9/11 was improving our ability to monitor terrorist communications. ... At my direction, the National Security Agency created the Terrorist Surveillance Program. Before 9/11, our intelligence professionals found it difficult to monitor international communications such as those between the al Qaeda operatives secretly in the United States and planners of the 9/11 attacks. The Terrorist Surveillance Program helps protect Americans by allowing us to track terrorist communications, so we can learn about threats like the 9/11 plot before it is too late. [...]"

http://georgewbush-whitehouse.archives.gov/news/releases/2006/09/20060907-2.html_

9. President Discusses Global War on Terror, Military Officers Association, Washington, DC, September 5, 2006

"Today we're releasing a document called the 'National Strategy for Combating Terrorism.' This is an unclassified version of the strategy we've been pursuing since September the 11th, 2001. This strategy was first released in February 2003; it's been updated to take into account the changing nature of this enemy. This strategy document is posted on the White House website—whitehouse.gov. [http://www.whitehouse.gov/nsc/nsct/2006/.] Our strategy for combating terrorism has five basic elements: First, we're determined to prevent terrorist attacks before they occur. So we're taking the fight to the enemy ... We're also fighting the enemy here at home ... Second, we're determined to deny weapons of mass destruction to outlaw regimes and terrorists who would use them without hesitation. ... Third, we're determined to deny terrorists the support of outlaw regimes. ... Fourth, we're determined to deny terrorist networks control of any nation, or territory within a nation. ... Fifth, we're working to deny terrorists new recruits. [...]"

http://georgewbush-whitehouse.archives.gov/news/releases/2006/09/20060905-4.html

10. *National Strategy for Combating Terrorism*, September 2006

"Today, we face a global terrorist movement and must confront the radical ideology that justifies the use of violence against innocents in the name of religion. As laid out in this strategy, to win the War on Terror, we will: Advance effective democracies as the long-term antidote to the ideology of terrorism; Prevent attacks by terrorist networks; Deny terrorists the support and sanctuary of rogue states; Deny terrorists control of any nation they would use as a base and launching pad for terror; and lay the foundations and build the institutions and structures we need to carry the fight forward against terror and help ensure our ultimate success."

https://2001-2009.state.gov/s/ct/rls/wh/71803.htm

11. President Bush Discusses Foreign Policy During Visit to State Department, August 14, 2006

> "Some say that America caused the current instability in the Middle East by pursuing a forward strategy of freedom, yet history shows otherwise. We didn't talk much about freedom or the freedom agenda in the Middle East before September the 11th, 2001; or before al Qaeda first attacked the World Trade Center and blew up our embassies in Kenya and Tanzania in the 1990s; or before Hezbollah killed hundreds of Americans in Beirut and Islamic radicals held American hostages in Iran in the 1980s. History is clear: The freedom agenda did not create the terrorists or their ideology. But the freedom agenda will help defeat them both."

http://georgewbush-whitehouse.archives.gov/news/releases/2006/08/20060814-3.html

12. President Bush Meets with Supporters of U.S. Military in Iraq and Afghanistan, June 26, 2006

> "The American people expect this government to protect our constitutional liberties and, at the same time, make sure we understand what the terrorists are trying to do. The 9/11 Commission recommended that the government be robust in tracing money. If you want to figure out what the terrorists are doing, you try to follow their money. And that's exactly what we're doing."

http://georgewbush-whitehouse.archives.gov/news/releases/2006/06/20060626-2.html

13. President Bush Delivers Commencement Address at the United States Military Academy at West Point, May 27, 2006

> "[...] The greatest threat we face is the danger of terrorists armed with weapons of mass destruction. To confront this danger, we launched the Proliferation Security Initiative, a coalition of more than 70 nations that are working together to stop shipments of weapons of mass destruction on land, at sea, and in the air, and to stop them from falling into terrorist hands ... we launched the most dramatic transformation of the NATO alliance since its founding in 1949. Working with allies, we created a new NATO Response Force that will allow NATO to deploy rapid reaction forces on short notice anywhere in the world. And together we transformed NATO from a defensive alliance focused on protecting Europe from Soviet tank invasion into a dynamic alliance that is now operating across the world in the support of democracy and peace. [...]"

http://www.presidency.ucsb.edu/ws/?pid=83

14. President Discusses War on Terror address to National Endowment for Democracy, Washington, DC, October 6, 2005

"[...] we're not facing a set of grievances that can be soothed and addressed. We're facing a radical ideology with inalterable objectives: to enslave whole nations and intimidate the world. No act of ours invited the rage of the killers—and no concession, bribe, or act of appeasement would change or limit their plans for murder.

"On the contrary: They target nations whose behavior they believe they can change through violence. Against such an enemy, there is only one effective response: We will never back down, never give in, and never accept anything less than complete victory. [...]"

http://georgewbush-whitehouse.archives.gov/news/releases/2005/10/20051006-3.html

15. President Discusses War on Terror at FBI Academy, Quantico, Virginia, July 11, 2005

"[...] In London last Thursday terrorists killed dozens of commuters and wounded hundreds more. Americans know what it's like to be attacked on our own soil. ... We have a comprehensive strategy in place ... We're working to improve our intelligence so we can uncover terrorist plots before they unfold. And we're staying on the offensive. We're fighting the enemy in Iraq and Afghanistan and across the world so we do not have to face them here at home ... The FBI efforts are central to our success in the war on terror ...We know that there is no such thing as perfect security and that in a free and open society it is impossible to protect against every threat. As we saw in London last week, the terrorists need to be right only once. Free nations need to be right a hundred percent of the time. The best way to defend America is to stay on the offense. When terrorists spread their—spend their days and nights struggling to avoid death or capture, they are less capable of arming and training and plotting new attacks. [...]"

http://georgewbush-whitehouse.archives.gov/news/releases/2005/07/20050711-1.html

16. President Addresses Nation, Discusses Iraq, War on Terror, Fort Bragg, North Carolina, June 28, 2005

"[...] as freedom takes root in Iraq, it will inspire millions across the Middle East to claim their liberty, as well. And when the Middle East grows in democracy and prosperity and hope, the terrorists will lose their sponsors, lose their recruits, and lose their hopes for turning that region into a base for attacks on America and our allies around the world. [...]"

http://georgewbush-whitehouse.archives.gov/news/releases/2005/06/20050628-7.html

17. President Bush's Press Conference, The Rose Garden, May 31, 2005

"[...] I am pleased that in less than a year's time, there's a democratically elected government in Iraq; there are thousands of Iraqi soldiers trained and better equipped to fight for their own country; that our strategy is very clear in that we will work to get them ready to fight, and when they're ready, we'll come home. And I hope that's sooner, rather than later. But, nevertheless, it's very important that we complete this mission, because a free Iraq is in our nation's long-term interests. A democracy in the heart of the Middle East is an essential part of securing our country and promoting peace for the long run. And it is very important for our country to understand that. A free Iraq will set such a powerful example in a neighborhood that is desperate for freedom. And, therefore, we will complete the mission and support this elected government. [...]"

http://georgewbush-whitehouse.archives.gov/news/releases/2005/05/20050531.html

18. President Discusses War on Terror at Naval Academy Commencement, Navy Marine Corps Memorial Stadium, Annapolis, Maryland, May 27, 2005

"[...] Our nation is pursuing a clear strategy for the war on terror: We're using every available tool to disrupt terrorists and their organizations. We are taking the fight to the enemy abroad so we do not have to face them here at home. We're denying the terrorists sanctuary, and making clear that America will not tolerate outlaw regimes that provide safe haven and support to terrorists. We're using all elements of national power to deny terrorists the chemical, biological and nuclear weapons they seek. We will not allow mass murderers to gain access to the tools of mass destruction. And we're stopping terrorists from achieving their ideological victories they seek, by working to spread the hope of freedom and reform across the broader Middle East. We understand that free nations do not support terrorists or invade their neighbors. We understand to make the world more peaceful and our country more secure, we will advance the cause of liberty. [...]"

http://georgewbush-whitehouse.archives.gov/news/releases/2005/05/20050527.html

19. President Bush's Press Conference, James S. Brady Briefing Room, March 16, 2005

"[...] Q Mr. President, can you explain why you've approved of and expanded the practice of what's called rendition, of transferring individuals out of U.S. custody to countries where human rights groups and your own State Department say torture is common for people under custody?"

"THE PRESIDENT: The post-9/11 world, the United States must make sure we protect our people and our friends from attack. That was the charge we have been given. And one way to do so is to arrest people and send them back to their country of origin with the promise that they won't be tortured. That's the promise we receive. This country does not believe in torture. We do believe in protecting ourselves. We don't believe in torture. [...]"

http://georgewbush-whitehouse.archives.gov/news/releases/2005/03/20050316-3.html

20. President Discusses War on Terror, National Defense University, Fort Lesley J. McNair, Washington, DC, March 8, 2005

"Our immediate strategy is to eliminate terrorist threats abroad, so we do not have to face them here at home. The theory here is straightforward: terrorists are less likely to endanger our security if they are worried about their own security ... We will keep the terrorists on the run, until they have nowhere left to hide."

http://georgewbush-whitehouse.archives.gov/news/releases/2005/03/20050308-3.html

21. State of the Union Address, Washington, DC, February 2, 2005

"In the long-term, the peace we seek will only be achieved by eliminating the conditions that feed radicalism and ideologies of murder. If whole regions of the world remain in despair and grow in hatred, they will be the recruiting grounds for terror, and that terror will stalk America and other free nations for decades. The only force powerful enough to stop the rise of tyranny and terror, and replace hatred with hope, is the force of human freedom. Our enemies know this, and that is why the terrorist Zarqawi recently declared war on what he called the 'evil principle' of democracy ... America will stand with the allies of freedom to support democratic movements in the Middle East and beyond, with the ultimate goal of ending tyranny in our world."

http://georgewbush-whitehouse.archives.gov/news/releases/2005/02/20050202-11.html

22. President's Remarks to the General Conference of the National Guard Association of the United States, Las Vegas, Nevada, September 14, 2004

"[...] Free societies in the Middle East will be hopeful societies, which no longer feed resentments and breed violence for export. Free governments in the Middle East will fight terrorists instead of harboring them ... So our mission in Afghanistan and Iraq is clear: We'll help new leaders to train their armies, move toward elections, and get on the path of stability and democracy as quickly as possible. And then our troops will return home with the honor they deserve. [...]"

http://georgewbush-whitehouse.archives.gov/news/releases/2004/09/text/20040914-23.html

23. President Bush Discusses Progress in the War on Terror, Oak Ridge National Laboratory, Oak Ridge, Tennessee, July 12, 2004

"[...] Although we have not found stockpiles of weapons of mass destruction, we were right to go into Iraq. We removed a declared enemy of America, who had the capability of producing weapons of mass murder, and could have passed that capability to terrorists bent on acquiring them. In the world after September the 11th, that was a risk we could not afford to take.

"Today, the dictator who caused decades of death and turmoil, who twice invaded his neighbors, who harbored terrorist leaders, who used chemical weapons on innocent men, women, and children, is finally before the bar of justice. Iraq, which once had the worst government in the Middle East, is now becoming an example of reform to the region. [...]"

http://2001-2009.state.gov/s/ct/rls/rm/2004/34309.htm

24. President Bush Speech on Terrorism, Afghanistan, and Iraq, Washington, DC, March 19, 2004

"[...] The war on terror is not a figure of speech. It is an inescapable calling of our generation. The terrorists are offended not merely by our policies—they are offended by our existence as free nations. No concession will appease their hatred. No accommodation will satisfy their endless demands. Their ultimate ambitions are to control the peoples of the Middle East, and to blackmail the rest of the world with weapons of mass terror. There can be no separate peace with the terrorist enemy. Any sign of weakness or retreat simply validates terrorist violence, and invites more violence for all nations. The only certain way to protect our people is by early, united, and decisive action. ... We are using every tool of finance, intelligence, law enforcement and military power to break terror networks, to deny them refuge, and to find their leaders. Over the past 30 months, we have frozen or seized nearly $200 million in assets of terror networks. We have captured or killed some two-thirds of al Qaeda's known leaders, as well as many of al Qaeda's associates countries like the United States, or Germany, or Pakistan, or Saudi Arabia, or Thailand. We are taking the fight to al Qaeda allies, such as Ansar-al-Islam in Iraq, Jemaah Islamiya in Indonesia, and Southeast Asia. [...]"

http://2001-2009.state.gov/p/nea/rls/rm/30633.htm

25. President Discusses America's Leadership in Global War on Terror, Roswell Convention and Civic Center, Roswell, New Mexico, January 22, 2004

"[...] We will continue our vital work to protecting American people, by protecting our ports and borders and safeguarding infrastructure, preparing for the worst. I mentioned the first responders. I can't tell you how pleased I am with the coordination now between the federal government, the state government, and local governments for preparing our homeland. I'm going to submit a budget to Congress next month, which will include spending of $30 billion for homeland security. That's—more than $30 billion—almost three times the amount that we were spending prior to September the 11th, 2001."

http://2001-2009.state.gov/s/ct/rls/rm/2004/28526.htm

26. The President's State of the Union Address to Congress, January 20, 2004

"[...] As long as the Middle East remains a place of tyranny and despair and anger, it will continue to produce men and movements that threaten the safety of America and our friends. So America is pursuing a forward strategy of freedom in the greater Middle East. We will challenge the enemies of reform, confront the allies of terror, and expect a higher standard from our friends. [...]"

http://georgewbush-whitehouse.archives.gov/news/releases/2004/01/20040120-7.html

27. President Bush Discusses the Economy and the War on Terror, San Bernardino, California, October 16, 2003

"Who can possibly think that the world would be better off with Saddam Hussein still in power? Surely not the dissidents who would be in his prisons or end up in his mass graves. Surely not the men and women who would fill Saddam's torture chamber or rape rooms. Surely not the families of victims he murdered with poison gas. Surely not anyone who cares about human rights and democracy and stability in the Middle East. There is only one decent and humane reaction to the fall of Saddam Hussein—good riddance. … America must never forget the lessons of September the 11th. America cannot retreat from our responsibilities and hope for the best. Our security will not be gained by timid measures. Our security requires constant vigilance and decisive action. I believe America has only one option: We will fight this war against terror until it is won."

http://2001-2009.state.gov/s/ct/rls/rm/2003/25258.htm

28. *War on Terror*; President George W. Bush; Address to the Nation, The White House, Washington, DC, September 7, 2003

"America and a broad coalition acted first in Afghanistan, by destroying the training camps of terror, and removing the regime that harbored al Qaeda. In a series of raids and actions around the world, nearly two-thirds of al Qaeda's known leaders have been captured or killed, and we continue on al Qaeda's trail. We have exposed terrorist front groups, seized terrorist accounts, taken new measures to protect our homeland, and uncovered sleeper cells inside the United States. And we acted in Iraq, where the former regime sponsored terror, possessed and used weapons of mass destruction, and for 12 years defied the clear demands of the United Nations Security Council. Our coalition enforced these international demands in one of the swiftest and most humane military campaigns in history. [...]"

http://2001-2009.state.gov/p/nea/rls/rm/23897.htm

29. *President Bush Announces Major Combat Operations in Iraq Have Ended*, Remarks by the President from the USS Abraham Lincoln, At Sea off the Coast of San Diego, California, May 1, 2003

"[...] The war on terror is not over; yet it is not endless. We do not know the day of final victory, but we have seen the turning of the tide. No act of the terrorists will change our purpose, or weaken our resolve, or alter their fate. Their cause is lost. Free nations will press on to victory. [...]"

http://georgewbush-whitehouse.archives.gov/news/releases/2003/05/20030501-15.html

30. President George W. Bush State of the Union Address, January 28, 2003

"[...] With nuclear arms or a full arsenal of chemical and biological weapons, Saddam Hussein could resume his ambitions of conquest in the Middle East and create deadly havoc in that region. And this Congress and the America people must recognize another threat. Evidence from intelligence sources, secret communications, and statements by people now in custody reveal that Saddam Hussein aids and protects terrorists, including members of al Qaeda. Secretly, and without fingerprints, he could provide one of his hidden weapons to terrorists, or help them develop their own. [...]"

http://www.washingtonpost.com/wp-

31. President George W. Bush Delivers Graduation Speech at West Point, *Remarks at 2002 Graduation Exercise of the United States Military Academy*, West Point, New York, June 1, 2002

"[...] The war on terror will not be won on the defensive. We must take the battle to the enemy, disrupt his plans, and confront the worst threats before they emerge. In the world we have entered, the only path to safety is the path of action. And this nation will act.

"Our security will require the best intelligence, to reveal threats hidden in caves and growing in laboratories. Our security will require modernizing domestic agencies such as the FBI, so they're prepared to act, and act quickly, against danger. Our security will require transforming the military you will lead—a military that must be ready to strike at a moment's notice in any dark corner of the world. And our security will require all Americans to be forward-looking and resolute, to be ready for preemptive action when necessary to defend our liberty and to defend our lives."

http://georgewbush-whitehouse.archives.gov/news/releases/2002/06/20020601-3.html

32. President George W. Bush State of the Union Speech, January, 2002

"[...] Our ... goal is to prevent regimes that sponsor terror from threatening America or our friends and allies with weapons of mass destruction. ... North Korea is a regime arming with missiles and weapons of mass destruction, while starving its citizens. Iran aggressively pursues these weapons and exports terror, while an unelected few repress the Iranian people's hope for freedom ... Iraq continues to flaunt its hostility toward America and to support terror.

"States like these, and their terrorist allies, constitute *an axis of evil*, arming to threaten the peace of the world. By seeking weapons of mass destruction, these regimes pose a grave and growing danger. They could provide these arms to terrorists, giving them the means to match their hatred. They could attack our allies or attempt to blackmail the United States. [...]"

http://georgewbush-whitehouse.archives.gov/news/releases/2002/01/20020129-11.html

33. President George W. Bush Announces Progress on Financial Fight against Terror The White House Rose Garden, December 4, 2001

"[...] Today we take another important step in the financial fight against terror. From the beginning of this fight I have said our enemies are terrorist networks of global reach; and all who harbor them and support them are our enemies as well. We began with Al Qaeda and the Taliban. We identified some of Al Qaeda's financial backers and we moved against their accounts.

"In November, we advanced further and identified 22 more global terrorist organizations. And now we are moving against their financing as well.

"At midnight yesterday the Treasury Department froze the assets and accounts of the Holy Land Foundation in Richardson, Texas, whose money is used to support the Hamas terror organization. [...]"

http://2001-2009.state.gov/s/ct/rls/rm/2001/6644.htm

34. President George W. Bush Discusses War on Terrorism, Address to the Nation, World Congress Center, Atlanta, Georgia, November 8, 2001

"To coordinate our efforts we've created the new Office of Homeland Security. Its director, my good friend and former Governor, Tom Ridge, reports directly to me—and works with all our federal agencies, state and local governments, and the private sector on a national strategy to strengthen our homeland protections. ... We've passed a new antiterrorism law which gives our law enforcement officers the necessary tools to track terrorists before they harm Americans. A new terrorism task force is tightening immigration controls to make sure no one enters or stays in our country who would harm us. We are a welcoming country, we will always value freedom—yet we will not allow those who plot against our country to abuse our freedoms and our protections."

http://2001-2009.state.gov/s/ct/rls/rm/2001/5998.htm

35. President Bush Signs Anti-Terrorism Bill, *Remarks at Signing of the Patriot Act*, Anti-Terrorism Legislation, Washington, DC, October 26, 2001

"[...] This legislation gives law enforcement officials better tools to put an end to financial counterfeiting, smuggling and money-laundering. Secondly, it gives intelligence operations and criminal operations the chance to operate not on separate tracks, but to share vital information so necessary to disrupt a terrorist attack before it occurs.

"As of today, we're changing the laws governing information-sharing. ... Countering and investigating terrorist activity is the number one priority for both law enforcement and intelligence agencies.

"Surveillance of communications is another essential tool to pursue and stop terrorists. The existing law was written in the era of rotary telephones. This new law that I sign today will allow surveillance of all communications used by terrorists, including e-mails, the Internet, and cell phones. [...]"

http://2001-2009.state.gov/s/ct/rls/rm/2001/5760.htm

36. *Presidential Address Announcing Military Strikes against the Taliban*, The Treaty Room, October 7, 2001

"[...] On my orders, the United States military has begun strikes against al Qaeda terrorist training camps and military installations of the Taliban regime in Afghanistan. These carefully targeted actions are designed to disrupt the use of Afghanistan as a terrorist base of operations, and to attack the military capability of the Taliban regime. We are joined in this operation by our staunch friend, Great Britain. Other close friends, including Canada, Australia, Germany and France, have pledged forces as the operation unfolds. More than 40 countries in the Middle East, Africa, Europe and across Asia have granted air transit or landing rights. Many more have shared intelligence. We are supported by the collective will of the world. [...]"

http://georgewbush-whitehouse.archives.gov/news/releases/2001/10/20011007-8.html

37. President Bush's Radio Address on Afghanistan, October 6, 2001

> "[...] The United States is presenting a clear choice to every nation: Stand with the civilized world, or stand with the terrorists. And for those nations that stand with the terrorists, there will be a heavy price. ... America is determined to oppose the state sponsors of terror. Yet we are equally determined to respect and help the men and women those regimes oppress. Our enemy is not the Arab world. Many friendly Arab governments are, themselves, the targets of extremist terror. Our enemy is not Islam, a good and peace-loving faith that brings direction and comfort to over 1 billion people, including millions of Americans. And our enemy is not the people of any nation, even when their leaders harbor terrorists. Our enemy is the terrorists themselves and the regimes that shelter and sustain them. [...]"

http://www.washingtonpost.com/wpsrv/nation/specials/attacked/transcripts/bushaddress_100601.html

38. President Meets with Congressional Leaders, The Oval Office, October 2, 2001

> "It is my desire to make sure that, as this war unfolds, that the leaders of both the Senate and the House are fully informed of what the government is doing. I can't think of a better way to conduct foreign policy than to consult regularly with the leadership.
>
> "[...] There is no time table for the Taliban, just like there are no negotiations. I have said that the Taliban must turn over al Qaeda organization [sic] living within Afghanistan, and must destroy the terrorist camps. And they must do so, otherwise there will be a consequence. There are no negotiations, there's no calendar. We'll act on our time, and we'll do it in a manner that not only secures the United States as best as possible, but makes the freedom in the world more likely to exist in the future. [...]"

http://georgewbush-whitehouse.archives.gov/news/releases/2001/10/20011002-1.html

39. President Freezes Terrorists' Assets, President Bush, Secretary of the Treasury O'Neill, and Secretary of State Powell, Washington, DC, September 24, 2001

> "[...] Today, we have launched a strike on the financial foundation of the global terror network. ... We will direct every resource at our command to win the war against terrorists: every means of diplomacy, every tool of intelligence, every instrument of law enforcement, every financial influence. We will starve the terrorists of funding, turn them against each other, rout them out of their safe hiding places and bring them to justice. ...

I've signed an executive order that immediately freezes United States financial assets of and prohibits United States transactions with 27 different entities. They include terrorist organizations, individual terrorist leaders, a corporation that serves as a front for terrorism, and several nonprofit organizations. [...]"

http://2001-2009.state.gov/s/ct/rls/rm/2001/5041.htm

40. President George W. Bush Address to the Nation on the 9/11 Terrorist Attacks, September 11, 2001

"[...] These acts of mass murder were intended to frighten our Nation into chaos and retreat, but they have failed. Our country is strong. ... A great people has been moved to defend a great nation. Terrorist attacks can shake the foundations of our biggest buildings, but they cannot touch the foundation of America. These acts shattered steel, but they cannot dent the steel of American resolve. America was targeted for attack because we're the brightest beacon for freedom and opportunity in the world. And no one will keep that light from shining. [...]"

http://www.presidency.ucsb.edu/ws/?pid=58057

Bush Pre-9/11

41. President George W. Bush, *Statement on Domestic Preparedness against Weapons of Mass Destruction*, May 8, 2001

"Protecting America's homeland and citizens from the threat of weapons of mass destruction is one of our Nation's important national security challenges. Today, more nations possess chemical, biological, or nuclear weapons than ever before. Still others seek to join them. Most troubling of all, the list of these countries includes some of the world's least responsible states—states for whom terror and blackmail are a way of life. Some non-state terrorist groups have also demonstrated an interest in acquiring weapons of mass destruction. ...

"Therefore, I have asked Vice President Cheney to oversee the development of a coordinated national effort so that we may do the very best possible job of protecting our people from catastrophic harm. [...]"

http://www.presidency.ucsb.edu/ws/index.php?pid=45592&st=weapons+of+mass+destruction&st1=

42. President George W. Bush Remarks to Troops and Personnel, Norfolk Naval Air Station, Norfolk, VA, February 13, 2001.

"[...] We have no higher priority than the defense of our people against terrorist attack. To succeed, America knows we must work with our allies. We did not prevail together in the cold war only to go our separate ways, pursuing separate plans with separate technologies. The dangers ahead confront us all. The defenses we build must protect us all. [...]"

http://www.presidency.ucsb.edu/ws/index.php?pid=45992&st=norfolk&st1=

President William J. Clinton

1. President Clinton, Remarks *On Keeping America Secure for The 21st Century*, National Academy of Sciences, Washington, DC, January 22, 1999

"We must be ready—ready if our adversaries try to use computers to disable power grids, banking, communications and transportation networks, police, fire, and health services, or military assets. More and more, these critical systems are driven by and linked together with computers, making them more vulnerable to disruption ... we already are seeing the first wave of deliberate cyber attacks, hackers break into Government and business computers, stealing and destroying information, raiding bank accounts, running up credit card charges, extorting money by threats to unleash computer viruses."

http://www.presidency.ucsb.edu/ws/index.php?pid=57688&st=&st1=

2. President Clinton, *Remarks to the Opening Session of the 53rd United Nations General Assembly*, United Nations, New York, September 21, 1998

"[...] If terrorism is at the top of the American agenda—and should be at the top of the world's agenda—what, then, are the concrete steps we can take together to protect our common destiny? What are our common obligations? At least, I believe, they are these: to give terrorists no support, no sanctuary, no financial assistance; to bring pressure on states that do; to act together to step up extradition and prosecution; to sign the global anti-terror conventions; to strengthen the biological weapons and chemical conventions; to enforce the Chemical Weapons Convention; to promote stronger domestic laws and control the manufacture and export of explosives; to raise international standards for airport security; to combat the conditions that spread violence and despair."

http://www.presidency.ucsb.edu/ws/index.php?pid=54944&st=opening+session+of+the&st1=

3. President Clinton Address to the Nation on Military Action against Terrorist Sites in Afghanistan and Sudan, August 20, 1998

"[...] America has battled terrorism for many years. Where possible, we've used law enforcement and diplomatic tools to wage the fight. The long arm of American law has reached out around the world and brought to trial those guilty of attacks in New York and Virginia and in the Pacific. We have quietly disrupted terrorist groups and foiled their plots. We have isolated countries that practice terrorism. We've worked to build an international coalition against terror. But there have been and will be times when law enforcement and diplomatic tools are simply not enough, when our very national security is challenged, and when we must take extraordinary steps to protect the safety of our citizens. [...]"

http://www.presidency.ucsb.edu/ws/print.php?pid=54799

4. President William J. Clinton, "*American Security in a Changing World*"

5. Remarks at George Washington University, Washington, DC, August 5, 1996

"[...] While we can defeat terrorists, it will be a long time before we defeat terrorism. America will remain a target because we are uniquely present in the world, because we act to advance peace and democracy, because we have taken a tougher stand against terrorism, and because we are the most open society on earth. [...]"

http://dosfan.lib.uic.edu/ERC/briefing/dispatch/1996/html/Dispatchv7no32.html

6. President William J. Clinton, *Statement on Signing the Antiterrorism and Effective Death Penalty Act of 1996*, April 24, 1996

"I have today signed into law S. 735, the 'Antiterrorism and Effective Death Penalty Act of 1996.' This legislation is an important step forward in the Federal Government's continuing efforts to combat terrorism. ... our law enforcement officials will have tough new tools to stop terrorists before they strike and to bring them to justice if they do. [including] broad new Federal jurisdiction to prosecute anyone who commits a terrorist attack in the United States or who uses the United States as a planning ground for attacks overseas; banning fundraising in the United States that supports terrorist organizations;

> "—allow U.S. officials to deport terrorists from American soil without being compelled by the terrorists to divulge classified information, and to bar terrorists from entering the United States in the first place; require plastic explosives to contain chemical markers so that criminals who use them can be tracked down and prosecuted; toughen penalties over a range of terrorist crimes;
>
> "—ban the sale of defense goods and services to countries that I determine are not 'cooperating fully' with U.S. anti-terrorism efforts. Such a determination will require a review of a country's overall level of cooperation in our efforts to fight terrorism, taking into account our counterterrorism objectives with that country and a realistic assessment of its capabilities."

http://www.presidency.ucsb.edu/ws/?pid=52713

President George H.W. Bush

1. President George H. W. Bush, *Remarks to the American Legion National Convention*, August 25, 1992

> "[...] Take Iraq as a test case for the most difficult security challenges we are likely to face in the future. We tried peaceful means to bring Iraq into the family of nations. Given the dangerous neighbors, given the vital interests at stake, it was right to try. Had we not made those efforts, had we not exhausted every peaceful means, we would never have been able to build the unprecedented United Nations coalition that stopped a tyrant in his tracks and rolled him back to Baghdad. [...]"

https://bush41library.tamu.edu/archives/public-papers/4713

2. President George H. W. Bush, *Remarks to the United Nations Security Council*, January 31, 1992

In a speech focusing on Iraq and Libya, President Bush said in part:

> "[...] progress comes from acting in concert, and we must deal resolutely with these renegade regimes, if necessary, by sanctions or stronger measures, to compel them to observe international standards of behavior. We will not be blind to the dangers we still face. Terrorists and their state sponsors must know there will be serious consequences if they violate international law. [...]"

https://www.gpo.gov/fdsys/pkg/PPP-1992-book1/html/PPP-1992-book1-doc-pg175.htm

President Ronald W. Reagan

1. President Ronald W. Reagan, *Address to the Nation on the Iran Arms and Contra Controversy*, November 13, 1986

"[...] Our government has a firm policy not to capitulate to terrorist demands. That no concessions policy remains in force, in spite of the wildly speculative and false stories about arms for hostages and alleged ransom payments. We did not—repeat—did not trade weapons or anything else for hostages, nor will we. Those who think that we have gone soft on terrorism should take up the question with Colonel Qadhafi. We have not, nor will we, capitulate to terrorists. We will, however, get on with advancing the vital interests of our great nation—in spite of terrorists and radicals who seek to sabotage our efforts and immobilize the United States. Our goals have been, and remain, to restore a relationship with Iran; to bring an honorable end to the war in the Gulf; to bring a halt to state-supported terror in the Middle East; and finally, to effect the safe return of all hostages from Lebanon. [...]"

https://reaganlibrary.archives.gov/archives/speeches/1986/111386c.htm

2. President Ronald W. Reagan, *Radio Address to the Nation on Terrorism*, May 31, 1986

"[...] Effective antiterrorist action has also been thwarted by the claim that—as the quip goes— 'One man's terrorist is another man's freedom fighter.' That's a catchy phrase, but also misleading. Freedom fighters do not need to terrorize a population into submission. Freedom fighters target the military forces and the organized instruments of repression keeping dictatorial regimes in power. Freedom fighters struggle to liberate their citizens from oppression and to establish a form of government that reflects the will of the people. Now, this is not to say that those who are fighting for freedom are perfect or that we should ignore problems arising from passion and conflict. Nevertheless, one has to be blind, ignorant, or simply unwilling to see the truth if he or she is unable to distinguish between those I just described and terrorists. Terrorists intentionally kill or maim unarmed civilians, often women and children, often third parties who are not in any way part of a dictatorial regime. [...]"

https://reaganlibrary.archives.gov/archives/speeches/1986/53186a.htm

3. President Ronald W. Reagan, *The "Terrorist Menace": Address to the Annual Convention of the American Bar Association*, July 8, 1985

   "[...] the greatest hope the terrorists and their supporters harbor, the very reason for their cruelty and viciousness of their tactics, is to disorient the American people, to cause disunity, to disrupt or alter our foreign policy, to keep us from the steady pursuit of our strategic interests, to distract us from our very real hope that someday the nightmare of totalitarian rule will end and self-government and personal freedom will become the birthright of every people on Earth. [...]"

   https://reaganlibrary.archives.gov/archives/speeches/1985/70885a.htm

4. President Ronald W. Reagan, *The Hijacking of TWA Flight 847: "America Will Never Make Concessions to Terrorists,"* June 18, 1985

   "[...] Let me further make it plain to the assassins in Beirut and their accomplices, wherever they may be, that America will never make concessions to terrorists—to do so would only invite more terrorism—nor will we ask nor pressure any other government to do so. Once we head down that path there would be no end to it, no end to the suffering of innocent people, no end to the bloody ransom all civilized nations must pay. [...]"

   http://www.presidency.ucsb.edu/ws/print.php?pid=38789

5. Larry M. Speakes, White House Principal Deputy Press Secretary, Statement by Larry M. Speakes, *International Terrorism*, April 17, 1984

   "[...] our paramount interest is in improving our ability to prevent terrorist attacks on our citizens, installations, and those foreign persons and facilities in the U.S. we are obligated to protect. We believe we can best achieve these results through a combination of improved information and better security and protection. This does not present any change in U.S. policy—rather, a refocused emphasis."

   https://reaganlibrary.archives.gov/archives/speeches/1984/41784d.htm

6. President Ronald W. Reagan, Transcripts of an Interview with *US News & World Report* on Foreign Government-Sponsored Terrorism, December 15, 1983

> "[...] the important thing about terrorism is not to be turned back by it. It is a worldwide threat, as we know. The threat is right here in our own country. It's everyplace in the world. ... But the one thing we can't do is what so many people, even here in our own country, are advocating in the face of the terrorist attacks against our forces in Lebanon. That is to bring home the marines from Lebanon. If terrorism can succeed in its goal, then the world is going to find itself under the control of the terrorists. You have to stand against that and not let it succeed. [...]"

https://reaganlibrary.archives.gov/archives/speeches/1983/121583d.htm

President James E. Carter

1. President James E. Carter, State of the Union Address to Congress, January 16, 1981

> "[...] We have no basic quarrel with the nation, the revolution or the people of Iran. The threat to them comes not from American policy but from Soviet actions in the region. We are prepared to work with the government of Iran to develop a new and mutually beneficial relationship.
>
> "But that will not be possible so long as Iran continues to hold Americans hostages, in defiance of the world community and civilized behavior. They must be released unharmed. We have thus far pursued a measured program of peaceful diplomatic and economic steps in an attempt to resolve this issue without resorting to other remedies available to us under international law. [...]"

http://www.presidency.ucsb.edu/ws/?pid=44541

2. President James E. Carter, State of the Union Address, January 23, 1980

> "[...] in Iran, 50 Americans are still held captive, innocent victims of terrorism and anarchy. Also at this moment, massive Soviet troops are attempting to subjugate the fiercely independent and deeply religious people of Afghanistan. These two acts—one of international terrorism and one of military aggression—present a serious challenge to the United States of America and indeed to all the nations of the world. Together, we will meet these threats to peace. [...]"

http://www.jimmycarterlibrary.org/documents/speeches/su80jec.phtml

3. President James E. Carter, Remarks at the 13th Constitutional Convention of the American Federation of Labor and Congress of Industrial Organizations, November 15, 1979.

   "[…] the Iranian Government and its leaders are fully responsible for the safety and well-being of our representatives in Iran, in Tehran, and they will be held accountable for that responsibility. It is unthinkable that any responsible government in today's modern world could regard the seizure and the holding of the diplomatic officials of another nation as a realistic means to advance any cause whatsoever. Terrorism is not an acceptable means to resolve disputes between individuals or between nations. […]"

   http://www.presidency.ucsb.edu/ws/index.php?pid=31691&st=&st1

President Richard M. Nixon

1. President Richard M. Nixon, Statement About Action to Combat Terrorism, September 27, 1972.

   "[…] There are those who would tell us that terror is the last resort of the weak and the oppressed, a product of despair in an age of indifference, and that it seeks only political justice. This is nonsense. The way to seek justice is through negotiation. We have sought in our own relations to turn from confrontation to negotiation. We believe that this is the only way for grievances to be resolved in a way that will contribute to peace and stability. […]"

   http://www.presidency.ucsb.edu/ws/?pid=3602

2. President Richard M. Nixon, Memorandum Establishing a Cabinet Committee to Combat Terrorism, September 25, 1972

   http://www.presidency.ucsb.edu/ws/?pid=3596

The Cabinets

1. Prepared Remarks of Attorney General Alberto R. Gonzales at the JAG Corps Leadership Summit, Lake Buena Vista, Florida, October 23, 2006

   "Because we are at war, we must govern our conduct by the law of war. And we must acknowledge that some of the limitations of the civilian justice system simply do not hold.

"In order to defend the security of our citizens, we must have the ability:

"*to detain terrorists and remove them from the battlefield;

"*to collect from them the vital intelligence that enables us to capture their associates and break-up future plots;

"*and to create effective and fair procedures that will allow us to prosecute and punish captured terrorists for their war crimes.

"The legal doctrines directed at achieving these ends are not the same as those we would employ during peacetime. The Supreme Court has recognized this in several of its decisions, including its recent Hamdan decision. And Congress has endorsed this view with the Military Commissions Act of 2006. [...]"

https://www.justice.gov/archive/ag/speeches/2006/ag_speech_061023.html

2. Prepared Remarks of Attorney General Alberto R. Gonzales at the World Affairs Council of Pittsburgh on Stopping Terrorists Before They Strike: *The Justice Department's Power of Prevention*, Pittsburgh, Pennsylvania, August 16, 2006

"[...] Prevention is the goal of all goals when it comes to terrorism because we simply cannot and will not wait for these particular crimes to occur before taking action. Investigating and prosecuting terrorists after they have killed our countrymen would be an unworthy goal. Preventing terrorism is a meaningful and daily triumph.

"At the Department of Justice, our strategy of prevention is built on four primary pillars of activity: First, aggressive criminal and intelligence investigations. Second, utilization of partnerships, information-gathering and collaboration at every level: international, national, state and local. Third, prosecution and incarceration of terrorists. And, finally, containment of the radicalization that leads to homegrown, al Qaeda-inspired terrorists. [...]"

https://www.justice.gov/archive/ag/speeches/2006/ag_speech_060816.html

3. *The Changing Face of Terror: A Post 9/11 Assessment*: Testimony by Ambassador Henry A. Crumpton, Coordinator for Counterterrorism, Before the Senate Committee on Foreign Relations, June 13, 2006

"Our strategy to defeat terrorists is structured at multiple levels—a global campaign to counter violent extremism; a series of regional collaborative efforts to deny terrorists safe haven;

and numerous bilateral security and development assistance programs designed to build partner CT capabilities, as well as liberal institutions that support the rule of law, and address political and economic injustice. ... This strategy is aimed to enhance our partners' capacity to counter the terrorist threat and address conditions that terrorists exploit. [...]"

http://2001-2009.state.gov/s/ct/rls/rm/2006/68608.htm

4. Prepared Remarks by Attorney General Alberto R. Gonzales at the International Institute for Strategic Studies, London, England, March 7, 2006

"I understand that our characterization of a 'global war against terrorism' has raised some questions here in Europe: for example, does the United States really believe it is engaged in a state of war against all terrorists in all places? To these questions, I should explain what we mean when we use this phrase. On a political level, we believe that all countries must exercise the utmost resolve in defeating the global threat posed by transnational terrorism. On a legal level, we believe that the United States is engaged in an armed conflict with al Qaeda. They have attacked our embassies, our military vessels and military bases, our capital city, and our financial center. On September 11th, they killed nearly three thousand people and the UN and NATO quickly passed resolutions acknowledging the right of the United States to self defense. It is appropriate and lawful to use all available tools, including our military forces, to defeat this brutal enemy."

https://www.justice.gov/archive/ag/speeches/2006/ag_speech_060307.html

5. U.S. Senate Judiciary Committee Hearing on *Wartime Executive Power and the NSA's Surveillance Authority*, Testimony by Attorney General Alberto R. Gonzales, February 6, 2006

Transcript of hearing on the terrorism surveillance program and its legal authorities.

"[...] The terrorist surveillance program allows us to collect more information regarding al Qaeda's plans, and, critically, it allows us to locate al Qaeda operatives, especially those already in the United States and poised to attack. ... the Department of Justice has thoroughly examined this program and concluded that the President is acting within his power in authorizing it. The Department of Justice is not alone in concluding that the program is lawful. Career lawyers at NSA and its Inspector General office have been intimately involved in the oversight of the program. The lawyers have found the program to be lawful and reviewed its conduct. [...]

"The terrorist surveillance program is firmly grounded in the President's constitutional authorities."

http://fas.org/irp/congress/2006_hr/nsasurv.html

6. *"U.S. Counterterrorism Strategy Update,"* Testimony by Ambassador Henry A. Crumpton, State Department. Coordinator for Counterterrorism, to the House International Relations Committee. Subcommittee on International Terrorism and Nonproliferation, October 27, 2005.

"Success in Iraq and all counterterrorism conflicts depends upon the success of our partnerships. The State Department, with the cooperation and support of other Federal agencies, works to build the political will and practical capacity of other governments and non-state actors, such as international organizations, to combat terrorism. We have intensified old relationships and built new ones with foreign militaries, intelligence services, law enforcement authorities, foreign ministries, and banking officials to advance our common counterterrorism goals. We are working with foreign civic groups, provincial officials, tribal authorities, business leaders, educators, and a growing array of private sector partners who have vested interests in political stability, liberal institutions such as free markets, and democracy."

http://2001-2009.state.gov/s/ct/rls/rm/55745.htm

7. Remarks as Delivered by Secretary Michael Chertoff, U.S. Department of Homeland Security, at the Woodrow Wilson School of Public and International Affairs' 75th Anniversary Celebration, Princeton University, October 1, 2005

"The Department has been working very closely with international partners to pinpoint vulnerabilities in our common international network, plug the gaps in the network, and we're doing it in every area of intercourse around the world, whether it be container security to biometrics that can be used to assess who's coming into the country and who's leaving the country, to secure travel documents, to making sure that our maritime and air domains remain free of terrorist activity. One example, through US VISIT, which is our system that gives us the capability to biometrically confirm the identity all visitors at our ports off entry using a simple fingerprint, we can now check people who are coming-in, in real time and have their fingerprint electronically matched against a database. [...]"

https://www.hsdl.org/?view&did=474589 https://www.hsdl.org/?view&did=474589

8. Remarks for Secretary Michael Chertoff, U.S. Department of Homeland Security, George Washington University Homeland Security Policy Institute, Washington, DC, March 16, 2005
Remarks as prepared

"[...] Risk management is fundamental to managing the threat, while retaining our quality of life and living in freedom. Risk management must guide our decision-making as we examine how we can best organize to prevent, respond and recover from an attack. For that reason, the Department of Homeland Security is working with State, local, and private sector partners on a National Preparedness Plan to target resources where the risk is greatest. [...] We all live with a certain amount of risk. That means that we tolerate that something bad can happen; we adjust our lives based on probability; and we take reasonable precautions. [...]"

https://www.hsdl.org/?view&did=474723

9. Remarks by Secretary of Homeland Security Tom Ridge at the Cargo Security Summit, Washington, DC, December 16, 2004

"[...] Cargo security is a linchpin issue, not only for the security of our homeland, but also for our economic security as well. ... The protection of this supply chain is vital. ... Over the past two years, much has been done to bolster our container and cargo security. And as a result of the cooperation and the hard work of our partners at the international level and within the private sector, new programs and technologies have been deployed and they have been put to use. We've added layer upon layer of security to tighten and close any gaps terrorists might seek to exploit.

"These new defenses begin thousands of miles away before a container is even loaded onto a cargo vessel bound for our shores, from the 24-hour rule that provides advance cargo manifests for all U.S.-bound containers to the Container Security Initiative that has U.S. Customs and Border inspectors stationed in 32 international ports."

https://www.hsdl.org/?view&did=474843

10. Ambassador Cofer Black, Coordinator for Counterterrorism, *Recommendations of the 9/11 Commission Report*: Statement before the House International Relations Committee, Washington, DC, August 19, 2004

Comments on two of the 9/11 Commission's recommendations: "[...] our actions to deny terrorists sanctuary around the world and our efforts to develop a comprehensive strategy against terrorism through multilateral mechanisms."

http://2001-2009.state.gov/s/ct/rls/rm/2004/35572.htm

11. Additional Prepared Statement to the August 19 Hearing

"[...] At the recent U.S.–E.U. Summit, we renewed our commitment to further develop our cooperation against terrorism and agreed to work together: to deepen the international consensus and enhance international efforts to combat terrorism; to prevent access by terrorists to financial and other economic resources; to develop measures to maximize our capacities to detect, investigate and prosecute terrorists and prevent terrorist attacks; to protect the security of international transport and ensure effective systems of border control; to develop further our capabilities to deal with the consequences of a terrorist attack. [...]"

http://2001-2009.state.gov/s/ct/rls/rm/2004/35684.htm

12. National Commission on Terrorism Report, *Countering the Changing Threat of International Terrorism*, July 2004

"After a thorough review, the Commission concluded that, although American strategies and policies are basically on the right track, significant aspects of implementation are seriously deficient. [...]" The report outlines a series of recommendations.

https://fas.org/irp/threat/commission.html

13. Testimony Prepared for Delivery to the National Commission on Terrorist Attacks upon the United States. Testimony Secretary of Defense Donald H. Rumsfeld, Washington, DC, March 23, 2004

Summary of the history of the counterterrorism strategy paper that was presented to the interagency Principals 4 days before 9/11 and later became National Security Presidential Directive-9.

"The more one studies terrorism, the more one becomes convinced that the approach to fighting it that had evolved over several decades wasn't working.

"That strategy was essentially to treat terrorism as a matter of domestic security; to combat it through national and international law enforcement techniques; and to try to take defensive measures against terrorist attacks.

"From the attack on the Marine barracks in Beirut, to the first World Trade Center attack, to the Embassy bombings in East Africa, and the attack on the U.S.S. Cole—that was the pattern.

"Reasonable people have to conclude that the value of that approach had diminished over the years. It had become increasingly clear that we could no longer afford to treat terrorism as a manageable evil that we needed an approach that treated terrorism more like fascism—as an evil that needed to be not contained, but fought and eliminated."

http://www.smh.com.au/articles/2004/03/24/1079939702817.html

14. *The Importance of Counterterrorism Cooperation in Regional & Sub-Regional Organizations*, Remarks by Ambassador Black, State Department Coordinator for Counterterrorism, to the Organization of American States, Inter-American Committee against Terrorism (CICTE), Washington, DC, October 7, 2003

Remarks as delivered

"[...] Effective counterterrorism cooperation means more than just attending meetings and sharing information. It means being committed to coordinating a broader counterterrorism agenda on the diplomatic, financial, military, intelligence, and law enforcement fronts. It means working together to identify needs and develop specific capacity-building programs to meet those needs. Most importantly, it means developing strong, continuous, and collaborative relationships to use shared resources and expertise to make real advances in the war on terror. And I think it is obvious that regional and multilateral organizations play a powerful role in all of the above. [...]"

http://2001-2009.state.gov/s/ct/rls/rm/2003/25128.htm

15. Attorney General John Ashcroft, *Preserving Life and Liberty,* American Enterprise Institute, August 19, 2003.

As prepared

"[...] in the Patriot Act, Congress began to tear down the walls that cut off communication between intelligence and law enforcement officials. The Patriot Act gave agencies like the FBI and the CIA the ability to integrate their capabilities. It gave government the ability to 'connect the dots,' revealing the shadowy terrorist network in our midst. ... the Patriot Act ... gave law enforcement improved tools to prevent terrorism in the age of high technology. For example, where before investigators were forced to get a different wiretap order every time a suspect changed cell phones, now investigators can get a single wiretap that applies to the suspect and various phones he uses. [...]"

https://www.justice.gov/archive/ag/speeches/2003/081903remarksataeifinal.htm

16. Ambassador J. Cofer Black, Coordinator for Counterterrorism, Remarks to the Eighth Annual Conference and General Meeting of the International Association of Prosecutors on *Combating Global Terrorism*, Washington, DC, August 11, 2003

> "[...] Cooperation and sharing of ideas is especially important on matters of law. Whether extraditing terrorists or controlling their money flow, identifying them before they act or punishing them afterwards—on each of these critical issues, the law is front and center. Over the past few years, there has been an upsurge in the number of laws—both domestic and international—that deal with terrorism-related issues. There are now more laws limiting terrorists' actions in more countries than ever before, and more governments are willing to enforce those laws. ... And yet, there is still too wide a gulf between the anti-terrorism laws of different countries. Often, the laws in our countries are based on varying—and sometimes, conflicting—views of how far a government should go to protect its citizens from terrorist attacks. On the one hand, this can be helpful and represents the diversity of legal, social, and political traditions that exist in the world today. But on the other hand, these contrasts too often create obstacles that hinder our efforts to combat terrorism. [...]"

http://2001-2009.state.gov/s/ct/rls/rm/2003/23256.htm

17. Testimony of John Ashcroft, Attorney General, United States Department of Justice before the Senate Judiciary Committee, March 4, 2003

> "Almost without exception the courts have endorsed the Justice Department's view of ordered liberty. For instance, appellate courts have upheld the Executive Branch's authority to detain enemy combatants, close sensitive immigration hearings, and coordinate our law enforcement and intelligence activities. We have been careful in our approach, ever mindful of constitutional liberties, and we are confident that we are striking the appropriate balance.
>
> "Perhaps the most effective provisions of the USA Patriot Act are those that altered outdated statutory restrictions so that intelligence and law enforcement agencies have greater freedom to coordinate their efforts and to share information gathered about terrorists. One important development, with which the Act's provisions amending the Foreign Intelligence Surveillance Act (FISA) were consistent, was dismantlement of the false 'wall' that had been built between intelligence and law enforcement."

https://www.justice.gov/archive/ag/testimony/2003/030403senatejudiciaryhearing.htm

18. Secretary of State Powell's Speech to the United Nations Security Council on Iraq WMD, New York City, February 5, 2003.

Secretary Powell laid out the US case that Saddam Hussein was pursuing nuclear weapons.

"[…] The facts and Iraqis' behavior, Iraq's behavior, demonstrate that Saddam Hussein and his regime have made no effort, no effort, to disarm, as required by the international community. Indeed, the facts and Iraq's behavior show that Saddam Hussein and his regime are concealing their efforts to produce more weapons of mass destruction. […]"

http://2001-2009.state.gov/secretary/former/powell/remarks/2003/17300.htm

19. Ambassador Francis X. Taylor, Coordinator for Counterterrorism, *The Global War against Terrorism: A Way Ahead*, Address to the Institute for National Strategic Studies, National Defense University, Washington, DC, October 23, 2002

"[…] military force alone will not suffice; indeed, for many phases of this long conflict, military power alone will *not* be the most important element of our campaign. We must also fight terror with every economic, law enforcement, diplomatic, and intelligence weapon we have in our arsenal. … We are using all these weapons in a coordinated, comprehensive campaign against the terrorist menace. Success will not come in one dramatic strike. Instead, it will come through the patient accumulation of many operations around the world whose effect will be cumulative until we break the back of terrorist organizations like al-Qaida. […]"

https://2001-2009.state.gov/s/ct/rls/rm/14570.htm

20. Vice President's Remarks at the United States Naval Academy Commencement, *Annapolis, Maryland,* May 24, 2002

"The war on terror has accelerated changes in thinking and strategy that were already in the making … any enemy conspiring to harm America or our friends must face a swift and certain and devastating response … There is no doubt that Saddam Hussein now has weapons of mass destruction. There is no doubt he is amassing them to use against our friends, against our allies, and against us. And there is no doubt that his aggressive regional ambitions will lead him into future confrontations with his neighbors—confrontations that will involve both the weapons he has today, and the ones he will continue to develop with his oil wealth. [...]"

http://georgewbush-whitehouse.archives.gov/news/releases/2002/05/20020524-25.html

21. Secretary Colin L. Powell, Senate Appropriations Subcommittee on Commerce, Justice, State, and the Judiciary, Washington, DC, March 12, 2002

"[...] The terrorist attacks of September 11 underscored the urgency of implementing an effective public diplomacy campaign. Those who abet terror by spreading distortion and hate and inciting others, take full advantage of the global news cycle. We must also use that cycle. Since September 11, there have been over 2,000 media appearances by State Department officials. Our continuous presence in Arabic and regional media by officials with language and media skills, has been unprecedented. Our international information website on terror is now online in seven languages. Internet search engines show it is the hottest page on the topic. ... 'Right content, right format, right audience, right now' describes our strategic aim in seeing that U.S. policies are explained and placed in the proper context in the minds of foreign audiences. [...]"

http://2001-2009.state.gov/secretary/former/powell/remarks/2002/8733.htm

22. *A Discussion on the Global Campaign against Terrorism*, Ambassador Francis X. Taylor, Coordinator for Counterterrorism, Remarks before the National Foreign Policy Conference For Leaders of Nongovernmental Organizations, Washington, DC, October 26, 2001

"[...] Another important tool in countering terrorist fundraising is the Antiterrorism and Effective Death Penalty Act (AEDPA) of 1996, which makes it a criminal offense for person subject to U.S. jurisdiction to knowingly contribute funds or other material support to groups that the Secretary of State has designated as Foreign Terrorist Organizations. U.S. law also allows freezing of the designated groups' assets and denial of visas for members as well as leaders of terrorist organizations. Last week, Secretary Powell designated 28 such groups, including al-Qàida.

"An important section in the AEDPA is worth repeating for the world at large: '[F]oreign terrorist organizations that engage in terrorist activity are so tainted by their criminal conduct that any contribution to such an organization facilitates that conduct.'

"This is a key point. Before they make a contribution to groups supporting terrorists, people around the world need to understand that by doing so they are assisting criminal conduct—and are themselves committing a criminal act. [...]"

http://2001-2009.state.gov/s/ct/rls/rm/2001/5773.htm

23. *The Bush Administration's Response to September 11th—and Beyond*

24. Richard N. Haass, Director, Office of the Policy Planning Staff, Remarks to the Council of Foreign Relations, New York City, October 15, 2001

"[...] Different tools will be used at different times as this sustained campaign progresses in the months and years ahead. ... We are using all the tools of statecraft in an integrated manner for maximum impact. The campaign began with intelligence and law enforcement cooperation; information was shared and suspects interrogated in the United States and abroad. We moved to choke off the financial lifeblood of terrorist networks. At the same time, we advanced on the diplomatic front, forging a robust, broad-based international coalition, opening lines of communications with the Afghan opposition to the Taliban, and laying the foundations for our military response by securing basing and overflight rights around the world. Eight days ago our military began striking al-Qàida and the forces of the Taliban inside Afghanistan in conjunction with a redoubling of our humanitarian assistance to the beleaguered Afghan people. [...]"

http://2001-2009.state.gov/s/p/rem/5505.htm

25. Secretary Colin L. Powell, Testimony on Counterterrorism before the Senate Appropriations Subcommittee on Commerce, Justice, State and the Judiciary, Washington, DC, May 8, 2001

Description of the many State Department counterterrorism programs: "[...] our diplomats deliver a consistent message on terrorism to foreign governments, reinforce that message with practical support to the willing, and we mobilize the international community to isolate, through political and economic pressure, those who support or use terrorism. [...]"

The testimony describes the many State Department counterterrorism programs

http://2001-2009.state.gov/secretary/former/powell/remarks/2001/2776.htm

26. *Drugs, Terrorism and Crime*, Statement of Michael A. Sheehan, Coordinator for Counterterrorism, U.S. Department of State, before the House Judiciary Committee, Subcommittee on Crime, December 13, 2000

> "[...] in looking at the broad picture of narcotics, terrorism and international crime, we should start with the basic fact that terrorism itself is a crime, not a political statement. Hijacking aircraft, kidnapping innocent people, and bombing busses, buildings or ships are all forms of a crime, which must be viewed separately from the so-called 'cause' that prompts some people to commit this crime. This is a long-standing U.S. policy, one that is shared by the international community and demonstrated in a dozen international conventions and treaties. [...]"

http://www.globalsecurity.org/security/library/congress/2000_h/001213-sheehan.htm

27. Secretary of State Madeline K. Albright, Statement Submitted to the Senate Appropriations Committee, Subcommittee on Foreign Operations, Export Financing, and Related Programs, April 13, 2000

> "[...] Through our diplomacy and training programs, we help friendly governments to improve border security and share information about those suspected of being affiliated with terrorist networks. We gather information to advise and warn Americans. We strive to forge international agreements and cooperation that will leave terrorists with no place to run, hide, operate or stash their assets. We do all we can to bring suspects before the bar of justice, as we have in several major cases, including the sabotage of Pan Am 103, and the tragic 1998 bombing of two U.S. embassies in Africa. [...]"

http://secretary.state.gov/www/statements/2000/000413-wr.html

28. Secretary of State Albright, Testimony before the Senate Appropriations Subcommittee on Commerce, State, the Judiciary and Related Agencies, Washington, DC, February 4, 1999

> "[...] the Five-Year Interagency Counter-terrorism and Technology Crime Plan serves as a baseline strategy for coordinating our response to terrorism in the United States and against American targets overseas."

https://www.justice.gov/sites/default/files/oip/legacy/2014/07/23/crime-plan.pdf

"[...] The Five-Year Plan is only the beginning. Certainly, no single arrest or shutdown of a terrorist operation will be sufficient. The advance of technology has given us new means to counter terrorists. But it has also enabled terrorists to develop more powerful weapons and to travel, communicate, recruit, and raise funds on a global basis. [...]"

http://secretary.state.gov/www/statements/1999/990204b.html

29. Secretary of State Madeleine K. Albright, Remarks on Designation of Terrorist Organizations, Washington, DC, October 8, 1997

"[...] Under a (Material Support) provision of the Anti-Terrorism Act of 1996, I'm designating 30 groups as foreign terrorist organizations. These designations have three main consequences.

"First, as of today, it is a crime to provide funds, weapons or other types of tangible support to any of the designated organizations. Second, members and representatives of these organizations are hereby ineligible for visas to enter the United States, and are subject to exclusion from the United States. And third, any funds that these organizations have in our country will be blocked.

"The Anti-Terrorism Act was designed to put a stop to fundraising in the United States by and on behalf of organizations that engage in or sponsor terrorist acts. [...]"

http://1997-2001.state.gov/www/statements/971008.html

30. Louis J. Freeh, Director, Federal Bureau of Investigation Before the House Appropriations Committee, Subcommittee on the Departments of Commerce, Justice, and State, the Judiciary, and Related Agencies, March 12, 1997

"There are four major cornerstones through which the government's policy on terrorism is to be implemented. These are:

"* To reduce the vulnerabilities of the United States to terrorism;

"* To deter terrorist acts before that occur;

"* To respond to terrorist acts that do occur, including apprehension and punishment of terrorists and management of the consequences of terrorist acts; and

"* To develop effective capabilities address the threat posed by nuclear, chemical, or biological materials or weapons.

http://fas.org/irp/congress/1997_hr/ss970513f.htm

31. Ambassador Philip C. Wilcox, Coordinator for Counterterrorism, Denver Council on Foreign Relations, September 12, 1996

> "[…] terrorism today is far more devastating than in the past because of the mass media. No story plays better, or longer, than a terrorist attack. Today's media, especially television, multiply the fear effect of terrorism by vividly conveying its horror. And this greatly increases our collective sense of vulnerability. The terrorists, of course, know this. And they seek to exploit media coverage to put us and our governments on the psychological defensive. […]"

The speech described the State Department's various counterterrorism efforts.

http://www.state.gov/www/global/terrorism/960912.html

32. Secretary of State Warren Christopher. *Fighting Terrorism: Challenges for the Peacemakers*, Address to the Washington Institute for Near East Policy Annual Soref Symposium, May 21, 1996

> "None of the challenges we now face is more pressing than the fight against terrorism. Terrorism destroys innocent lives. It undermines a society's sense of security—and with it the very foundation upon which a lasting peace must be built. Through our diplomacy and training programs, we help friendly governments to improve border security and share information about those suspected of being affiliated with terrorist networks. We gather information to advise and warn Americans. We strive to forge international agreements and cooperation that will leave terrorists with no place to run, hide, operate or stash their assets. We do all we can to bring suspects before the bar of justice, as we have in several major cases, including the sabotage of Pan Am 103, and the tragic 1998 bombing of two U.S. embassies in Africa. […]"

http://dosfan.lib.uic.edu/ERC/briefing/dossec/1996/9605/960521dossec.html

33. Secretary of State Warren Christopher address to the 50th session of the United Nations General Assembly, New York, September 25, 1995

> "[…] Terrorists should be treated as criminals and there must be no place where they can hide from the consequences of their acts. States that sponsor terrorists should feel the full weight of sanctions that can be imposed by the international community. Let us not deceive ourselves: Every dollar that goes into the government coffers of a state sponsor of terrorism such as Iran helps

pay for a terrorist's bullets or bombs. Iran's role as the foremost state sponsor of terrorism makes its secret quest for weapons of mass destruction even more alarming. We must stand together to prevent Iran from acquiring such threatening capabilities."

http://dosfan.lib.uic.edu/ERC/briefing/dossec/1995/9509/950925dossec.html

34. Timothy E. Wirth, Counselor of the Department of State, Testimony to the House Foreign Affairs Committee Subcommittee on International Security, International Organizations, and Human Rights, March 1, 1994

"[...] we believe the basic U.S. policy of no concessions, pressure on state sponsors and application of the rule of law is a sound one. ... I want to emphasize that regardless of the political claims of terrorists, their actions are in violation of domestic and international law and should be treated as criminal by the world community. [...]"

https://archive.org/stream/uscounterterrori00unit/uscounterterrori00unit_djvu.txt

Bibliography

Yonah Alexander. 2010. ed. *Terrorists in Our Midst*. Santa Barbara, CA: Praeger Press.

Yonah Alexander and Michael B. Kraft. 2008. *The Evolution of U.S. Counterterrorism Policy*. Westport, CT: Praeger Security International.

Gabriel A., Almond, R. Scott Appleby, and Emmanuel Sivan. 2002. *Strong Religions: The Rise of Fundamentalisms Around the World*. University of Chicago Press.

Stewart Baker. 2010. *Skating on Stilts: Why We Aren't Stopping Tomorrow's Terrorism*. Stanford, CA: Hoover Institution Press.

Peter L. Bergen. 2016. *United States of Jihad: Investigating America's Homegrown Terrorists*. New York: Crown Publishers.

Peter L. Bergen. 2012. *Manhunt: The Ten-Year Search for Bin Laden from 9/11 to Abbottabad*. New York: Crown Publishers.

Conrad C. Crane. 2016. *Cassandra in Oz: Counterinsurgency and Future War*. Annapolis, MD: Naval Institute Press.

Richard A. Clarke. 2004. *Against All Enemies: Inside America's War on Terror*. New York: Free Press.

Martha Crenshaw and Gary Lafree. 2017. *Countering Terrorism*. Washington DC. Brookings Institution Press.

Henry A. Crumpton. 2013. *The Art of Intelligence: Lessons from a Life in the CIA's Clandestine Service*. [Reprint Edition] New York: Penguin Books.

Michael T. Flynn and Michael Ledeen. 2016. *The Field of Fight: How We Can Win the Global War against Radical Islam and Its Allies*. New York: St. Martin's Press.

James J.F. Forrest. 2015. ed. *Essentials of Counterterrorism*. (Praeger Security International).

Joshua Alexander Geltzer. 2010. *US Counter-Terrorism Strategy and al-Qaeda: Signaling and the Terrorist World-View*. New York: Routledge.

Garrett M. Graff. 2011. *The Threat Matrix: The FBI at War in the Age of Global Terror*. New York: Little, Brown and Company.

Bruce Hoffman. 2017. *Inside Terrorism., Third Edition*. New York: Colombia University Press.

Brian Michael Jenkins and John Paul Godges. 2011. ed. *The Long Shadow of 9/11: America's Response to Terrorism*. Santa Monica, CA: RAND Corporation.

Brian Michael Jenkins. 2006. *Unconquerable Nation: Knowing Our Enemy, Strengthening Ourselves*. Santa Monica, CA: RAND Corporation.

David Kamien. 2012. ed. *The McGraw-Hill Homeland Security Handbook, 2nd edition*. New York: McGraw-Hill Press.

Fred Kaplan. 2014. *The Insurgents: David Petraeus and the Plot to Change the American Way of War*. New York: Simon & Schuster Paperbacks.

Ronald Kessler. 2003. *The CIA at War: Inside the Secret Campaign against Terror*. New York: St. Martin's Press.

Ronald Kessler. 2007. *The Terrorist Watch: Inside the Desperate Race to Stop the Next Attack*. New York: Crown Forum, 2007.

David Kilcullen. 2016. *Blood Year: The Unravelling of Western Counterterrorism*. New York: Oxford Press.

Michael B. Kraft and Edward Marks. 2012. *U.S. Government Counterterrorism: A Guide to Who Does What*. Boca Raton, FL: CRC Press.

Walter Laquer. 2004. *Voices of Terror: Manifestos, Writings and Manuals of Al Qaeda, Hamas, and Other Terrorists from Around the World and Throughout the Ages*. New York: Reed Press.

Walter Laquer. 2009. *The New Terrorism*. New York: Oxford University Press.

Matt Levitt. 2015. ed. *The Rise of ISIL, Series of Counterterrorism Lectures*. Washington, DC: Institute of Near East Policy.

Matt Levitt. 2013. *Hezbollah: The Global Footprint of the Party of God*. Washington, DC: Georgetown University Press.

George C. Lovewine. 2014. *Outsourcing the Global War on Terrorism: Private Military Companies and American Intervention in Iraq and Afghanistan*. New York: Palgrave Macmillan.

Philip Mudd. 2013. *Takedown: Inside the Hunt for Al Qaeda*. Philadelphia, PA: University of Pennsylvania Press.

John Mueller and Mark G. Stewart. 2016. *Chasing Ghosts: The Policing of Terrorism*. New York: Oxford University Press.

William McCants. 2016. *The ISIS Apocalypse: The History, Strategy and Doomsday Vision of the Islamic State*. New York: St. Martins Press.

Timothy Naftali, 2005. *Blind Spot: The Secret History of American Counterterrorism*. New York: Perseus Books.

Paul R. Pillar. 2011. *Intelligence and U.S. Foreign Policy: Iraq, 9/11, and Misguided Reform*. New York: Columbia University Press.

Dr. Jerrold M. Post. 2007. *The Mind of the Terrorist.* New York: Palgrave-McMillan.

Greg C. Reeson. 2011. *Stalemate: Why We Can't Win the War on Terror and What We Should Do Instead* (Lanham), MD: Government Institutes/An Imprint of The Scarecrow Press, Inc.

Linda Robinson. 2013. *One Hundred Victories: Special Ops and the Future of American Warfare.* New York: Public Affairs.

Jose A. Rodriguez, Jr., with Bill Harlow. 2012. *Hard Measures: How Aggressive CIA Actions After 9/11 Saved American Lives.* New York: Threshold Editions.

Marc Sageman. 2008. *Leaderless Jihad.* Philadelphia, PA: University of Pennsylvania Press.

Eric Schmitt and Thom Shanker. 2011. *Counterstrike: The Untold Story of America's Secret Campaign against al Qaeda.* New York: Times Books/Henry Holt & Company.

Michael A. Sheehan. 2008. *Crush the Cell: How to Defeat Terrorism Without Terrorizing Ourselves.* New York: Crown Publishers.

Joshua Sinai, *The United States of America: Domestic Counterterrorism since 9/11.* Chapter 55 in Andrew Silke, editor, Routledge Handbook of Terrorism and Counterterrorism. New York, NY: Routledge.

Frank Shanty. 2012. ed. *Counterterrorism: From the Cold War to the War on Terrorism.* Santa Barbara, CA: ABC-CIO.

Jessica Stern and J.M. Berger. 2015. *ISIS, the State of Terror.* New York: HarperCollins.

Strobe Talbott and Nayan Chanda 2001. ed. *The Age of Terror.* New York: Basic Books.

Gregory F. Treverton. 2009. *Intelligence for an Age of Terror.* New York: Cambridge University Press.

Gabriel Wineman. 2005. *Terrorism in Cyberspace: The Next Generation.* New York: Woodrow Wilson Center press and Colombia University Press.

Laurence Wright. 2016. *The Terror Years: From al-Qaeda to the Islamic State.* New York: Knopf/Borzoi Books.

Robin Wright. 2012. *Rock the Casbah: Rage and Rebellion Across the Islamic World.* New York: Simon and Schuster.

William Zartman and Buy Olivier Faure. 2011. ed. *Engaging Extremists.* Washington, DC: US Institute of Peace.

Juan C. Zurate. 2013. *Treasury's War.* New York City: Public Affairs.

Index

For Product Safety Concerns and Information please contact our EU
representative GPSR@taylorandfrancis.com
Taylor & Francis Verlag GmbH, Kaufingerstraße 24, 80331 München, Germany

www.ingramcontent.com/pod-product-compliance
Ingram Content Group UK Ltd.
Pitfield, Milton Keynes, MK11 3LW, UK
UKHW022132190926
475702UK00013B/1759

* 9 7 8 0 3 6 7 7 7 8 7 8 1 *